DEPARTMENT OF EDUCATION AND SCIENCE

EDUCATIONAL PRIORITY

VOLUME 1: E.P.A. PROBLEMS AND POLICIES

Edited by

A. H. HALSEY

Director of Department of Social and Administrative Studies,
University of Oxford

Report of a research project sponsored by
the Department of Education and Science and
the Social Science Research Council

233025

LONDON

HER MAJESTY'S STATIONERY OFFICE

1972

SBN 11 270295 3

Contents

List of Figures

List of Tables

CONTRIBUTORS

National Director	A. H. Halsey
The Oxford Team	Joan Payne Keith Hope Constance Rollett
The Birmingham Team	Randall Lines Paul Widlake Lorna Bell
The Liverpool Team	Eric Midwinter Keith Pulham Eleanor Connor Tom Lovett Trilby Shaw
The London Team	Charles Betty Alan Little Jack Barnes Jim Stevenson Karen Lyons
The West Riding Team	Mike Harvey George Smith Teresa Smith Caroline Moseley Geoffrey Poulton Lin Poulton Gina Armstrong
H.M.I. responsible for liaison	John Gregory

Preface

This book has its origins in the immediate aftermath of the publication of the Plowden Report in 1967 when Anthony Crosland was the Secretary of State at the D.E.S., I was his part-time adviser, Michael Young was the Chairman of S.S.R.C., and the informal seminars on problems of educational policy described elsewhere by Crosland[1] were in full swing.

Two things particularly impressed me in the Plowden Report—the principle of positive discrimination as applied to slums and the call for action–research. The Plowden Committee had drawn attention to the schools in run-down areas which had grim buildings, high staff turnover, and teachers liable "to become dispirited by long journeys to decaying buildings to see each morning children among whom some seem to have learned only how not to learn".[2] Positive discrimination was advocated "to make schools in the most deprived areas as good as the best in the country". Within the limits of the tiny resources made available to us the first aim of the programme reported here was to do just that, and much of our report is made up of descriptions of our successful and unsuccessful efforts.

This aim of action may be thought of as the primary interest of the D.E.S., backed by a grant of up to £100,000. But the second aim, which perhaps belongs more properly to the S.S.R.C. and its £75,000, was to transform action into action–research. The Plowden Committee had made a plea for "research to discover which of the developments in the educational priority areas have the most constructive effects so as to assist in planning the longer term programme" which they hoped was to follow. The evaluations (a term with a range of strong and weak senses), which appear at various points in this book and subsequent volumes, are our contribution to Plowden's plea. In the context of the programme as a whole they constitute a pioneering effort in the use of the action–research method in Britain.

The Programme

The slow progress of negotiating a grant began after the "Plowden seminar" in 1967 and involved correspondence and discussion between Michael Young, Anthony Crosland, Sir Lionel Russell, the S.S.R.C.'s Educational Research Board and various Chief Education Officers of the local education authorities. The Secretary of State declared willingness to consider an action–research proposal in October 1967 and the E.R.B. approved the idea of an E.P.A. programme the next month. Protracted

---

[1]Edward Boyle and Anthony Crosland in conversation with Maurice Kogan, *The Politics of Education*, Penguin Education Specials, 1971.

[2]*Children and their Primary Schools*, Central Advisory Council for Education, Vol. I, p. 51.

negotiations with L.E.A.s and nearby universities[1] followed in 1968. An H.M.I., John Gregory, was seconded to us from May 1968. The districts in London, Birmingham, Liverpool and the West Riding were chosen, parallel Scottish arrangements were made at Dundee,[2] and a grant for the English programme of up to £175,000 for a three-year programme was made at the end of May 1968.

The next few months were taken up with negotiating detailed arrangements with the L.E.A.s and the appointment of staff. The Liverpool project director, Eric Midwinter, took up his post in September 1968, Charles Betty went to Deptford in October, and Randall Lines and Mike Harvey to Birmingham and the West Riding respectively on 1st January 1969. There was thus a staggered start in the four areas but the National Steering Committee fixed a common terminal date—the last day of 1971.

While staffing arrangements were being made in the autumn of 1968 George Smith had been looking closely at the American literature on "compensatory education". Then, in January 1969, Mr. Smith, Dr. Alan Little and I attended a conference under the auspices of the Centre for Educational Research and Innovation of O.E.C.D. and the Ford Foundation at which we discussed with experienced Americans the relevance of their programmes for the E.P.A. programme on which we were about to embark. Mr. Smith and Dr. Little subsequently visited a wide range of American projects with a view to preparing an extended report for O.E.C.D.[3].

By this time we were reaching the end of a series of plenary conferences attended by the staff of all the projects as they were appointed, by the Dundee project group, by Alan Brimer and his colleagues from the University of Bristol and by Michael Young and Jack Tizard from the E.R.B.. There were also smaller conferences especially between the research staffs. The general character of our collective approach is fairly accurately reflected in my summary of the concluding plenary conference in January 1969, and this document appears as Appendix 1. It is worth including not only because it shows how early we focused on the idea of the multiplier of educational effort from our own initial input and on the idea of the community school, but also because of the divisions within the project teams concerning the balance between action and research. Already I had become convinced that local autonomy and initiative could not and should not be subjugated to central direction in the interests of evaluation in its strongest sense, i.e. within the rigorous constraints of a national experimental design. Rather was it that five case studies with evaluation in the weak sense of orderly description of the area, the schools and the action programme were assured and beyond this I encouraged co-operation towards inter-project co-operation and comparison. The main fruits of this persuasion are

---

[1]It turned out in the end that, apart from helpful contacts with particular individuals, the university departments as such offered little or no help to the local project teams. By contrast colleges of education were, in many cases, extremely helpful.

[2]The Scottish project is not dealt with in this book. It will be reported in Vol. V of this series of E.P.A. books which will be entitled *E.P.A.: Dundee* and edited by Charles Morrison in collaboration with Joyce Watt and Terence R. Lee.

[3]G. A. N. Smith and A. Little, *Strategies of Compensation: A Review of Educational Projects for the Disadvantaged in the United States*, O.E.C.D., 1971.

presented in our account of the pre-school experiment (Chapter 7) and the baseline surveys of teacher attitudes, parents' attitudes and children's test performances (Chapter 5).

The differences between the teams were a function of both situation and personality. Charles Betty came to London from a primary school headship and was strongly teacher-oriented in an organisational setting which was unfamiliar to him and where a strong research department existed within the L.E.A.. Randall Lines was an experienced chief education officer with a strong sense of the financial constraints on educational innovation, and he was partnered in Birmingham by a teacher and psychologist, Paul Widlake, with passionate interests in children who have to struggle with the elementary skills of language and number. Eric Midwinter came from a college of education and with a deep knowledge of the culture of Liverpool 8 and the E.P.A. school. His research officer, Keith Pulham, had had planning experience and, with the other members of the team, worked loyally and closely to Midwinter's leadership. Their co-operation with the L.E.A. was powerfully supported by the Chief Inspector, Tom MacManners. Mike Harvey was a young man with successful experience in the teaching of "difficult" children, and his research officer, George Smith, was a classicist turned sociologist who had taught in India and whose wife was a trained social worker. The team was thrown closely together by the circumstances of an isolated and close-knit mining community at some distance from the centre of educational administration in Wakefield whence Sir Alec Clegg generated benevolent interest.

At all events differences of conceptions or priorities were obvious in the four projects from the beginning. Liverpool was action dominated from the start. The problem in Eric Midwinter's view was to get something done. As he wrote at the end of his interim report, "so pressing is the need, both for the practical purpose of avoiding permanent social dislocation and for the moral purpose of ensuring an elementary system of social justice, that it would have been preferable to have come up with an answer in three weeks". In fact and plan however, the projects went on to the end of their three years with increasing pressure from the centre towards strengthening the evaluation side of the programme. An interim report was submitted to the D.E.S. and S.S.R.C. via the National Steering Committee in the autumn of 1970 at which point the budget for the final year was allocated.

During the third and final year, while the main effort has, of necessity, been concentrated on the action and research programmes which had been developed in the first two years, we have also done what we could to ensure that what has been successful among our innovations should not end with our formal departure from the four districts. The result so far lies between the height of our hopes and the depression of our expectations. Our attempt to persuade the S.S.R.C. to finance continuation of action–research in Birmingham, Liverpool and the West Riding failed despite the backing of the National Steering Committee—a bad omen for both the realisation of Plowden reform and for the progress of action–research. The only gain on this front was a small grant towards the completion of the Home Visiting and follow-up testing programmes in the West Riding.[1] On the other hand

---

[1] In effect this was a time extension only as we had not spent all the original grant.

we have been encouraged by another arm of government—the Community Development Projects of the Urban Programme which have increasingly incorporated E.P.A. elements into their development, especially in the Vauxhall district of Liverpool and at Coventry. Moreover, after our final report was submitted, the D.E.S. gave us serious and sympathetic interest leading to discussions with officials and the Secretary of State which are continuing.

Important parts of the work in all four areas will continue to be financed by the Exchequer under the Urban Programme for at least five years. The I.L.E.A. will continue its action programme and will benefit, as do all the innovations of that Authority, from the established existence of Alan Little's research department.[1] The West Riding (regrettably to be broken up in 1974) will carry on its support to Red House, thereby essentially continuing the project. Birmingham is continuing some of the work in Balsall Heath, and Liverpool is contributing towards a new organisation for the national promotion of E.P.A. policy and practice, *Priority*. *Priority* promises to be a notable success and is owed first and foremost to the ceaseless and infectious enthusiasm of Eric Midwinter. Given our claim to have put substance on to the skeleton of the Plowden conception of the community school, it was essential to provide for the dissemination of successful practice to all E.P.A. schools, indeed to all schools, in the country. That is the essential function of *Priority*. In Dundee the education authority and other agencies have made provision for carrying on and extending E.P.A. work.

Meanwhile we can reasonably claim that a more or less permanent mark has been left on the schools, the communities, the teachers and the colleges of education where our action programme has taken us. The desirability of an evaluative revisit in, say, two years' time is almost too obvious to mention.

The other gain which deserves a mention is that the programme has developed experience and expertise in the skills of action–research which scarcely existed before the D.E.S. and S.S.R.C. financed this first venture. Some of the staff, and especially the younger research workers, are now highly valuable resources. They are the first generation of what I hope will become an important branch of the social sciences with its great potential utility for government, administration and constructive social criticism. We have now established a "Social Evaluation Unit" in the Department of Social and Administrative Studies at Oxford which is concerned with the study of action–research methods and their application to various fields of public policy.

Our thanks are due to all those teachers, administrators, parents and their children whose participation made our work both possible and enjoyable. For my own part I want to record that the result which appears below owes much more to the labour of my colleagues than to me. The field work was enjoyable and enjoyed but it was nonetheless arduous: but despite the solemn warning of American experience we never lost a single member of the team before the study was completed.

---

[1]Dr. Little has since left the I.L.E.A. to join the Community Relations Commission.

Finally we are grateful to the D.E.S. for arranging publication for us through the Stationery Office. The opinions expressed in this and subsequent volumes are, of course, ours and in no way represent policies or commitments of Her Majesty's Government.

A. H. HALSEY
Oxford
15.5.72

Part One

The E.P.A. Problem

CHAPTER 1

Political Ends and Educational Means

To find a strategy for educational roads to equality! That has been a central theme of educational discussion from the beginning of the twentieth century. It has produced a prolific sociology of education over the last generation in which the centrality of educational systems to the structure and the functioning of industrial societies has become a commonplace. In the nineteen fifties education in these societies was seen as having a crucial role for economic growth and change. More recently the emphasis has shifted to the part played by formal educational organisations in defining what is and what is not knowledge, and as selective agencies allocating individuals to social positions, moulding their social personalities and their definitions of the world around them. But the underlying question is whether, and if so under what circumstances, education can change society.

The answer, whatever its form, has been controversial in two apparently different ways. Debate has turned on the *desirability* of using educational means for political ends. But also, and much more fruitfully, it has turned on the feasibility of different educational means towards agreed ends. Thus "keeping education out of politics" can be a crude evasion of the incontrovertible fact that, in a modern or a modernising society, educational arrangements are an important determinant of the life and livelihood of individuals: education is a social distributor of life chances. In its more subtle forms, however, this political or moral stance may be a protest against narrow definitions of the social consequences of educational reform. As such it belongs neither to the political right nor to the political left. It is of course associated with such writers as T. S. Eliot,[1] Professor Bantock[2] and the authors of the Black Papers,[3] but there are equally important radical criticisms of narrowness in the sociological imagination; for example reform in the direction of meritocracy may fail to take account of those ramified consequences which Professor Bernstein has referred to as "the individualisation of failure" and there is a good deal of current writing from an interactionist or phenomenological point of view which insists on the importance of education as structuring reality for those exposed to it in broader terms than that associated with a definition of schooling as the agency through which individuals are allocated to the labour force.

The problem of the entanglement of analysis with value assumptions is intrinsic to sociological study. To get it straight we must first distinguish the "scientific" from the "value" problem: to ask separately what is possible and thereby, with the issues and alternatives sharply defined, to decide on

---

[1] See *Notes Towards a Definition of Culture*.
[2] G. H. Bantock, *Education and Values*, Faber, 1965, especially Chapter 7.
[3] C. B. Cox and A. E. Dyson (eds), *Fight for Education*, and T. E. B. Howarth, *Culture, Anarchy and the Public Schools*, Critical Quarterly Society, 1969.

preferences and priorities. In this way the challenge to social science becomes clear and the task for the sociologist is, literally, to inform the political debate. Of course the distinction between sociology and politics is much less easy than a naive positivism would presuppose. It is necessary at every step to try to make explicit what are the implicit assumptions of political aims and the value premises of sociological analysis. There is no final or ready-made procedure for either of these tasks. We have only imperfect aids beyond the injunction to constant vigilance.

One aid of particular relevance to our problem in this book can be taken from John Goldthorpe's discussion of futurology.[1] Goldthorpe distinguishes between futurology as *prediction* and futurology as *design*. Conventional futurology is essentially extrapolation to the future of trends from the recent past. It therefore tends to carry with it the value assumptions of the status quo and is in that sense conservative. That is why the book covers of this literature (*U.S.A.*2000) are, as Raymond Aron has remarked, so much more exciting than the pages. The future is only the present, usually writ slightly larger. Futurology as *design* is quite another matter, and not only because it is inherently more radical in its political possibilities. It is scientifically much more challenging in that it directly requires the social scientist to state clearly what he knows or does not know about the possibility of moving from the present state to a postulated, presumably desired, future state.

Political aims and programmes in general and the aim of educational equality in particular, together with the various programmes for its attainment, lend themselves fairly readily to translation into futurology as design. The translation can be used to define the critical and constructive role of the social scientist, in this case with relation to the problems of educational reform through political and administrative action. And action–research, as we understand it, is an experimental or quasi-experimental version of futurology as design. Ends are stated together with means to their achievement. In this case the ends are greater social equality of educational opportunity and attainment and the means are Plowden's positive discrimination for educational priority areas. Ends and means are modified and explicated in a programme of action and the relation between them is analysed by research monitoring of the action programme.

A second and related aid to understanding the social science task is the Popperian distinction between holistic and piecemeal reform. The general arguments against holism cannot be rehearsed here. What is relevant however is not a debate over the dichotomy but over the appropriate scale of the piecemeal. It is not so much a question of whether education can change society: it is a question of the level of ambitiousness of social engineering which may be required to change an undesired state of affairs. The Plowden analysis of low educational standards in E.P.A.s points to causes outside the school in the neighbourhood structure of life and therefore calls for a widely based programme of social reform alongside positive discrimination in education. Within this framework Plowden postulates that

[1]J. Goldthorpe, 'Theories of Industrial Society: Reflections on the Recrudescence of Historicism and the Future of Futurology', *European Journal of Sociology*,Vol.XII, 1972, pp. 263–88.

"what these deprived areas need most are perfectly normal, good primary schools". There is in other words a belief here in educational cures for educational evils. Some of the early American compensatory education programmes seem to have gone much further and approached the belief that poverty can be completely abolished through educational reform. Others take an opposing and more radical view of the changes necessary to ameliorate either poverty in general or educational poverty in particular. K. Coates and R. Silburn have expressed this view in a recent comment on the Plowden ideas.

". . . the schools themselves could become, to a degree, centres of social regeneration: growth points of a new social consciousness among the poor, which might at last bring poverty under attack from its sufferers, no less than from the all-too-small battalions of liberal welfare workers and social administrators.

"Obviously many of these are sensible aims. Yet it is important at the same time to state baldly what these aims could *not* achieve. Education, in itself, will not solve the problem of poverty. The social structure that generates poverty generates its own shabby education system to serve it; and while it is useful to attack the symptom, the disease itself will continually find new manifestations if it is not understood and remedied. The solution to poverty involves, of course, the redistribution of effective social power. Self-confidence, no less than material welfare, is a crucial lack of the poor, and both can only be won by effective joint action. More contentiously, it seems to us that educational provision alone cannot solve even the problem of educational poverty, if only because in this sphere there are *no* purely educational problems."[1]

Our own view in undertaking the E.P.A. action–research was cautiously open-minded on the capacity of the educational system to reform itself, dubious about an educational approach to the abolition of poverty, but at least as optimistic as Plowden about the primary school and pre-schooling as points of entry for action–research aimed at inducing changes in the relation between school and community.

In principle action–research can approach the holistic end of the continuum. In practice it usually operates at the other extreme though often with implicit holistic expectations of the kind reflected in the early euphoria and rhetoric of the American Headstart programme. Perhaps it is mainly the confused contradiction between astronomical ends and miniscule means that underlies the asperity of such criticisms as Bernstein's "education cannot compensate for society". We have to know what is sociologically and politically possible. In part the answer to both questions turns on the willingness and power of a society to define education imperiously in relation to the other social organisations which carry educative or culturally transmitting functions, especially the family but also classes, neighbourhoods, ethnic groups and local communities. This depends again in part on economic and technical means. Obviously the feasibility of education as the dominant means to a particular social design is eased by wealth and growth, but the crucial factor here is political—the political structure and the will of political leadership.

Perhaps the importance of the economic and technical base for educational development is exaggerated. There are conspicuous variations in the level of educational development between countries of similar income and wealth

---

[1] K. Coates and R. Silburn, "Education in Poverty" in David Rubinstein and Colin Stoneman (eds), *Education for Democracy*, Penguin Education Special, 1970.

per capita. And the remarkably durable success of classical China in using her educational system to create and maintain a ruling administrative class of mandarins was, it should be remembered, the invention of a pre-industrial society. Perhaps also the serviceability of education as an agent of social selection and distribution is exaggerated until one examines the evidence: for example it was shown in the Robbins Report that two-thirds of *middle-class* children with I.Q.s of 130+ who were born in 1940/41 did not go on to a university education. Nevertheless it still remains a crucial question as to how seriously a society determines to realise the values in which the use of the educational system as a means is involved. That is the crux of the problem of educational inequality and the ultimate determinant of whether or not Plowden's positive discrimination will bring about its intended effects.

What, then, are the sought ends in the politics of education in modern Britain? The dominant slogans are combinations of efficiency and equality. Efficiency for modernity. Equality for efficiency and justice. But both the meaning of these combined ends and the means postulated as adequate to their attainment remain dubious and confused. Thus the combination of equality of educational opportunity with the goal of national efficiency has led to policies designed to create and maintain a meritocracy—a principle which by no means commands universal acceptance.

However the essential fact of twentieth century educational history is that egalitarian policies have failed. This must be the starting point for understanding the significance of our studies and to reach it we must review past principles and policies. There appears to us to have been a developing theoretical and practical debate in three stages about the way education can be used as a means towards the political and social end of equality.

In the first phase, from the beginning of the century to the end of the nineteen fifties, the definition of policy was liberal—equality of opportunity. It meant equality of access to the more advanced stages of education for all children irrespective of their sex or social origin in classes, religious and ethnic groups or regions. It therefore expressed itself in such measures as building the scholarship ladder, abolishing grammar school fees, doing away with a system of separate secondary education for the minority and elementary education for the majority and substituting a system of common schooling with secondary schools "end-on" to primary schools. In the later years of this phase it also meant expansion of higher education.

The logical end of the first phase, when equality of opportunity is combined with national efficiency, is meritocracy. In its most advanced educational expression this essentially liberal principle is to be found in the Preface to the Newsom Report written by the then Minister for Education, Sir Edward (later Lord) Boyle: "The essential point is that all children should have an equal opportunity of acquiring intelligence, and of developing their talents and abilities to the full." But the inexactitudes of psychometrics, the capriciousness of late developers, the survival of the private market in education along with the continuous renewal of non-educational avenues to higher social positions—all these factors together have prevented the emergence of an educationally based meritocracy.

The liberal notion of equality of opportunity dominated discussion at least until the nineteen fifties. But it was never unchallenged by those who wrote in the tradition of R. H. Tawney and it was effectively lampooned in

Michael Young's *Rise of the Meritocracy*. Writers like Tawney and Raymond Williams[1] always sought for an educational system which would be egalitarian in the much broader sense of providing a common culture irrespective of the more or less inescapable function of selection for different occupational destinies. There is a broad distinction of political and social aims here which, in the end, come to the most fundamental issue of the purposes of education in an urban industrial society and about which judgements are explicitly or implicitly made in any action–research programme of the type we have undertaken. One way of putting the distinction is that the liberal goal of efficient equality of opportunity is too restrictive: we have also to consider liberty and fraternity. Properly conceived the community school, an idea which we discuss in detail below, reflects the attribution of value to these other two great abstractions of the modern trilogy of political aims.

All this is to say nothing about the problem of feasibility of either narrowly or broadly conceived egalitarian aims. Tawney took it for granted that the processes of parliamentary democracy, serviced by the British type of civil administration, would be adequate as means to these ends. There is less confidence now and much more questioning as to what it might mean politically to achieve what Coates and Silburn have referred to as "the redistribution of effective social power". Questioning of this kind comes from many sources, but not least from recognition of the failures of past policies directed towards a greater equality of educational opportunity.

The essential judgement must be that the "liberal" policies failed even in their own terms. For example, when, in a large number of the richer countries during the nineteen fifties, a considerable expansion of educational facilities was envisaged, it was more or less assumed that, by making more facilities available, there would be a marked change in the social composition of student bodies and in the flow of people from the less favoured classes into the secondary schools and higher educational institutions. This has certainly not happened to the degree expected. While expansion of education was accompanied by some increase in both the absolute numbers and the proportions from poor families who reached the higher levels and the more prestigious types of education, nevertheless progress towards greater equality of educational opportunity as traditionally defined has been disappointing. It is now plain that the problem is more difficult than had been supposed and needs, in fact, to be posed in new terms.[2]

Too much has been claimed for the power of educational systems as instruments for the wholesale reform of societies which are characteristically hierarchical in their distribution of chances in life as between races, classes, the sexes and as between metropolitan/suburban and provincial/rural populations. The typical history of educational expansion in the nineteen fifties and nineteen sixties can be represented by a graph of inequality of attainment between the above-mentioned social categories which has shifted markedly upwards without changing its slope. In other words

---

[1]See, for example, Raymond Williams, *Culture and Society*, Penguin Books, 1966; *The Long Revolution*, Penguin Books, 1965.

[2]Cf. Charles Frankel's and A. H. Halsey's introduction to *Educational Policies for the 1970s*, O.E.C.D., 1971, p. 14ff.

relative chances did not alter materially despite expansion. No doubt, the higher norms of educational attainment contributed something towards raising the quality of life in urban industrial society—that, at least, is the faith of the educationist. But in terms of relative chances of income, status and welfare at birth, the impact of the educational system on the life of children remained heavily determined by their family and class origins. From the same point of view, what appears to have happened was a general adjustment of the occupational structure such that entry to it was in process of continuous upward redefinition in terms of educational quali- fications. The traditional social pattern of selection remained remarkably stable. The school is only one influence among others, and, in relation to the phenomenon of social stratification, probably a fairly minor one. Attitudes towards schooling, and actual performance in school, reflect children's general social milieu and family background, and, probably most important of all, the expectations, built in by constraining custom, of his teachers. School reform helps but the improvement of teacher/pupil ratios, the building of new schools and even the provision of a wider variety of curricula have at best a limited effect as counterweights.

Moreover there has been a tendency to treat education as the waste paper basket of social policy—a repository for dealing with social problems where solutions are uncertain or where there is disinclination to wrestle with them seriously. Such problems are prone to be dubbed "educational" and turned over to the schools to solve. But it was now increasingly plain that the schools cannot accomplish important social reforms such as the demo- cratisation of opportunity unless social reforms accompany the educational effort. And it also became more evident that the schools are hampered in achieving even their more traditional and strictly "educational" purposes when, in societies changing rapidly in their technologies and in the aspira- tions of their populations, a comparable effort to make the required change in social structures and political organisation is lacking.

In summary, it may be said that liberal policies failed basically on an inadequate theory of learning. They failed to notice that the major deter- minants of educational attainment were not schoolmasters but social situations, not curriculum but motivation, not formal access to the school but support in the family and the community.

So the second phase began with its new emphasis on a theory of non- educational determination of education. In consequence of the experience of the first phase in trying to bring about greater equality of educational opportunity, there had to be a change in the meaning assigned to the phase. Its earlier meaning was equality of access to education: in the second phase its meaning gradually became equality of achievement. In this new inter- pretation a society affords equality of educational opportunity if the proportion of people from different social, economic or ethnic categories at all levels and in all types of education are more or less the same as the proportion of these people in the population at large. In other words the goal should not be the liberal one of equality of access but equality of outcome for the median member of each identifiable non-educationally defined group, i.e. the *average* woman or negro or proletarian or rural dweller should have the same level of educational attainment as the average male, white, white-collar, suburbanite. If not there has been injustice.

This important social-cum-educational principle, with its radical implications for both social and educational policies, was graphically illustrated in the findings of the American Coleman Report[1] where educational attainments were compared as between northerners and southerners of white and non-white race. The graph below shows that schooling between ages 6 and 18 (Grades 1–12 in American schools) is associated with a divergence of the mean attainment of four categories of children who are not directly defined in educational terms.[2] The radical goal of educational equality of opportunity would, if realised, produce converging as opposed to diverging lines.

Figure 1.1   Patterns of Achievement in Verbal Skills at Various Grade Levels by Race and Region

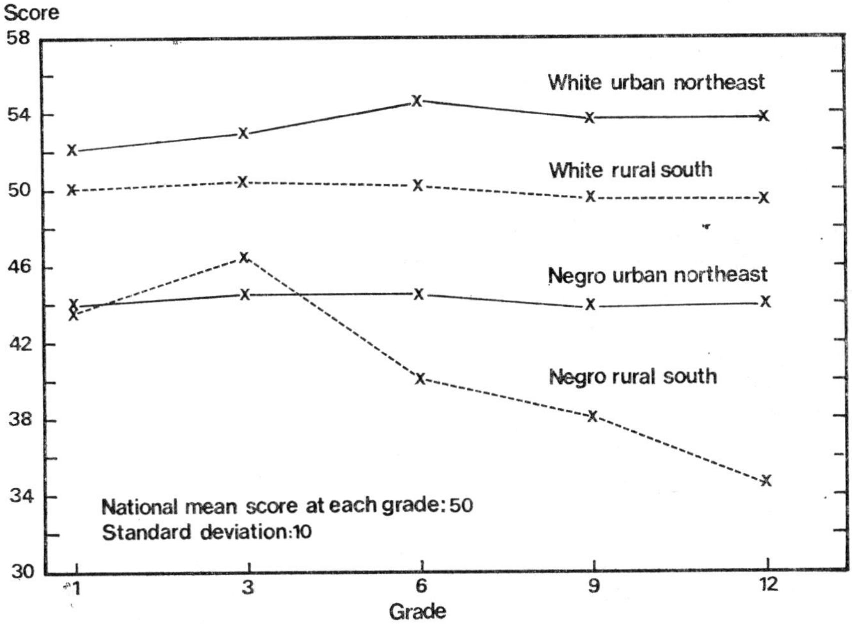

The Plowden Report belongs to this phase in the development of our understanding of the egalitarian issues in education and relates them to the social setting of the school.

With Plowden the close relationship of social deprivation, in neighbourhood and home, and educational attainment was well-founded in research. Equally valid is the corollary that, if social conditions and parental interest could be improved, achievement might be expected to rise. One or two

[1]James S. Coleman et al., Equality of Educational Opportunity, U.S. Government Printing Office, Washington D.C., 1966.

[2]We found some evidence, discussed in Chapter 5, of similar patterns in our E.P.A. schools.

examples must suffice. J. W. B. Douglas in 1964 set the attainment scores of a large sample of upper primary children against a number of social factors.[1] From this survey certain extreme cases might be extrapolated. At eleven years of age and with 50 as the average mark, lower manual working class children in unsatisfactory housing were scoring on average 46·66 as against the 56·91 of upper middle class children in satisfactory accommodation; as between the same groups divided by low and high levels of parental interest the scores were 46·32 and 59·26; polarised by "very disturbed" and "undisturbed" assessments, the two groups averaged 44·49 and 57·53; while the seventh child of the lower bracket of parents obtained 42·19 over against the 59·87 of the first child in the higher social category. Eleven per cent of the lower manual group and 54·3 per cent of the upper middle group obtained grammar school places. Only 4·8 per cent of the children in a poorly assessed lower working class school as opposed to 53·22 per cent of those in a highly assessed upper middle class school obtained places in grammar schools. Just below the cut-off point for selection, 1·4 per cent only of the "lower manual" children and as many as 42·9 per cent of "upper middle" children were in grammar, technical or independent schools.

These admittedly are deliberately extracted extremes, but the E.P.A. projects were planned to consider one of these extremes. A very disturbed child of unskilled parents, who showed no interest in his schooling and who lived in unsatisfactory accommodation was, for example, no rarity in Liverpool 7. In 1967, the Ministry of Social Security reported that 7 per cent of families were at or below the poverty line. Either figure would include a large number of the study area's population; indeed, in 1968, the Merseyside Child Poverty Action Group found that one in three in Liverpool 8 were living in poverty as defined by the Ministry of Social Security, while, in 1971, the Child Poverty Action Group claimed that one in every six children in the nation was on or below the poverty line.[2]

Professor Wiseman argued convincingly that "'home' variables have, pro rata, twice the weight of 'neighbourhood' and 'school' variables put together" when correlated with educational attainment.[3] His research indicated that it was parental attitudes rather than social levels which were more important in the home. Again, the National Child Development Study showed that parents in the highest occupational grouping were much readier to initiate school contacts than those in the lowest grouping, and there was a similar social gap in terms of adjustment to school.[4] A recent examination of truancy suggests that gross absenteeism is solidly linked with unsatisfactory home life and uninterested parents.[5]

We are not here, it must be added, embracing the view that the pre-Plowden literature had over-emphasised the part played by class in determining educational performance. On the contrary we agree with the

---

[1] J. W. B. Douglas, *The Home and the School*, MacGibbon and Kee, 1964.

[2] R. Boyson (ed), *Down with the Poor*, C.P.A.G., 1971.

[3] S. Wiseman, "The Manchester Survey", App. IX, *Plowden Report*, ii.

[4] 1st Report of the National Child Development Study (1958 Cohort), April 1966, App. X, *Plowden Report*, ii, *Research and Surveys*, 1967.

[5] M. J. Tyerman, *Truancy*, University of London Press, 1968.

sociological critique of the Plowden Report by B. Bernstein and B. Davies, in which they expressed the view that, by its concentration on child centredness, Plowden had underestimated class distinctions.[1] As these writers argue, "evidence suggests a strong relationship between social class and the extent of the mother's preparation of her child for school" and that "one would wish to guard against an argument that avoided including attitudes as a dimension of class differences".

At all events, in reading the Plowden Report, one could hardly escape the view that equality of opportunity was without equality of conditions, a sham. Home circumstances were obviously critical and these in turn were adversely affected by class and neighbourhood patterns. The school, where, after all, the children spent only five hours of the day, seemed comparatively powerless to alter matters radically of its own volition. Assuredly, a decision to consider the E.P.A. school in its communal setting was a wise one, and the Plowden Committee had been well advised to recommend that community schools should be developed in all areas but especially in E.P.A.s.

Our own definition of the problem in 1968 was consonant with the debate up to this point and was in accord with the Plowden approach accepting that positive discrimination held out the hope of further steps towards the new definition of equality of opportunity.

But in the early months of our work we began to realise that there were unsolved issues behind the equality debate even in its advanced formulation and especially when applied to the children of the educational priority areas. The debate could be taken beyond equality of educational opportunity to a third phase which involves reappraisal of the functions of education in contemporary society. Education for what? The debate over equality as we have summarised it—a movement from preoccupation with equality of access towards concern with equality of outcomes as between social groups —is essentially a discussion about education for whom and to do what. In planning our intervention in schools we were forced sooner or later to consider both questions and in doing so to question whether an E.P.A. programme is anything more than a new formula for fair competition in the educational selection race.

What assumptions could or should be made about the world into which our E.P.A. children would enter after school? Were we concerned simply to introduce a greater measure of justice into an educational system which traditionally selected the minority for higher education and upward social mobility out of the E.P.A. district, leaving the majority to be taught, mainly by a huge hidden curriculum, a sense of their own relative incompetence and impotence—a modern, humane and even relatively enjoyed form of gentling the masses? Or could we assume a wide programme of social reform which would democratise local power structures and diversify local occupational opportunities so that society would look to its schools for a supply of young people educated for political and social responsibility and linked to their communities not by failure in the competition but by rich opportunities for work and life? Even short of the assumption of extra-educational

---

[1]B. Bernstein and B. Davies, "Some Sociological Comments on Plowden", R. S. Peters. (ed), *Perspectives on Plowden*, Routledge & Kegan Paul, 1969, pp. 58–77.

reform how far should we concentrate on making recognition easier for the able minority and how far on the majority who are destined to live their lives in the E.P.A.? And if the latter did this not mean posing an alternative curriculum realistically related to the E.P.A. environment and designed to equip the rising generation with the knowledge and skills to cope with, give power over and in the end to transform the conditions of their local community?

It was, and is, commonly felt that a discriminatory boost was needed in the backward areas to bring education up to scratch so that, for instance, the thousands leaving school at fifteen who had the potential to benefit from advanced schooling might stay on. The Plowden Report argued this respectable and widely held thesis with admirable spirit. It detailed a programme of "positive discrimination" and "a new distribution of educational resources", through priority building and minor works, improved staffing and auxiliary help, supplemented salaries and so on. This was designed to cater for "a great reservoir of unrealised potential", for "what these deprived areas need most are perfectly normal good primary schools". Twice over Plowden decreed that the E.P.A. schools should be as good as the best in the land.[1]

Because the national system of education was seen not to operate efficiently in its uniform application across the country, it was accepted that a differential application would help close, to quote Plowden again, "the gap between the educational opportunities of the most and least fortunate children . . . for economic and social reasons alike." But, logically, an alternative existed. It was worth considering that what was wrong was a uniform system, and that differing areas required differing educational formats.

This viewpoint, Eric Midwinter insisted in our early conferences, does no disservice to the pioneers who campaigned for parity of opportunity. They doubtless imagined that equality of opportunity would beget conditions in which forthcoming generations would automatically start at par. This has not, unhappily, transpired. Those working in a deprived area are typically sympathetic to the egalitarian tradition and find the alarums and the postures of the anti-egalitarian commentators laughable.[2] They shout before they are hurt. One might recall the words of R. H. Tawney: of the nation's children, he wrote ". . . if, instead of rejuvenating the world, they grind corn for the Philistines and doff bobbins for the mill-owners, the responsibility is ours into whose hands the prodigality of nature pours life itself".[3] Eventually an E.P.A. community must stand on its own feet like any other and rejuvenate its world, and that is a dogma which might hold good on both political wings.

---

[1]Plowden, *op. cit.*, Ch. 5, especially paras. 136–152 and 158–173.
[2]For instance, C. B. Cox and A. E. Dyson (eds), *op. cit.*
[3]R. H. Tawney, *The Acquisitive Society*, Bell, 1921, republished 1961 (Fontana), p. 81.

CHAPTER 2

Poverty and American Compensatory Education

The failure of past policies for more equal educational opportunities in Britain was an essential background to the inauguration of our work in four educational priority areas. But so too was the transatlantic hubbub which followed President Johnson's declaration in 1964 of "unconditional war on poverty in America", followed by a plethora of legislation, government programmes and social science literature. A new generation had rediscovered poverty and educational remedies were fashionable. But there was no guarantee that either new politics or new social science or their partnership would banish poverty from unprecedentedly rich societies.

On the political side we were working within assumptions concerning the attainment of the welfare society through the welfare state which were increasingly questioned. As we saw it, the project was a pioneering venture in Britain in experimental social administration, or futurology as design, in which the partnership of ourselves as social scientists and educationalists with politicians and administrators was assumed to be viable. But we were under no illusions. We were well aware that only in the loosest sense could the projects be described as experimental. The laboratory for testing "Plowden hypotheses" was natural, not experimental. There were political as well as academic determinants of the districts which were chosen. The desired outcomes of action were not always precisely defined and in some cases resistant to precise measurement. We could not hope for complete control of relevant inputs to the local social and educational systems and so the relation between our input and the outcomes was to that extent bound to be uncertain. Nevertheless we took up the challenge—to contribute to developing a theory of poverty in its educational aspects and to test it in the very real world of the urban twilight zones.

The Theory of Poverty

What then is a viable explanation of poverty? First, poverty is not adequately conceived in the singular, either in its manifestations or its causes. We must speak of "poverties" and we must recognise multiple if related causes with the implication that a war on poverty is indeed a war and not a single battle. A panel of the Social Science Research Council recently produced a discussion of current research which identified six types of poverty:—

(a) crisis poverty;
(b) long-term dependency;
(c) life-cycle poverty;
(d) depressed area poverty;
(e) down-town poverty; and
(f) "the culture of poverty".[1]

---

[1]S.S.R.C. *Research on Poverty*, Heinemann, 1968, p. 9.

The classification put forward by the committee, and the fact that the six types are not clearly distinguishable in practice, may help us to relate the American experience of "compensatory education" to our own work in the four E.P.A.s. Three of these projects addressed themselves primarily to the fifth type, "down-town" poverty, and all assumed the validity of a description of the poor which permits effective intervention using "communities" or local administrative units as the appropriate arena of battle. On this view the problem is formulated as one where under modern urban conditions, social deprivation tends to be geographically concentrated, especially in the decaying inner ring of conurbations, in such a way as to reduce the quality of environmental service and opportunity. All local institutions, it is argued, are defective—the family, the school, the welfare agencies, the job market and the recreational organisation. Moreover the situation is seen as self-perpetuating; those most capable of doing so move out to take advantage of the opportunities provided elsewhere, be they residents moving to better jobs or better houses or be they school teachers or social workers who live in more salubrious districts and are concerned with this problematic territory only in their professional capacities. And the least capable move in, those most in need of and least able to avail themselves of education, housing, jobs and other publicly provided amenities and opportunities (e.g. immigrants and the downwardly mobile). Thus the inhabitants of the priority areas are thought of, correctly or incorrectly, as a sub-working class formed by selective migration with a distinctive set of economic, social and cultural attributes.

The theory of "down-town" poverty begins with an elaboration of this description. Its factual base is surprisingly little explored in Britain. In America the description is heavily influenced by concern with the social conditions of negro ghettoes in the northern industrial cities, and the question therefore arises of how far it is relevant to British cities, either generally or more particularly to the districts inhabited by immigrants whose origins and characteristics cannot be equated with those of American negro migrants from the south. It is significant that the label given to this kind of poverty by the S.S.R.C. panel is clearly a transatlantic importation: and though Americans have, in the past few years, begun to produce a description of their version of the sub-working class,[1] to transplant the description without careful enquiry could be disastrous for both analysis and remedy.

On the basis of a review of American social science literature, Rossi and Blum have summarised the characteristics of the poor as follows.

"1. *Labour-Force Participation.* Long periods of unemployment and/or intermittent employment. Public assistance is frequently a major source of income for extended periods.

"2. *Occupational Participation.* When employed, persons hold jobs at the lowest levels of skills, for example, domestic service, unskilled labour, menial service jobs, and farm labour.

---

[1]See the essays by P. H. Rossi and Z. D. Blum, Oscar Lewis, H. J. Gans, L. Rainwater and W. Miller in D. Moynihan (ed), *On Understanding Poverty*, Basic Books, 1969. See also H. Gans, 'Urban Poverty and Social Planning' in Lazarsfeld *et al.*, *The Uses of Sociology*, Free Press, 1967, pp. 437–476.

"3. *Family and Interpersonal Relations.* High rates of marital instability (desertion, divorce, separation), high incidence of households headed by females, high rates of illegitimacy; unstable and superficial interpersonal relationships characterised by considerable suspicion of persons outside the immediate household.

"4. *Community Characteristics.* Residential areas with very poorly developed voluntary associations and low levels of participation in such local voluntary associations as exist.

"5. *Relationship to Larger Society.* Little interest in, or knowledge of, the larger society and its events; some degree of alienation from the larger society.

"6. *Value Orientations.* A sense of helplessness and low sense of personal efficiency; dogmatism and authoritarianism in political ideology; fundamentalist religious views, with some strong inclinations towards belief in magical practices. Low "need achievement" and low levels of aspirations for the self."[1]

As a general description of the poor in any advanced industrial society this summary would command the assent of most social scientists. However the description of down-town poverty which developed during the nineteen sixties in relation to the American poverty programme is more dubious. It is well expressed by H. Gans, who distinguishes between a working class and a lower class. "The former is distinguished by relatively stable semi-skilled or skilled blue-collar employment and a way of life that centres on the family circle, or extended family. The lower class is characterised by temporary, unstable employment in unskilled—and the most menial— blue-collar jobs and by a way of life equally marked by instability. Largely as a result of a man's instability, the lower class family is often matrifocal or female-based. This is most marked among the negro population, in which the woman has been the dominant figure since the days of slavery, but it can also be found in other groups suffering from male occupational instability. Although this type of family organisation has some stable and positive features, especially for its female members, the hypothesis has been suggested that it raises boys who lack the self-image, the aspiration, and the motivational structure that would help them to develop the skills necessary to function in the modern job market. Also it may prevent boys from participating in a "normal" family relationship in adulthood, thus perpetuating the pattern for another generation. These conditions are, of course, exacerbated by racial and class discrimination, low income, slum and overcrowded housing conditions, as well as illness and other deprivations which bring about frequent crises."[2]

The matrifocal family is also described in English studies, for example Madeline Kerr's *Ship Street* in Liverpool, but the essential point here is the juxtaposition of uncertain occupational opportunities with an unstable family structure. In this connection S. M. Miller has drawn the contrast between W. F. Whyte's *Street Corner Society* which described men in

[1]Z. D. Blum and Peter Rossi, "Social Class Research and Images of the Poor: A Bibliographical Review" in D. Moynihan (ed), *op. cit.*, pp. 351–2.

[2]H. Gans, *loc. cit.*, (1967).

an Italian slum in Boston in the late nineteen thirties and Elliott Liebow's *Tally's Corner* (1967) which offers a vivid portrait of a Washington negro ghetto in a blighted section of the inner city in the early nineteen sixties. "Whyte's men were unemployed casualties of the Depression, and members of strongly-knit families. Most of them went on later to employment. On Tally's Corner the men have much less favourable relationships with each other and with their families; their hopes for a different and better future are constantly frustrated. The shift in these two books from the emerging Italian temporarily blocked by an economic depression to the thwarted negro of the affluent society captures the change in the social issues facing American society."[1]

The theory is then, that of a vicious cycle of lack of opportunity and lack of aspiration, so that the "pathologies" of rejection of the world and the search for gratification in alcohol and drugs, the apathy, drifting and dependence on public aid, are to be seen as adaptations to a life of exclusion from the main stream of society.

It is an open question as to how far British city slums resemble either those of Boston in the nineteen thirties or Washington D.C. in the nineteen sixties, though the signs that coloured immigrants are developing into a "thwarted social stratum" are clear enough in E. J. B. Rose's *Colour and Citizenship*. But whether or not the theory can be properly applied to the British scene, it corresponds in many respects to the S.S.R.C.'s sixth type —the "culture of poverty"—and as such has been the subject of a developing debate in America during the nineteen sixties. All agree that the poor are different. But the explanation of these differences by those who insist on a situational rather than a cultural theory have profoundly different implications for the strategies of action against poverty.

The culture of poverty[2] insists in its simplest form that the poor are different not primarily because of low income but because they have been habituated to poverty and have developed a sub-culture of values adapted to these conditions which they then pass on to their children. It was this definition of the problem which dominated the war on poverty in America and the Economic Opportunity Act of 1964—providing a convenient rationalisation for the emphasis on community action and social work rather than on employment policies and the redistribution of income.[3] Recent contributors however have returned in one form or another to a situational approach. Thus O. D. Duncan asserts that "if there were any chance that the slogan-makers and the policy-builders would heed the implications of social research, the first lesson for them to learn would be that *poverty is not a trait but a condition*."[4]

---

[1]S. M. Miller, "Invisible Men", *Psychiatric and Social Science Review*, Vol. II, No. 5, May 1968, p. 14.

[2]See Oscar Lewis, "The Culture of Poverty" in Moynihan (1969), pp. 187–200.

[3]Thus in presenting the case for the Economic Opportunity Act to Congress in 1964, Sargent Shriver argued that "being poor . . . is a rigid way of life. It is handed down from generation to generation in a cycle of inadequate education, inadequate homes, inadequate jobs and stunted ambitions. It is a peculiar axiom of poverty that the poor are poor because they earn little, and they also earn little because they are poor."

[4]Otis Dudley Duncan, "Inheritance of Poverty or Inheritance of Race" in D. Moynihan (ed), *On Understanding Poverty*, p. 88.

Out of this debate so far we must conclude that the "poverties" to which urban industrial populations are prone must be understood to have their origins in both situational and cultural characteristics of those minorities which suffer disadvantage and discrimination and to have their cures in both economic and cultural reform, not only at the local or community level but also in the total structure of society.

Application of the Theory

In social action–research theory is applied in a political context. Within the framework of the theoretical discussion of poverty there are large political implications according to whether the emphasis is put on changing the structure of opportunities or raising levels of motivation. Clearly our E.P.A. programme was so conceived—in being confined to small geographical areas and endowed with very limited resources—that it had to focus mainly on the second alternative. A possible assumption of the E.P.A. programme is that the most effective point at which to break into the vicious poverty circle is in early childhood, in the primary school or in the pre-school period: and this approach tends to lead to considerable emphasis on work with families, thus raising fundamental questions about the right of the state, through its agencies, to intervene in the relation between parents and children.

But quite apart from this fundamental issue there are three partial interpretations of the general theory which may be distinguished and which have political consequences. On a first view, the cause of poverty is "cultural deprivation" in the sense of inadequate social parenthood, and the cure consists of improved socialisation with the implication that the main thrust must be towards family casework. In the E.P.A. context this means that the sub-working class family is held to be the major villain of the piece, failing to provide the early training in literacy, numeracy, and acceptance of work and achievement habits which constitute the normal upbringing of the middle class child and which prepare the child to take advantage of the opportunities provided in school. An example and an elaboration of this point of view, directed towards the more pathological aspects of "cultural deprivation", would be Sir Alec Clegg and Barbara Megson's *Children in Distress* with its description of neglectful, cruel and workshy parents.

The second interpretation focuses on the other socialising institution—the school. It is the theory that the cause of poverty is educational deprivation. The blame is transferred here to the school teacher who fails to provide adequate educational stimulus to the sub-working class child. Although they both concentrate on the socialisation process these two interpretations of the theory are often opposed in practice, at least in their emphases.

For our own part we have linked these two interpretations, emphasising both pre-schooling and the development of the so-called community school. Pre-schooling is a possible means of arousing community support for improved education: to reverse the process whereby the deprived child is one who has been prepared not for learning but for failure. Here is one of Clegg's infant school head-teachers:

"We have children starting school for whom the words 1, 2, 3, 4, 5 represent a new language, children who are so unawakened to the world around them that the meaning of the colour words, red, blue, etc., is not known. Of the 19 children admitted in September this year there are eight who could not fit red to a red jersey or blue to a blue bead. Looking at a book, having someone read a story from it, or talk to them about it, is a new experience, as is the handling of a pencil or crayon. For some, communication by speech is an art to be acquired in school, toilet training has not been established, and the handling of cutlery needs to be taught. . . ."

Playgroups, nursery classes and nursery schools can directly repair these deficiencies; and the effect can multiply. If there is forbearance from the professional teachers and charity from their trade unions, then parents can learn to teach and the primary schools can begin their own task without a crippling handicap of ineducability among their five-year-olds.

A force possibly more significant is the community school. It is typical that contacts in slum schools between parents and their children's teachers are either non-existent or farcical. At worst the teacher drives through enemy-occupied territory at 9 a.m. to withstand siege until the 4 p.m. withdrawal. At best the occasional "open evening" attracts the respectable and aspiring mother, sometimes accompanied by an embarrassed father, to a ritual and uncomprehending inspection of the pupils' exhibits while they queue for an inhibited account of their child's progress from the class teacher. Odd exceptions here and there suggest that it is possible to over-come this travesty of partnership between parent and teacher. The Plowden Committee found one school in its national survey where "there is after-school activity on almost every evening during the year when groups of children meet voluntarily for pottery, drama, recorder playing, gardening . . . football, athletics, jumping and agility work. Parents are welcome."[1] *Genuine* participation could provide the multiplier here. The traditional isolation of school from community reflects the uneasy relation between, on the one hand, the legally protected autonomy of the family and, on the other, the political state committed to the provision of individual oppor-tunity through selective education. Within the traditionally isolated school, chances could be given to the exceptionally able or highly motivated individual, but all too often by subversion of the family (a process as rarely successful as it is inefficient).

The community school holds out the promise of peace and co-operation between teacher and parent. The first dove must be flown by the teacher, ideally one who is appropriately trained. The development of courses designed for teachers intending to go to E.P.A. schools and their link to community oriented curriculum change was an innovation we were keen to test. But the teacher cannot reconstruct the community unaided. If he is successful at all, the needs of the neighbourhood for health, housing, employment and other services will be found to impinge directly on his teaching tasks. The implication is clear: educational priorities must in the end be integrated into community development. The E.P.A. school is impotent except in the context of a comprehensive organisation of social services in the community.

---

[1] Plowden, para. 122.

The third interpretation of the theory of poverty, however, puts the emphasis on the opportunity structure of society and in this sense is opposed to both of the first two interpretations. On this view, high achievement orientation and performance on the part of the sub-working class child would be irrational until the structure of opportunities for jobs, and indeed all the other elements of citizenship in the affluent society, are provided equally for all, independently of their social, familial and racial origins. There was very little that could be done directly in order to apply this side of the theory within the framework of an E.P.A. action programme. All that can be said is that no amount of success with work on either the cultural poverty of the home or the educational poverty of the school will result in anything but frustration if socialisation cannot be translated into opportunity at the end.

All these three interpretations are explanations of poor school performance. A parallel can, however, be drawn with independence or dependence on the social services. The view may be taken first, that cultural deprivation leads to both dependence on and incapacity to use the social services intelligently. For example, failure to take up the statutory entitlements may be regarded as a failure on the part of the individuals concerned. A second view, equivalent to the educational deprivation view, regards these services as inadequate for the needs of slum dwellers, for example, the gap between need and supply is interpreted as a failure of comprehension and communication on the part of the welfare bureaucracies. Another example would be that housing services are too narrowly defined, concerning themselves with the letting of council tenancies and not with the search for accommodation, mortgages, etc. in the private as well as the public market. Then the third and radical interpretation would suggest that social services are no more than a palliative while the structure of opportunity, especially opportunities for employment, and discrimination against coloured immigrants, continue. This third point of view may be taken to the point of seeing the whole apparatus of E.P.A. as a diversion from the pursuit of genuine egalitarian policy into the obscurities of unnecessary research.

We were prepared to take this risk. But we by no means accepted the idea that either the inner rings of the conurbations or all of the designated E.P.A.s were wholly inhabited by a sub-working class approximating to American descriptions of the poor. This reservation is amply borne out by the description of the four areas and their schools which follows in Chapter 5. We expected to find, and found, the recognisable descendants of Hoggart's Hunslet[1] as well as the hopelessly downtrodden, the shiftless and the abandoned. Moreover one of our districts, and the one most community-like, was in the mining towns and villages of South Yorkshire, far removed from the inner ring of a conurbation.

American Compensatory Education

That "compensatory education" in the United States has failed is a well-established belief in this country: indeed for some people it is almost the only thing known about American compensatory programmes. Many

[1]Richard Hoggart, *The Uses of Literacy*, Chatto and Windus, 1957.

refer to the failure of compensatory education without having grasped the complex variety of educational developments and innovations loosely grouped under this heading.

When we were exploring the American experience in 1968–69, morale among those connected with the American poverty programmes had probably reached its nadir. Moynihan's *Maximum Feasible Misunderstanding*[1] gives a clear account of the politics of disillusionment felt by those who had been involved in the early, optimistic stages of the war on poverty. And at the same time the massive Westinghouse Report on the national pre-school programme Head Start[2] completed a series of negative findings on the long-run effects of pre-school programmes. The Report showed that the project did not make any substantial long-term impact on children's intellectual and social development. And evaluation of other programmes, both national and local, had not produced much clear-cut evidence of success. A study of a thousand selected projects[3] identified only 21 studies where there was clear evidence of success—and many of these were small-scale research projects affecting only a few children.

It was this series of negative findings that stimulated Jensen[4] to reopen the debate on the relative importance of genetic and environmental factors in intelligence and to question a basic assumption of compensatory educational programmes—that the differences between social and ethnic groups on measures of educational attainment were primarily caused by environmental factors and could be influenced by educational programmes.

Meanwhile social and educational programmes connected with the war on poverty had their funds reduced as the war in Vietnam expanded. Race relations in many of the northern cities had worsened sharply, and race riots were common. Schools had become centres of conflict. The pressure was for increasingly radical solutions to the problems of poor educational attainment by deprived children—for free schools run by the community,[5] for community control of state schools and for decentralisation and desegregation. Demand for these changes led in turn to increased conflict between parents, community groups, teachers and administrators, resulting in teachers' strikes, school lockouts and boycotts.

Thus, in the years 1965–69, there had been a rapid shift from high optimism to profound pessimism. It is these extreme positions that have most successfully penetrated into this country and there is probably far less knowledge of what actually took place, or its detailed results.

---

[1]D. P. Moynihan, *Maximum Feasible Misunderstanding: Community Action in the War on Poverty*, Arkville Press, New York, 1969.

[2]V. G. Cicirelli *et al.*, "The impact of Head Start on children's cognitive and affective development", Westinghouse Learning Corporation, Washington D.C., O.E.O., 12th June 1969, mimeo (The Westinghouse Report).

[3]D. G. Hawkridge *et al.*, *A Study of Selected Exemplary Programs for the Education of Disadvantaged Children*, U.S. Department of Health, Education and Welfare, September 1968 (2 vols.).

[4]A. R. Jensen, "How much can we boost I.Q. and scholastic achievement?", *Harvard Educational Review*, 1969.

[5]See for example George Dennison, *The Lives of Children*, Penguin Education Special, 1972.

The difficulties of making any overall assessment of compensatory education in the United States are formidable. Certainly the early optimistic expectations have not been realised. And there are many who would share Professor Bernstein's distaste for the notion of compensation on the grounds that it is difficult "to talk about offering compensatory education to children who in the first place have not, as yet, been offered an adequate educational environment"[1] as well as the argument that the phrase tends to direct attention away from the internal organisation and the educational context of the school and to focus attention on the shortcomings of families which is a partial interpretation of the general explanation of poverty that we have outlined above.[2] Moreover where rigorous evaluation has been conducted, results have often been disappointing, or where significant, have not been maintained for any length of time. As Light and Smith note, "our ability to detect failure has outrun our power to instil success".[3] They attribute part of the problem to the "make or break" method of the traditional evaluation approach, and suggest the need for "improved development and evaluation strategies". Others would lay most of the blame on the design of the action programmes, for inadequately using research evidence, or working within a limited frame of reference that neglects the child's wider experience outside school. And others would criticise the overall level of resources and the short time span within which measurable return was expected. More fundamentally, it may be argued that the educational system alone has little independent effect as an agent of social change, and that improvements, however radical, in educational facilities could never achieve the kind of objectives that were set; for even if these objectives were apparently "educational" themselves, for example, an increase in pupil performance, the influence of the other social factors far outweighed the influence that schools could wield. In the face of such basic criticisms, it may well be asked whether the whole compensatory education movement has not in fact been a series of "paper programmes" founded on inadequate assumptions and poorly articulated theory.

Some programmes have set themselves unrealistic objectives. This problem is particularly marked where vague non-educational goals are put forward—for example "breaking the poverty cycle"; and in general, the more extensive and varied the programme, the more likely it is to have such objectives. Thus "umbrella" programmes such as Head Start or Title I of the Elementary and Secondary Education Act of 1965 almost inevitably become associated with broad objectives as a way of including the varied components of such programmes. The relationship between these objectives and the educational changes promoted by the programmes was never spelt out, and, as in the case of the "poverty cycle", the theories on which such relationships were based were often very inadequate. Yet it would be wrong to dismiss compensatory education as a series of "paper programmes" because of weaknesses at this level of theory. Clear knowledge about such

---

[1] Basil Bernstein, "A Critique of the Concept of Compensatory Education" in David Rubinstein and Colin Stoneman, *op. cit.*, p. 111.

[2] Supra, pp. 13–17.

[3] R. J. Light and P. V. Smith, "Choosing a future: strategies for designing and evaluating new programs", *Harvard Educational Review*, 1970, 40(1), 1–28.

relationships is inadequate on any analysis, and it is perhaps only by experiment and research in this way with educational change that better theory will be developed.

At a lower level, there is no doubt that several compensatory programmes have demonstrated that the findings of social research can be used to produce more effective educational experiences for disadvantaged children. Though no single panacea has been discovered and it seems unlikely that any will, a number of promising innovations have been developed and tested. If several of these were tried out on an extensive scale, it is possible that educational performance would improve, and that the educational system would become more responsive to changing social needs.

In summarising the American experience of compensatory education, it is important not to underestimate the social changes which accompanied its development. These were primarily changing patterns of urbanisation as negroes moved in to central urban areas, and whites moved to the suburbs. Between 1950 and 1960 the city centres of the 24 largest metropolitan areas lost nearly $1\frac{1}{2}$ million whites to their suburbs, and gained more than 2 million negroes. These rapid movements were reflected in changing school populations in the inner cities. One consequence was that the differences in school performance between black and white pupils were underlined as teachers were faced with changing school populations. Lower school performance, however, was only one aspect of a series of social and economic inequalities experienced by the black population, by other ethnic minorities and by low-status whites, many of whom also came from depressed rural areas.

Though educational performance was only one aspect of such disparities, it appeared to be one where improvement could be achieved, with some hope that better job opportunities would result and thus a general reduction in inequality. Educational theory, too, was beginning to indicate ways in which basic changes in ability might be achieved, if the right kinds of educational environment could be created. The child's early years were isolated as those in which such changes were most likely to occur. The work of Hunt[1] and Bloom[2] was particularly influential in this respect. Other educational research was documenting, with increasing precision, the ways in which the child's experience outside the school, particularly in the home, affected his development in school. This suggested that the school could somehow "compensate" for inadequate external experiences, or could influence the home in such a way as to bring about change for the better.

The Coleman Report[3] added extensive information about the disparities in educational performance between black and white children and the factors that were most highly correlated with school performance, indicating that the effects of home background and the characteristics of fellow pupils were far more marked than variations in school or teacher quality. These findings underlined the three general strategies of action that could be taken to improve educational outcomes: improvements within the school, increased educational influence in the home, or changes in the background

---

[1] J. McV. Hunt, *Intelligence and Experience*, Ronald Press, New York, 1961.
[2] B. S. Bloom, *Stability and Change in Human Characteristics*, Wiley, New York, 1964.
[3] J. S. Coleman *et al.*, *op. cit.*

of fellow pupils that could be achieved by altering pupil composition to include a more socially and ethnically heterogeneous group. Also, as we have noted in Chapter 1, the Coleman Report gave impetus to the conception of equality of educational opportunity as equality of outcome rather than equal chances of access to educational facilities—and this implied policies of positive discrimination as well as desegregation.

The terms that came to be adopted to describe such programmes, "compensatory education" and "the disadvantaged", are essentially vague in reference. Neither clearly indicates an underlying theory, though several critics have restricted the term "compensatory education" to strategies which confine change to the school curriculum. Such terms, though helpful in focusing attention on the problem and eliciting funds, have added confusion. Thus the use of the term "disadvantaged" has tended to give a spurious unity to a group distinguished on broad social and economic criteria: it has concealed the diversity between groups, and, more importantly, the diversities of individuals within any group so classified.

Compensatory educational programmes in one way embody a continuing debate about educational change, with particular reference to social groups which have benefited least from previous educational development. Each new project has therefore tended to mark a point in the debate at which new assumptions were introduced or new theories came into fashion. It is difficult to offer a clear but brief chronology of a debate so confused and conflicting. As Deutsch[1] notes, no orthodoxy of compensatory education has yet emerged. The sudden increase in resources available for special programmes positively encouraged experiment and diversity. A strong motive for many participants was a desire to "get into the action" and demonstrate that they had solutions and innovations to offer. The risk, and indeed the reality, was of a mass of small independent schemes which impeded the necessary replication and extension of successful programmes.

However, for purposes of exposition, the American projects can be grouped into three broad strategies of change. First there were changes within the school, particularly the development of new curricula, and the extension of formal schooling to younger age groups. Second there were changes in the relationship between schools and their social setting, for example improved home-school links; and third, as a special case of the second type, there was the strategy of integrating schools racially or socially when the communities themselves were not integrated. Each of these strategies has its own pattern of development as the initial belief that the problem would be quickly solved by goodwill, better communication and a small increase in resources, has had to be abandoned in favour of more complex and radical solutions.

Though pre-school education has not turned out to be as effective as many hoped, there are consistent indications that certain types of programme can produce gains in cognitive abilities. The more intensively the programme is geared to such intellectual development as language skills, the more substantial the gains that have been achieved. The work of Bereiter

---

[1] M. P. Deutsch, Preface to J. Hellmuth (ed), *The Disadvantaged Child*, Brunner-Mazel, Boston, 1967.

and Engelmann[1] is among the best known in this field, but several other research studies have shown considerable gains in children's ability at the end of the programme, for example, the Early Training Project in Nashville[2], the work of Deutsch and his associates at the Institute for Developmental Studies in New York, the various pre-school projects run at Ypsilanti, Michigan by Weikart and his colleagues, the individual tutorial scheme carried out by Marion Blank in New York[3], and many others.

In general, traditional pre-school methods have not compared favourably with more structured programmes of intervention, though the findings of Weikart,[4] who compared three different pre-school approaches, the traditional and two structured methods, suggest that where planning time, resources, and teacher motivation are equal, very similar results can be achieved with different types of programme. The overall results of large scale pre-school programmes such as Head Start have proved to be disappointing, in comparison to those of smaller experimental projects. These differences must in part reflect the problem of mounting a large-scale programme and the uneven quality of people and approaches to be found in Head Start centres. In its first summer of operation, more than 560,000 pre-school children were enrolled for an eight-week summer programme; and by 1967, about 215,000 children were enrolled in more than 13,000 different centres for a full year programme.

Follow-up studies of children who have attended pre-schools have also produced disappointing findings; in general gains are not maintained significantly for any length of time. These findings have indicated the need to look closely at whether pre-school work has made a real impact on development, and suggested that programmes will have to be maintained into the elementary grades if the negative effects of later schooling are to be counteracted. The child who moves from a well staffed reception pre-school atmosphere to a conventional school class with a high pupil-teacher ratio may be more at a disadvantage than one who has not been to pre-school. Equally these findings indicated the need for even earlier intervention— home visiting for very young children, and, as a logical extension, "parent training" programmes for teenagers.

At school level, programmes have in general not been able to achieve the type of gains in performance seen in the small pre-school projects. One reason may be that changes at this level often have been too piecemeal. No overall change in curriculum and method has been made. However the strategy of the "Follow-Through" programme, the extension of Head Start to the elementary grades, is geared to bring about this overall change by providing curricula along the lines of the experimental pre-school projects. But at this level too there have been spectacular failures, with projects such

[1]C. Bereiter and S. Engelmann, *Teaching Disadvantaged Children in the Pre-school*, Prentice Hall, N.J., 1966.
[2]S. W. Gray and R. A. Klaus, "An experimental pre-school program for culturally deprived children", *Child Development*, 1965, 36, 887–898.
[3]M. Blank and F. Solomon, "A tutorial language program to develop abstract thinking in socially disadvantaged pre-school children", *Child Development*, 1968, 39(2), 379–389.
[4]D. P. Weikart, "A comparative study of three pre-school curricula", Ypsilanti Public Schools, Michigan, 1970, mimeo.

as the "More Effective School" programme in New York which sought to increase substantially the school's resources by virtually doubling the numbers of teachers. The evaluation[1] of this project indicated that despite changes in teaching ratios, teachers were using the old methods only with smaller classes. As the researchers pointed out, what may have been a dramatic change for the adults involved may have made little impact on the children in the school. However, at higher levels, programmes which have provided college entrance courses have at times been successful in achieving substantial advances in academic skills. Thus the College Board programme in New York was able to demonstrate that the students had made considerable gains in a short space of time.

Many programmes have avoided involvement with the existing teaching force in schools by working outside schools or by appointing new staff specifically for the project. However, such programmes have uncovered a number of ways in which the teaching staff can be supplemented and reinforced. The use of aides or sub-professionals, often from depressed areas themselves, is common both at pre-school and school level. Students in training have also been involved in several projects. An alternative method of increasing the "teaching force" and one that begins to undermine the traditional distinction between "teacher" and "pupil" is to use one student to teach others. This can either take the form of older children working with younger groups—for example teenage girls in pre-school—or genuine "peer teaching" within the same class or age-group. Plans for a "tutorial community project"[2] outline a school organisation in Los Angeles built on this concept of older pupil and peer teaching, using a wide variety of different teaching techniques involving different age-groups in the teaching and learning relationship.

The second broad strategy is to change the relationship between the school and its social setting. Here there is evidence that carefully worked out programmes of parental involvement, as for example in the Nashville pre-school project[3] and the Bloomingdale family programme[4] can produce measurable change in parental behaviour and attitudes towards education, and even produce I.Q. gains among the parents as well. The development of home visiting schemes, initially as an adjunct to pre-school work, for example in Nashville and Ypsilanti, but later as an alternative strategy, has also produced successful results. The "diffusion effect" noted in the Nashville "Early Training Project", whereby younger siblings of the children in the project and other children in the community appeared to progress more rapidly, may well indicate an effect of home visiting. Where the mother is closely involved in the teaching programme, it is possible that the long-term impact can be maintained by periodic visits. This suggests an

---

[1]D. J. Fox, 'Expansion of the More Effective School Program", Center for Urban Education, September, 1967, mimeo.

[2]R. J. Melaragno and G. Newmark *et al.*, "Tutorial community project: Progress Report 1968", Systems Development Corporation, Santa Monica, California, 1968, mimeo.

[3]S. W. Gray and R. A. Klaus, *op. cit.*

[4]A. B. Auerbach, "Parent development through active involvement with their children in an integrated pre-school education and family recreation program", paper presented to the American Orthopsychiatric Association, 21st March 1968.

alternative strategy to concentrating resources in the formal educational system, and deploying them instead to make a direct impact on the child's educational experience in the home. Many argue that such programmes may well be more effective than those based within the school system. Successful programmes are reported by Gordon in Florida,[1] Weikart and Lambie in Ypsilanti,[2] and Shaefer[3] in the Infant Education Project in Washington D.C.. Generally these home visiting programmes have concentrated on younger children, either from birth or in the infancy period from 18 to 36 months.

Another way to increase educational influences within the home is to change school organisation and control in such a way that it is more open to the influence of the community. As the school becomes more involved in the community through the development of community study and programmes of parental involvement, further changes may occur. Thus several projects, notably the Head Start group in Mississippi, have argued that schools must be concerned with general community progress, rather than education alone. The idea of the community school as an agency concerned with general community welfare and development is closely related to this approach. Community oriented curricula for such schools have emphasised the need to inform students as to how change in their community can be achieved. "A Book about New York City and How to Change It" is the title page of one such community textbook.

More radically, such links with the community are taken to imply that formal control over the school should be vested in the community rather than in a central authority. This is the method of "community control" or "decentralisation". The results of such changes in control are not, so far, clear. Schools involved have become centres of conflicting groups of parents, teachers and administrators. In the past, schools have been insulated from strong social and political pressures; the traditional expectation of an orderly ₁learning environment held by both teachers and parents does not respond well to the unpredictable and sudden changes that many "community schools" or "community controlled" schools have experienced. Such changes in the organisation and control of schools are more closely concerned with wider issues of political power than with programmes to improve the outcomes of schooling for disadvantaged groups. Many, however, argue that until such groups are given more control over institutions which shape the lives of citizens, programmes of educational reform will continue to be ineffective.

Schemes to integrate schools or school systems entail a very different conception of the relationship between school and community; here "community" represents a much wider cross section of society than that normally found in the catchment area of a single school. To achieve this balanced group within schools, children have to be bussed to other areas,

---

[1] I. J. Gordon, "A parent education approach to provision of early stimulation for the culturally disadvantaged", Final Report to the Fund for the Advancement of Education of the Ford Foundation, 30th November 1967, mimeo.

[2] D. P. Weikart and D. Z. Lambie, "Pre-school intervention through a home teaching project", Paper presented at the American Education Research Association convention, 1968, mimeo.

[3] D. G. Hawkridge et al., op. cit.

catchments re-zoned, massive new schools or educational parks have to be built. The belief that the performance of deprived children will improve once they join an integrated school has been a powerful factor in developing such programmes. In fact, the evidence of research studies on this issue is not clear cut, and where pupil performance has increased it may be that the new schools to which they are bussed are of generally higher quality. Many integration programmes have only been able to move a token number of pupils, and there are few schemes as comprehensive as that of Berkeley, California, which planned to integrate all its elementary schools. Other areas have planned more comprehensive schemes, involving "educational park" complexes, which are large enough to draw from integrated catchment areas, though the more residential segregation there is, the larger such institutions have to be.

The building of new institutions has been another response to the problems of getting schools to adopt innovations: "model" or "demonstration" schools are a way of showing the feasibility and effectiveness of new ideas, at a relatively local level. Such development can apply equally to curriculum innovation and to more general changes in school organisation and control. Thus the "free" schools demonstrate that members of minority groups can run schools effectively; while another type of "model school" emphasised the working of new curriculum approaches or organisational methods.

Examples of free schools are to be found in many large city centres: model or demonstration schools have also been tried in a number of areas—for example the "World of Inquiry" school in Rochester which aims to take a cross-section of the city population and makes extensive use of activity methods and flexible organisation. Another much publicised example is the Parkway project in Philadelphia, a school without a building for those who have left school, which uses the resources of central Philadelphia, libraries, museums, research institutes, commercial and industrial firms to provide courses for students. Another method is the "model district", for example the Cardozo district of Washington D.C., where a small team works with a number of schools, introducing teachers to new methods and providing the necessary materials, workshop sessions, and classroom support, so that teachers can experiment in their own schools.

Compensatory programmes have drawn on research, both to design and to evaluate new educational programmes. The experience of combining action and research in this way has at times been uncomfortable for both parties. Each exposes vulnerable positions in the other; the methods of research introduce uncertainty into action, and undermine the needs of the decision-making process for clear cut results. And involvement in action by research may challenge the basic distinction between fact and value that underlines many research procedures. Many of the requirements of research for control over the development of the action and for the systematic allocation of children to one group or another cannot be met in large-scale action programmes for social and political reasons. Though small-scale studies, for example at pre-school level, have managed to approximate to experimental design and have produced relatively clear cut results, there is need for more information about the reasons for such results—for the study of "process variables". In the context of large-scale programmes such as the Head Start pre-school project there are strong arguments that overall evaluation of the final outcomes is in many cases premature; there is need for detailed examination of whether the programme has been adequately implemented, and for research strategies that identify successful elements in the programme. Overall evaluation of final outcomes tends to encourage an over-simplified response to programmes in sharp success or failure terms. Evaluation of educational programmes for the disadvantaged has increased the demand on research resources, and new research and evaluation centres have been created to respond to this need. Basic research has also been stimulated, and a hopeful development has been the increasing interaction between basic research findings and the evaluation and development of action programmes.

Running through both action and research approaches to the problems of education for deprived groups, there appear to be two contrasting themes, based on different assumptions about the potential for development. Illustration of these approaches will serve to round off this summary of American experience in this field. The first example concerns the length of time a child should ideally take part in special programmes. One response to the apparent failure of short-term intervention projects has been to press for more total programmes; for the child to join almost at birth, and ideally to be in some form of residential care. The aim, here, is clearly to minimise the effects of other influences on the child. He is in a "controlled environment" for as long as possible. A different response to the problem of ineffective short-term programmes is to try to change the dynamic forces in the child's experience—to "multiply" the effects of the programme. A home visiting strategy that seeks to improve the educational content of interaction between mother and child in the home is clearly of this kind. Programme effects may be maintained through the mother with a relatively low level of support from the home visitor.

Similar differences of standpoint can be seen in the methods of introducing new curriculum to teachers: one approach here is to work out a complete curriculum package, where the teacher only has to monitor its operation in the classroom; for example the Individually Prescribed Instruction Programme developed at Pittsburgh, where each child follows a set course of study, only calling upon the teacher when he cannot understand something in the programme, or to have his work checked. Another method seeks to involve teachers in the development of the curriculum, accepting that each teacher will introduce her own variations. These differences of approach are reflected in the methods of organisation set up to stimulate innovation on a wider basis; the "model school" approach can be similar to the development of a "package"; teachers in effect are asked whether they wish to adopt the approach or not. In the "model district" strategy, however, there is an attempt to build a curriculum with teacher involvement at the start; there is in fact no precise "model" or "package"—but a series of ideas and guidelines within which teachers are free to develop their own approaches.

In research strategy, too, similar distinctions can be seen. A major requirement of "experimental" procedures is that action develops in a predictable way; such an approach is more closely in accord with the development of curriculum "packages". Yet the experience of using such methods in evaluation has indicated the need for more information about how the programmes actually developed, for this is not always in accordance with the predicted course. Teachers, for example, may use kits or "curriculum packages" in quite different ways, and consequently with different effects. This possibility underlines the need for alternative research strategies to aid in programme development, and to identify successful programme elements. Such research strategies are likely to be more amenable to the more "organic" methods of curriculum development outlined above.

This summary of American experience has deliberately selected some of the more optimistic outcomes of compensatory programmes. These developments occurred at a time of worsening race relations in the cities, and it would be easy to outline a more depressing picture. Changing political conditions have made it impossible in some areas to revert to earlier methods of compensatory education. Black militant groups may block programmes aimed at the cognitive "deficits" of the disadvantaged child, and both black and white militants oppose integration programmes that involve bussing.

Though there have been some "paper programmes", it would be wrong to use this description to cover "compensatory education" in general; for there are a set of positive findings. If this is thought to be a small return for the amount of money invested in such programmes, it would be interesting to compare the "return" from the general educational budget. The range of innovations in curriculum and school organisation must be hard to parallel in any comparable period of time. Indeed the extent and diversity of programmes, as we have noted, makes any overall assessment extremely difficult.

Compensatory education has not produced clear cut answers to such questions as the relative importance of genetic or environmental factors in intelligence, or the relationship between education and the occupational structure. It is interesting that the genetic-environmental controversy has been opened again, at a time when experimental pre-school programmes, part of "compensatory education", have demonstrated that considerable improvements in intelligence test scores can be achieved and maintained. Attempts to improve the educational experience and qualifications of disadvantaged groups may well help to clarify the complex relationship between education and the occupational structure, particularly if research and evaluation are a part of them.

To simplify our description of American compensatory education programmes we can say that the movement began with what appeared to be a simple educational problem, the fact that certain social groups on average had a lower level of educational performance. Attempts to solve that problem were forced to go further and further outside the educational system, as the ramifications of the initial problem were uncovered. In this process the most basic questions are raised about the nature of social organisation, and about the reasons why lower social status should be associated with lower educational performance. These developments indicate that a purely educational response to the initial problem is unlikely to succeed. Action programmes have tended to follow this pattern, first seeking to introduce changes in the child's experience in the formal school setting, and then increasingly to widen their approach, so that larger areas of the child's experience are affected. Educational underachievement has become merely one manifestation of a series of social and economic disparities experienced by disadvantaged groups. The long-term solution must be a comprehensive policy which strikes at these political, social and economic inequalities. Nevertheless many participants at the New York conference, while recognising the need for comprehensive programmes of this kind, underlined the important role that educational reform would have to play. It is possible, too, that educational programmes may make considerable impact on the political consciousness of the poor, a process that has certainly accompanied the development of compensatory education in the United States. Such political awakening may be the most effective means of ensuring that the gross inequalities between social and ethnic groups are eradicated.

CHAPTER 3

The Governmental Response to Plowden

The idea of educational priority areas, as formulated in 1966 in the report by the Plowden Committee, was widely acclaimed both in Parliament and among the professional and administrative bodies concerned with education, though the welcome accorded it by the D.E.S. was tempered by extreme caution and refusal to commit the government to the increased spending recommended.

In introducing the concept of educational priority areas the committee was trying to formulate a scheme for helping those schools and neighbourhoods in which children were most severely handicapped. In distinguishing E.P.A.s for special attention the committee recognised that the benefits of economic advance were not automatically and evenly spread throughout all social groups nor would they, given the present pattern of public services, secure for every child "increasing opportunities of contributing to the nation's progress". Thus the argument for special treatment for poor areas came in two parts; first to compensate for the poor living conditions which affected the children's progress in the schools and drastically reduced their chances of further education and, second, to enable children to develop their abilities in order to contribute to economic progress. ". . . From the earliest stages of education, the schools enlarge or restrict the contribution their pupils can make to the life of the nation. Money spent on education is an investment which helps to determine the scope for future economic and social development".[1] The E.P.A. proposal represented both a measure of social justice and a way of improving the efficiency of the educational system as a means to economic advance.

The help to be concentrated on schools in poor areas was not designed only to bring them up to the level of those in better off areas in terms of buildings, equipment and teachers. The committee insisted on the compensatory principle. "We ask for 'positive discrimination' in favour of such schools and the children in them, going well beyond an attempt to equalise resources. Schools in deprived areas should be given priority in many respects. The first step must be to raise the schools of low standards to the national average; the second, quite deliberately to make them better. The justification is that the homes and neighbourhoods from which many of their children come provide little support and stimulus from learning. The schools must supply a compensating environment. The attempts so far made within the educational system to do this have not been sufficiently generous or sustained, because the handicaps imposed by the environment have not been explicitly and sufficiently allowed for. They should be."[2] The aim was equal opportunity for all and this could only be achieved if some children had "unequally generous" treatment.

---

[1]Plowden, p. 54.
[2]*Ibid.*, p. 57.

The E.P.A. scheme was to be translated into administrative terms by identifying schools needing special help in accordance with agreed criteria which it was hoped would provide a measure of educational and social need. The Plowden Committee suggested a tentative list of significant factors relating to occupation, family size, the receipt of state benefits, housing conditions, poor school attendance, the proportion of handicapped children in ordinary schools, incomplete families and children unable to speak English. On the basis of information supplied by local authorities the Minister would designate schools or groups of schools as priority schools or areas and they would then qualify for particularly favourable treatment. The form such treatment might take and the way in which it could be guaranteed was not precisely specified in the report, but a number of suggestions were made. More experienced and better qualified teachers should be recruited, there should be extra allowances for teachers serving in the difficult areas and teachers' aides should be provided. Efforts should be made to develop links between teachers in training and the E.P.A. schools. Money available for minor works should be concentrated on improving the most dilapidated schools. Nursery education should be provided to allow all children between four and five to attend part-time and 50 per cent of them full-time. Social work should be developed in association with the schools, and the schools themselves should be developed as community schools.

In making their proposals for implementing an E.P.A. programme the committee envisaged two stages. The period up to 1972 was to be in some ways experimental. The special measures suggested were to be introduced in those areas and schools containing the 10 per cent of most deprived children (two per cent in the first year, rising to 10 per cent by 1972): and research was to be planned to evaluate the success of different innovations and so to provide some guide to the most appropriate future developments.[1] The initial stage would add an extra £11 million to the current costs of maintained primary schools. The second stage, the more long-term programme, would depend to some extent on the discoveries of the experimental years. The committee envisaged that compensatory measures should continue for 10 per cent of the population, though left open the possibility of including a higher proportion. In any case the policy would call for additional resources over and above those then allocated to education. "Positive discrimination . . . calls both for some redistribution of the resources devoted to education and, just as much, for an increase in their total volume. . . . It would be unreasonable and self-defeating—economically, professionally and politically—to try to do justice by the most deprived children by using only resources that can be diverted from more fortunate areas".[2]

Professional reactions to the E.P.A. idea

The Plowden Report was debated in the Lords on 14th March 1967 and in the Commons two days later. It was received enthusiastically by all who spoke, though Mrs. Shirley Williams noted that the attendance of members

---

[1]The projects reported in this and subsequent volumes are, in effect, a small-scale realisation of the Plowden recommendations for evaluated innovations.
[2]Plowden, p. 65.

in the Commons was very poor. The recommendation about E.P.A.s to which the Plowden Committee had given first importance was singled out by speakers for special welcome, though many pointed out that there would be problems of definition. Only Lord Newton qualified his acceptance of the principle of positive discrimination: "But I do not think ... (it) ... should be pushed too far .. I do not think that more generous staffing in priority areas ... should be allowed to result in levelling down over the whole field."[1] He believed the socialists had placed themselves in a dilemma in arguing against selection for clever children for a privileged education but in favour of selection for children from poor homes for such treatment. "What I want to see is the widening of opportunity without loss of excellence".[2] On the whole however the Conservatives in both houses were more inclined to welcome the idea of positive discrimination as consistent with and expressing their own convictions about the need for selectivity throughout the public services generally and for distributing benefits according to some kind of need or means test. Lord Plowden particularly emphasised the importance of the E.P.A. idea, insisting that it should be put into practice if necessary by diverting resources from other parts of the educational budget. The Commons followed the Lords in endorsing the E.P.A. principle though doubts were raised about the procedure for defining and designating the areas and about the proposal to give extra allowances to teachers in priority schools.

Here for the moment the matter rested, the government refusing to commit itself to any definite statement of what it intended to do about the Plowden recommendations until it had considered the views of the various professional and administrative bodies concerned with education policy. These were submitted to the Department over the next few months. The National Union of Teachers gave an enthusiastic welcome to the report and a resolution at the 1967 conference called on the government to make available the resources necessary to carry out the major proposals. The union agreed that E.P.A.s should have highest priority, that education should attempt to compensate for social deprivation, and it welcomed the idea of positive discrimination. The definition of areas should proceed experimentally, however, and local education authorities and teachers should be responsible. If the D.E.S. were formally responsible for designation this should follow automatically on the recommendations of the local authorities. The National Association of Head Teachers were especially interested in the proposed extra payment for teachers in E.P.A.s and sceptical as to whether this was the best way of attracting and retaining suitable staff. The actual teaching conditions were seen as more significant in encouraging teachers to work in the deprived areas. The Headmasters' Association had some reservations about the proposals for positive discrimination in E.P.A.s, envisaging scarce resources for education and pointing to the claims of newly established comprehensive schools for specially favourable treatment. The Association of Head Mistresses on the other hand were insistent on the need to give special help to the deprived areas, welcomed the proposals for attracting teachers to them, but went on to urge that improving the schools

---

[1] *Parliamentary Debates, Commons*, 14th March 1967, cols. 177–8.
[2] *Ibid.*

was only one element in the reform of such districts, "in which youth and community work and all the facets of the social services should also be involved". The Assistant Mistresses were more cautious about the E.P.A. strategy, agreeing that schools in poor districts should have special treatment but questioning the desirability of extra payments to teachers and placing more hope in positive efforts to make teachers more aware of the needs of such areas and the opportunities for service within them. In accepting the idea of E.P.A.s the Assistant Masters' Association argued that the case for special treatment applied with equal force to secondary schools. The Association also insisted that extra help for deprived areas should not be to the detriment of other areas and should be financed by additional grants and by the recruitment and training of extra teachers. The Assistant Masters went on to stress that the problems of the poor areas could not be solved by the schools alone but would have to be tackled by all the social services.[1] Teachers in colleges and departments of education followed school teachers in generally welcoming the report and the proposals for special treatment for priority areas. They also approved the suggestion relating particularly to themselves, for establishing close links between the colleges of education and the schools in the poor districts.

There were varied reactions from the administrative bodies. The Association of Education Committees was notably restrained, pointing out that implementing the report must be a long-term project which would involve determining relative priorities and that recent decisions of the Secretary of State had ruled out the possibility of carrying out all Lady Plowden's proposals. The Association did not think it practicable to define E.P.A.s precisely or objectively and thought that the best way to help schools in difficulties would be by making extra money available to local authorities for building purposes. Given the problems of defining E.P.A.s the Association of Education Committees opposed extra payments to teachers working within them. Nor did the Association think extra payments could be justified unless the schools were designated as schools for handicapped pupils and this they thought neither necessary nor desirable.[2] The official journal of the A.E.C., *Education*, argued that the E.P.A. proposals presented a dilemma; they implied more resources for education than would be forthcoming.[3] In a later issue Sir William Alexander elaborated the argument. It was not realistic to think that more money would be available for education and the government must determine its priorities. Sir William's priorities were clear: ". . . it is hard to avoid the conclusion that those parts of the education service which impact most directly on increased productivity must take priority over any proposals, however desirable, in the field of social welfare which do not have such direct impact on our economic problems".[4] The real need, he said, was to increase the wealth of the nation so that it could carry the burden of increased spending on education. There

---

[1]Other professional bodies than the teachers submitted their views to the Department. The Council for Training in Social Work declared itself "much interested" in the idea of E.P.A.s though considered that it had raised important matters of principle which should be further discussed since it had implications for other services than education.

[2]A.E.C. Executive Committee minutes, March 1967.

[3]*Education*, 13th January 1967, editorial.

Ibid., 20th January 1967.

had been suggestions, he went on, that extra charges for school milk and meals might help to pay for the Plowden proposals, but such charges were, he insisted, essential to help to meet existing commitments.

The local authority associations were more favourably disposed. The County Councils Association welcomed the proposal for positive discrimination for deprived areas as "a generous one which must command everyone's sympathy and support". Like the teachers, though, they pointed out that other services must be involved in the approach to the priority areas and emphasised that possibilities for discrimination within the limits of existing resources were very small. They also stressed the problems involved in defining E.P.A.s.[1] The Association of Municipal Corporations agreed with the priority given to aid for deprived areas but, at the same time, raised queries about the criteria for identification, the period for which designation should last and the possibility of help for schools which were deprived though not officially designated.

The proposals for teachers' aides in the priority schools was seen as a threat to some of the interests of the professional bodies and, to a much lesser extent, the administrative authorities. The suspicions of the professional bodies were concentrated on the possibility that aides or ancillaries might be involved in actual teaching. The N.U.T. thought the recommendations of the Plowden Committee about the conditions of employment and the period of training for aides implied that they would have some teaching functions and this the union opposed. The joint executive committee of the Association of Head Mistresses, the Association of Head Masters, the Association of Assistant Mistresses and the Association of Assistant Masters was more welcoming to the idea of ancillary helpers but also stressed that they should work in a non-teaching capacity and under the direction of teachers. The National Association of Head Teachers were more uncompromising. "The N.A.H.T. can support the principle of teachers' aides only if they are used *in addition* to the school's proper establishment".[2] Thus professional welcome for the idea of teachers' helpers was tempered by anxiety to regard professional status through insistence that terms of employment and training should distinguish very clearly between the aide and the qualified teacher.

The fears of the teachers were echoed to some extent by the administrative bodies. The A.E.C. thought that the proposed two-year training for ancillaries was too long and likely to establish a new grade of teacher which would be unacceptable. The A.M.C. however gave unqualified approval to the recruitment of aides, accepting the two-year training, and had doubts only about the possibility of attracting enough suitable trainees.

The Plowden Committee had also emphasised the importance of introducing parents into the work of the schools in priority areas and in fact of developing the community school. This notion, vague as it was, received widespread support, though the N.U.T. was careful to point out that there was a limit to the time teachers could spend on community relations, given the variety of ways in which they contributed already to the life of the community in other respects. The Union also insisted that no activities be

---

[1]County Councils Association, *Observations on the Plowden Report*, July 1967.
[2]N.A.H.T., Commentary on the Plowden Report, May 1967.

proposed without full consultation with the profession, and there was a general feeling among the teachers that the profession itself was in the best position to judge what particular kinds of programme were most useful and appropriate in their areas.

The third major recommendation was an increase in nursery schooling— particularly in the deprived areas. Again this received general approval though the A.E.C. pointed out that the establishment of nursery classes must be limited in order to restrict calls on teaching manpower.

The progress of the idea

Action over the Plowden Committee's proposals was a slow business. On 19th January 1967 the Secretary of State, Mr. Anthony Crosland, was asked to make a statement on the report and in a written answer he welcomed it as "a major contribution to educational thinking". He also pointed out however that some of the proposals would involve substantial expenditure and even legislation and that, although the government had begun to study them, the formulation of policy would inevitably take time. On 4th April it was announced that £3 million out of £54 million to be devoted to school building in 1968–69 was to go to areas likely to emerge as E.P.A.s. But later in the month Mr. Crosland refused to make any statement about his intentions about nursery education.[1]

In July the government announced a special allocation of £16 million for building in priority areas over the following two years.[2] The E.P.A.s were not at this point formally designated by the Department. Mr. Crosland believed that local authorities were well placed to judge special needs, though he told the local authorities that he would attach particular importance to evidence that children were suffering from a number of disadvantages and to the general quality of the physical environment. Action was to be concentrated in urban areas since, although the problems of rural areas were recognised, the Secretary of State believed deprivation to be greatly accentuated in densely populated districts. The kinds of projects envisaged were replacement of unsatisfactory schools, improvements to existing schools including better staff and amenities, additions related to planned educational development and measures designed to associate the schools directly with the life of the local community. Circular 11/67 (issued by the Department on 24th August) invited local authorities to submit argued proposals for action which would amount to claims on the £16 million. The government was rather hesitant about pressing the general E.P.A. notion on local authorities. On 7th December 1967 the new Secretary of State, Mr. Gordon Walker, reported that 92 local education authorities had applied for grant for priority areas. He was asked whether he would give "strong and detailed" advice to the local authorities about discriminating in favour of E.P.A.s in their current expenditure, over and above the capital allocations agreed by the Department, but Mr. Gordon Walker avoided committing himself and asserted that local authorities must have discretion in spending their money. When pressed he rather reluctantly agreed to encourage local authorities to do all they could.

---

[1]*Parliamentary Debates, Commons*, 20th April 1967, col. 781.
[2]D.E.S. circular 11/67.

This unwillingness to try to influence or impinge upon the responsibilities of the local education authorities to implement the Plowden proposals was evident in other ways. Questioned about the steps he was taking to improve contact between home and school in E.P.A.s, the Secretary of State replied that this was mainly a matter for the local authorities, though the Department did intend to publish a pamphlet on home/school relations.[1] And there was a similar response to an enquiry about what was being done to increase the number of teachers' aides in priority areas. "It is for the local education authority to decide on the employment of teachers' aides, in the light of the resources available and the needs of the area . . .".[2]

Early in 1968 the Secretary of State was asked what the government was doing about the Plowden recommendations apart from the allocation of the £16 million for building. He replied that some £10 million of the normal major building programme had been allocated to E.P.A. schools and also some of the additional £8 million a year recently announced for 1968 and 1969. Further, in the quota calculations a number of teachers were being held back for service in priority areas. Protests that the government was being too dilatory were rejected. "Quite a lot of the proposals of the Report are being . . . carried out, but some . . . will be very expensive . . . restrictions on central and local government expenditure will hold up these and other desirable reforms".[3]

The government had persistently refused to commit itself to expanding nursery education and at this point, in reply to a further question, Mr. Gordon Walker argued that, apart from problems of cost, more nursery classes would simply take teachers from the primary schools. Later replies to questions in the House confirmed that the government had no intention of making extra funds available to develop nursery education in general, though they might sanction proposals for extra classes which were included in the schemes being submitted by the local authorities with priority areas.[4] The Secretary of State was also questioned about the possibility of changing the weighting of the rate support grant to help areas of high population density, a matter which, he replied, was being considered.

From 1st April 1968 teachers employed in schools of exceptional difficulty were to receive an extra £75 a year—such schools to be recognised by the Secretary of State on the recommendation of the local authority. Criteria for selection were to be the social and economic status of parents, the absence of amenities in children's homes, the proportion of children receiving free meals or whose families received supplementary benefits and the proportion of children in the schools with serious linguistic difficulties. Problems arose, however, over the matter of designation for purposes of the extra allowances for teachers. In 1967 the Burnham Committee had allotted £75 to teachers in schools of special difficulty on the understanding that local education authorities should apply to the Secretary of State for the schools to be so recognised. But in July 1968 the Secretary of State maintained that he could not select from the lists submitted by local authorities

---

[1]*Parliamentary Debates, Commons*, 3rd March 1968, cols. 1602–3.
[2]*Parliamentary Debates, Commons*, 19th November 1970, col. 435.
[3]*Parliamentary Debates, Commons*, February 1968, cols. 1534–5.
[4]*Parliamentary Debates, Commons*, 8th February 1968, cols. 629–30 & 637–8.

without creating "serious anomalies" and asked the Burnham Committee to consider other ways of distributing the £400,000 set aside for the purpose. The Committee did not however wish to consider alternatives, and in November the Minister again agreed to be responsible for selection.

By April the allocation of the £16 million had been settled and distributed among over 150 school building programmes. Altogether 51 authorities in England and six in Wales shared in the programme. The English regions benefiting most were the north-west, the north-east, the Midlands and London, all being authorised to spend between £3 million and £4 million while Wales was allowed £1 million. In a comment on these arrangements the Secretary of State remarked that government action in going ahead with the programme despite the country's economic difficulties was a measure of the importance it attached to improving school conditions. "The concept of E.P.A.s is one of the most imaginative proposals of the Plowden Report. This building programme together with the special allowances for teachers . . . is evidence of the government's determination to follow up the Plowden recommendation as fast as resources allow".[1]

In fact at the beginning of 1968 there were 424 schools containing 104,431 children in England, 143 with 40,144 children in London and five with 1,226 children in Wales which were recognised for purposes of special payments to teachers. This meant a total of 572 schools with 145,801 children. The schools so designated corresponded roughly though not exactly with those benefiting from the building programme. The schools distinguished as meriting special treatment thus accounted for 145,801 children out of a total of 3,694,975—very far short of the 10 per cent envisaged in the Plowden Report for designation by 1972.

The identification of schools needing priority treatment was rather an arbitrary procedure and in practice reflected not so much the circumstances of the schools as the amount of money the government chose to make available for improving them. This was made very clear by the Minister of State in reply to a question about what estimates the Department had made of the number of schools needing priority treatment. The answer was as follows: "None. It is not practicable to try and list such schools centrally. The procedure adopted has been to decide centrally the resources available and the criteria of need, and then to seek bids from local education authorities and to select from among them those schools where the needs are judged to be most urgent".[2]

Meanwhile, the question of expanding nursery education continually engaged the attention of M.P.s. In the summer of 1968 the Minister of State refused to withdraw the circular preventing local authorities setting up nursery classes, but added that she was considering the possibility of limited expansion.[3] It was also reported that 23 of the proposals approved under the £16 million building programme included plans for replacing existing nursery classes or building new ones.

Possibilities of further advance in nursery education were re-opened by the Urban Programme, announced by the government at the end of July 1968,

---

[1]Press notice by the D.E.S., 4th April 1968.
[2]*Parliamentary Debates, Commons,* 22nd July 1968, col. 39.
[3]*Parliamentary Debates, Commons,* 27th June 1968, cols. 785–6.

which embodied an attempt to tackle some of the problems of the most severely deprived areas through increased expenditure on education, housing, health and welfare. A new grant was to be introduced, payable retrospectively on expenditure incurred by local authorities on schemes approved under the Urban Programme. The government declared itself ready to sanction immediately expenditure up to £25 million over the succeeding four years. It planned to select a number of local authorities showing clear evidence of urgent need and to agree with them projects which could start without delay. The Home Secretary added that he expected that in the first year the projects would be mainly concerned with nursery education and child care.[1]

In October a joint circular from the Home Office, the D.E.S., and the Ministry of Health[2] explained the details of the Urban Programme to the 34 selected local authorities and invited them to submit their proposals— specifically limited for the initial phase (the remaining months of the financial year) to nursery classes and children's homes which might be approved up to a value of £3 million.

In February 1969 the second phase of the Urban Programme was intro- duced covering the period up to the end of 1970 and involving expenditure up to a further limit of about £2 million. At this point all local authorities were invited to submit proposals, the rate of government grant being fixed at 75 per cent of approved expenditure, and schemes were no longer limited to nursery schools and children's homes. The government indicated to the local authorities that it would give specially favourable consideration to plans for teacher centres, for in-service training courses, for language classes for immigrants, for family advice centres, for aid to voluntary societies and for expenditure on educational materials, equipment and transport.[3]

A year later, in June 1970, a third joint circular[4] set out the government's future plans for the Urban Programme and the arrangements for the third phase. The original four-year programme was to be extended for a further four years up to March 1976, it being anticipated that local authority expenditure between 1972 and 1976 would amount to between £35 and £40 million. During the third phase the government was prepared to approve plans for capital expenditure up to the value of £4 million for the period up to March 1973 and for new revenue items up to £400,000 for the year 1970–71. All local authorities were invited to submit proposals along the lines suggested in previous circulars and were informed that, although the Urban Programme had too small resources to be able to contribute to housing development, grants would be available for extra staff to deal with housing problems in areas of special need.

The joint circular also contained a review of progress to date under the earlier phases of the Urban Programme. Altogether expenditure amounting to £8·5 million had been approved which was to provide over 10,000 new places in nursery classes, over 2,000 new places in day nurseries and 20

---

[1]*Parliamentary Debates, Commons*, 22nd July 1968, cols. 40–1.
[2]Joint Circular, Home Office 225/68, D.E.S. 19/68, Ministry of Health 35/68.
[3]Joint Circular, Home Office 34/69, D.E.S. 2/69, D.H.S.S. 2/69.
[4]Home Office 117/70, D.E.S. 9/70, D.H.S.S. 9/70.

more homes for children in care. A variety of other approved schemes, listed in an annexe to the circular, were concerned with the development of playgroups and community work, aid to voluntary bodies of different kinds, holiday projects for children, centres for different groups of handicapped children and adults, and the appointment of advisory staff.

Meanwhile, it became clear in reply to questions in the House that the government did not propose to make any further specific capital allocations for priority areas beyond the £16 million for 1968–70.[1] The Department did however propose to concentrate the resources available for building and improvements in the priority areas: "The Secretary of State believes that the principle of E.P.A.s is now widely accepted; and although he does not underestimate the claims of other areas, he proposes to allocate most of the resources available in 1971–72 to projects in urban areas of acute social need".[2]

In November 1969 the Secretary of State was asked about progress in the priority areas—about pupil/teacher ratios, about the amount of money allocated and attempts to measure its effectiveness and about the number and proportion of children attending nursery schools or classes. Mr. Short reported that 86 local education authorities had benefited from the £16 million special building allocation, the £75 allowance for teachers in schools of exceptional difficulty (£0·4 million per annum) and from the educational element in the Urban programme (£3·4 million up to date). He pointed out that no areas were designated as E.P.A.s as such. The Department's information related to those authorities who had qualified for a share of the £16 million building allocation or within which schools had been recognised as of exceptional difficulty or which had had schemes approved under the Urban Programme. Figures about pupil/teacher ratios and the proportion of children in nursery classes were available for the whole local authority areas and these were supplied. But the Secretary of State maintained it was too soon to attempt to measure the results of the expenditure. Further information about nursery education in the 86 authorities was provided in December.[3] The increase of 10,000 nursery school places under the Urban Programme meant that there would be a total of 107,000 places in these areas.

By January of 1971 further expenditure of £4·4 million was authorised under the Urban Programme for capital spending over the next two years with an additional £600,000 for non-capital projects. It was to cover an additional 5,219 places in nursery schools and classes, and other schemes for day nurseries, centres for the old and handicapped, community work, special facilities for immigrant children and housing advisory centres. The approved expenditure was in respect of 530 projects submitted by 107 local authorities. In all 135 local authorities had proposed 1,530 schemes. At the end of the year the government allocated a further £1·2 million to provide 3,000 more nursery places,[4] thus bringing the total of new places approved

---

[1]*Parliamentary Debates, Commons*, 24th April 1969, cols. 639–40; 17th July 1969, col. 874.

[2]Letter from the D.E.S. to local education authorities, 13th November 1969.

[3]*Parliamentary Debates, Commons*, 11th December 1969, cols. 163–4.

[4]*Parliamentary Debates, Commons*, 18th November 1971, cols. 659–60.

under the Urban Programme to over 18,000. Plowden recommended an increase of over 500,000 places for the country as a whole by 1975.

Conclusion

During 1971 the experiments in action–research which this book describes were drawing to a close. It had always been hoped that the projects developed in the different districts would be of lasting value in persuading the government of the need for a policy of positive discrimination and in suggesting the most effective ways of pursuing such policies. These hopes have yet to be fulfilled so far as the response of the government is concerned, though the work begun under the research programme will survive locally, supported by some local authorities and by voluntary funds.

At the end of our action–research programme in December 1971, government interest in the E.P.A. idea remained very uncertain with only one more year of the present Urban Programme to run and with a history of only half-hearted support by either political party for the proposals spelled out in the Plowden Report. On the hustings in 1970 both Mr. Short and Mrs. Thatcher promised priority for primary education; smaller classes, better buildings and more nursery provision. There had been some progress in the five years since 1966 but it had been slow.

The Plowden Committee aimed to improve the ratio of teachers to children in E.P.A.s to a point at which no class in those areas exceeded 30. By 1970 the Chief Education Officer of Manchester reported that in his 38 E.P.A. schools there were 237 classes among which 107 were up to that standard with 29 children or less, 89 with between 30 and 40 children, and only 12 with 40 or more. Reporting from Wolverhampton in *The Times* (December 1971) Mrs. Rene Short remarked that the borough had nearly 2,500 primary school children being taught in classes of 40 or more. She also complained that Wolverhampton was being allowed to build only 2 out of 11 primary projects in the period 1972–74. Again, while there had been some gesture towards a national building plan it fell short of the recommendation in the Plowden Report that approximately £5,000 be allocated for minor works for every E.P.A. school. There had also been some move to increase nursery education against a background of total inactivity from 1944, but the majority of E.P.A. children still had no such provision.

One of the first of the government's responses to the Plowden Report was to introduce a £75 a year increment for E.P.A. teachers, which is now raised to £83, but the Committee had recommended £120. Meanwhile little or nothing has been heard of the proposal to add teachers' aides in the priority schools to a ratio of 1 to every 2 infant and junior classes. There were also proposals to link students in training with priority schools and to set up teachers' centres for in-service training. Our study has shown that a very valuable contribution can be made by the colleges of education, but little has been done to develop such schemes nationally. Local projects have also concentrated on trying to develop the notion of the community school to which the Plowden Committee attached great significance, and enterprising and ingenious experiments have been introduced in efforts to establish the schools as centres of local interest and activity which form an essential part of the life of the neighbourhood.

In general, the efforts to turn the idea of the priority area into reality and to devise ways of following up the recommendations of the Plowden Committee have derived largely from the enthusiasm and commitment of a small group of people. Local experience has undoubtedly opened up a great range of possibilities and the Urban Aid Programme has allowed some significant advances. The question now is whether the British government is prepared to launch a full-scale national policy. In the chapters which follow we describe and discuss our own experience in four educational priority areas and finally, in Chapter 14, outline the policy to which our action–research has led us.

CHAPTER 4

The Definition of E.P.A.

In this chapter we pose the problem of definition as it has been inherited from Plowden and we report on the London study in search of an adequate formula.

Both theoretically and administratively the definitions we inherited from Plowden were not in terms of individual children, nor classes, nor streams, nor even primarily schools but *areas*. From the theoretical side this definition has been challenged as a false conception of the problem of inequality in education. We have referred to Bernstein's criticism of compensatory education—that it distracts attention from educational to cultural deprivation. The point was well taken. There is no doubt that the danger exists. But at the same time it is important not to misrepresent Plowden. They certainly speak of a "vicious circle", which has all the echoes of the theory of a cultural cycle of poverty. Nevertheless their emphasis is on the schools.

"Thus the vicious circle may turn from generation to generation and the schools play a central part in the process, both causing and suffering cumulative deprivation.

"We have ourselves seen schools caught in such vicious circles and read accounts of many more. They are quite untypical of schools in the rest of the country. ... tiny playgrounds; gaunt looking buildings; often poor decorative conditions inside; narrow passages; dark rooms; unheated and cramped cloakrooms; unroofed outside lavatories; tiny staff rooms; inadequate storage space with consequent restriction on teaching materials and therefore methods; inadequate space for movement and PE; meals in classrooms; art on desks; music only to the discomfort of others in an echoing building; non-soundproof partitions between classes; lack of smaller rooms for group work; lack of spare room for tuition of small groups; insufficient display space; attractive books kept unseen in cupboards for lack of space to lay them out; no privacy for parents waiting to see the head; sometimes the head and his secretary sharing the same room; and, sometimes all around, the ingrained grime of generations. . . .

"What these deprived areas need most are perfectly normal, good primary schools alive with experience from which children of all kinds can benefit. What we say elsewhere about primary school work generally applies equally to these difficult areas. The best schools already there show that it is absurd to say, as one used to hear, 'it may be all very well in a nice suburb, but it won't work here.' But, of course, there are special and additional demands on teachers who work in deprived areas with deprived children. They meet special challenges. Teachers must be constantly aware that ideas, values and relationships within the school may conflict with those of the home, and that the world assumed by

teachers and school books may be unreal to the children. There will have
to be constant communication between parents and the schools if the aims
of the schools are to be fully understood."

But even if the emphasis is on schools it can still be argued that it is
fundamentally misconceived in that the appropriate "unit" is the individual
child. An example of this criticism, which in one form or another usually
comes from those who are pessimistic about the Plowden approach and
suspicious of its origins in American thinking on compensatory education,
comes from Mr. Henry Acland. His major point is that not all low academic
achievement is concentrated in E.P.A. schools. He then goes on to scorn
the vague generality of Plowden conceptions of what schooling is about
and to recommend "concentrating on the narrow issue of school achievement".[1] He warns us that "imprecisely defined programmes tend to
evaporate leaving little behind" and that "teaching an E.P.A. child about the
way his local government works may put him even further behind in the
conventional scholastic race".[2]

Again these points are well taken insofar as they refer directly either to
the vagueness of the aims set by Plowden for E.P.A.s or to the danger of
preparing children for a world which will not exist unless radical reforms
are also carried through to ensure that after his education the child will be
confronted by adequate opportunities for work and for the exercise of
power and influence over his environment. But whether these criticisms have
any relevance to what Acland calls the "E.P.A. demonstration projects" he
could not know in advance of the publication of our results. Two points
can however be made about his essay before we come to the description and
findings of our projects. First Acland's conception of the aims of schooling
in E.P.A.s is narrow and contentious, and we do not accept it. Nevertheless,
even if we did, it should certainly not be assumed, nor can it be inferred
from any research evidence, that changes in curriculum, better and more
stable teaching staffs, parental involvement or pre-schooling will be necessarily ineffective in relation to achievement standards. Second, Acland's
argument about the distribution of low achievers is not confirmed by our
own evidence. He reanalysed national survey data collected on behalf of
the Plowden Committee, defining E.P.A. schools as those schools in the
sample which had scores in the lowest 10 per cent on two out of five
indicators (social class, family size, incomplete families, parents from abroad,
too few bedrooms), and defining under-achievement as a score in the lowest
10 per cent of the test score range. On the basis of this analysis he concluded
that "for the special E.P.A. pupils only one fifth or less were under-achievers,
compared with one tenth for the whole sample . . . In other words, there is
some concentration of 'slower' children in the E.P.A. schools. But the
difference is not educationally exceptional."[3] Using the same definition of
under-achievement we found that Acland had grossly underestimated the
proportion of under-achievers in the E.P.A. project schools. Although only
16 per cent of children were under-achievers in the junior departments of
the West Riding E.P.A. schools, there were 23 per cent in Deptford, 33 per
cent in Liverpool, and 49 per cent in Birmingham. These proportions are

[1] Henry Acland, "What is a Bad School?", *New Society*, 9th September 1971.
[2] *Ibid.*
[3] *Ibid.*

undoubtedly inflated by the large numbers of immigrants with language problems in many of the schools, but they nevertheless represent a problem for the E.P.A. teacher which is, on any terms, "educationally exceptional".

The difference between Acland's estimate and our own is not surprising when we consider how they were reached. He defined as E.P.A. those schools falling in the bottom 10 per cent on certain social criteria of a national sample of 173 schools. However in England and Wales as a whole only 570, or 2·5 per cent of maintained primary schools, were recognised as schools of exceptional difficulty in 1968, and it was from among these that the E.P.A. project schools were largely selected. It follows that those which Acland took to represent E.P.A. schools must have been, on the whole, considerably better off than the schools which are officially regarded as E.P.A.

But, whatever the distribution of low achievers may be, the point is that programmes directed at individual needs are not in conflict with the area approach: indeed the two are complementary. The area approach is based on recognising the complex forces in school and community which determine the meaning and effectiveness of educational experience including attainment. It also recognises that schooling is more than the transmission and competitive testing of academic skills. To take the wider approach is admittedly more difficult, especially for "hard-nosed" evaluation. Nothing less than a generation would be necessary to test some of the Plowden hypotheses, however refined by research designs. But, as we shall see, some elements in the actual designs of the four projects made precise testing of achievement hypotheses possible, and our conclusions in Chapter 8 do not support Acland's pessimism.

Returning now to the Plowden conceptions we may note that the Newsom Report, published in 1963, had already hinted at the idea of E.P.A.s.[1] Newsom and his colleagues wrote about education in the slums though with care to write of "schools in slums", not of "slum schools", and they added "there is no satisfactory objective criterion of a slum".[2] With the advent of Plowden there was an attempt at closer definition. The key word is deprivation and the plea was for "objective criteria for the selection of educational priority schools and areas".[3] Plowden was quite categorical in demanding that the "criteria required must identify those places where educational handicaps are reinforced by social handicaps" and suggested the eight characteristics we have listed in Chapter 3.[4] They were aware that "an infallible formula cannot be devised" and called for "wise judgement and careful interpretation".[5]

Most L.E.A.s would claim that they could pick out schools in an E.P.A. category without a complicated analysis based on specific indices and there is some element of truth in this claim. For example, the Birmingham L.E.A.,

---

[1] Their *Half Our Future:* Report of the Central Advisory Council for Education (England), H.M.S.O., 1963, has a chapter 3 with the title "Education in the Slums".
[2] *Ibid.*, paragraph 62.
[3] Plowden, paragraph 153.
[4] See above, Chapter 3, p. 32.
[5] Plowden, paragraph 155.

faced in 1967 with a possible E.P.A. experiment backed by A.C.E. and the Ford Foundation, named a number of schools in Balsall Heath and Spark-brook which might be included. Eventually these became the schools suggested for experiment and evaluation in the Birmingham project. One of them failed to qualify as a school of exceptional difficulty by a substantial margin and one (an infant school) failed by a small margin, but the others were very near to the top of the list of deprived schools. We shall argue below that local diagnosis and flexible formulae are essential, but the desirability of seeking more precise and widely acceptable criteria is also obvious.

The reference in the Plowden definition to both schools and areas indicates a muddle which still remains and which was not disentangled by the D.E.S. Circular 11/67 dealing with a supplementary building programme for educational priority areas. It was recognised in this circular that there must be an identification first of districts which would satisfy the Plowden criteria and second of schools within these districts to be replaced or improved. However, the Secretary of State went on to say that he "does not intend to designate or define educational priority areas . . . (and) that the authorities themselves are well placed to judge to what extent their areas contain districts which suffer from the social and physical deficiencies which the Plowden Council had in mind".

In many ways the response to circular 11/67 was a familiar exercise for L.E.A.s in submitting building programmes, though in this case the criteria were not, as in the past, a matter of the need for new schools on new housing estates nor of additional accommodation required because of an increase in the birth rate. The claims had to be based on an assessment of the degree of deprivation in different districts.

It was the second part of the Plowden exercise which identified schools (i.e. Schools of Exceptional Difficulty) in which there should be additional allowances for the staffs (£75 for qualified teachers). The amending order to The Remuneration of Teachers (Primary and Secondary Schools) 1968 gave statutory authority to these payments and Section R of the Burnham Report 1969 set out the criteria for recognising these schools:—

 (i) the social and economic status of parents of children at the school;

 (ii) the absence of amenities in the homes of children attending the school;

 (iii) the proportion of children in the school receiving free meals or belonging to families in receipt of supplementary benefits under the Ministry of Social Security Act 1966;

 (iv) the proportion of children in the school with serious linguistic difficulties.

The standard of school building was not in this case a primary factor.

Local authorities tended to name all schools in the areas identified in accordance with circular 11/67, and, in order to ensure that none which might conceivably have a claim was excluded, a number of border-line cases was usually added.

Certain criteria were applied to all the schools and points awarded. Thus, in Birmingham, the L.E.A. and the teachers thought 191 schools deserved to be considered by the Secretary of State and 50 were approved as schools of exceptional difficulty for the purpose of additional allowances for teachers. Clearly recognition by the D.E.S. was bound to be somewhat limited because, in the first instance, the cost of the £75 allowances for the country as a whole was to be restricted to £400,000 per annum. If all the schools named by Birmingham had been recognised the additional cost in teachers' salaries in a full year would have been around £177,000. In fact, the 50 approved cost the authority about £46,000.

This serious gap between schools where deprivation was substantial and those recognised officially as schools of exceptional difficulty was certainly not peculiar to Birmingham. A survey of the five county boroughs adjacent to Birmingham to the North West and collectively described as the Black Country, showed that the variations between expectancy and reality was broadly similar. These six large urban authorities (including Birmingham) with a total population of over 2 million, submitted 278 schools out of a total of 976 for recognition as schools of exceptional difficulty but only 78 were accepted by the D.E.S. Put another way the L.E.A.s in this vast conurbation considered that over 25 per cent of their schools were of E.P.A. type but only 8 per cent were so recognised. Allowing for overstatement by L.E.A.s and the national limitation placed on allowances for schools of exceptional difficulty, it would be reasonable to suggest that at least 15 per cent of the schools in these urban areas would have satisfied the Plowden criteria for positive discrimination.

Limited resources combined with the administrative procedures involved in the local application of multiple criteria and the vetting of L.E.A. submissions by the D.E.S. inevitably resulted in the creation of local anomalies. For instance 10 schools in Birmingham were one point only (maximum 100) below the last school admitted for recognition by the D.E.S.; and one case is known of an infant school on the same site as a junior school failing to get recognition while the junior school was approved. On the criteria used the most likely source of this anomaly was the percentage of children with serious language difficulties. But, in any case, there ought to be some common criteria other than the broad headings indicated by the D.E.S.

The D.E.S. recognised the problems involved in attempting to identify schools which were to be recognised as of exceptional difficulty, and attempted to ensure some standardisation in interpretations of the Burnham criteria.[1] They were asked for information under four broad headings, two of which related to the socio-economic status of the child's home and parents, one to the incidence of free school meals (and therefore an extension of the socio-economic factor) and the other to linguistic difficulties but not necessarily to immigrants: sources of data were indicated. The age and/or condition of school buildings were not relevant in this context.

Our study of five attempts by L.E.A.s to define E.P.A. schools showed a relatively common pattern of criteria, though there were some interesting differences in detail including quite substantial difference in the "weighting" given to various indices in order to arrive at a "points" total capable of being set in an order of priority.

---

[1] The details are set out in the D.E.S. letter to local authorities dated 28th March 1968.

In several cases it was made clear that catchment areas were not easily defined and the use of statistics based on enumeration districts of the 1966 Census were sometimes seriously out of date, as in areas of recent development, or distorted by overlap. Free choice of school was another hazard, as it was possible for various children living in the same road to attend a number of different primary schools, sometimes on religious grounds. Truancy is difficult to define and to quantify, and attendance figures may fluctuate widely for other than socio-economic reasons. Staff turnover can be suspect unless carefully adjusted to reflect a genuine flight of teachers from repellent areas. However, such factors as standards of housing, large families, unemployment, social class, living density, immigrants and free meals were common to most lists of criteria.

It is widely acknowledged that the I.L.E.A. index was the most sophisticated of those used by L.E.A.s and we look at this in detail below. Some other authorities arranged their indices to total to ten with each index scoring ten points while one authority scored 25 points for free school meals and dropped social class to five points. In many ways the non-take up of statutory benefits like free school meals is a sound indicator of deprivation as it can cover such factors as large families, broken families and unemployment and, to this degree, to weight it heavily merely reinforces other factors already taken into account. But such variations in weighting, from as low as ten points to as high as 25 points out of 100 for free school meals, suggest a need for the development of agreed national criteria.

The I.L.E.A. Index[1]

Alan Little and his colleagues in London began work on the construction of an index in the spring of 1967, after the appearance of the Plowden Report, conducting a pilot enquiry with a view to measuring and weighting the eight Plowden criteria[2] to which were added two others, pupil turnover and teacher turnover. The index was intended to relate to schools rather than to areas.

On the basis of the pilot study a general study was begun later in 1967, collecting data from all I.L.E.A. primary schools but limiting it to those criteria which were felt to be both satisfactory and readily measurable. This meant that the criteria of truancy and inability to speak English were rejected as unsatisfactory and that those relating to size of family, incomplete families, and proportion of disturbed or physically handicapped children were eliminated as not readily and adequately measurable.

At this point circular 11/67 (August 1967) intervened. Consequently, the criteria mentioned in the circular were added and considerations of national comparability were also brought into the problem. Thus for the general study the following criteria were used:

(a) Occupation

(b) Supplements in cash from the state

---

[1] This section is taken from the paper prepared by Alan Little and Christine Mabey for I.L.E.A. under the title, "An Index for Designation of Education Priority Areas", I.L.E.A., March 1971.

[2] See above, Chapter 3, p. 32.

(c) Overcrowding of houses

(d) Lack of basic housing amenities

(e) Poor attendance

(f) Proportions of handicapped pupils

(g) Immigrant children

(h) Teacher turnover

(i) Pupil turnover

Poor attendance was included because specifically asked for in the circular, although the research group had originally thought it not a meaningful index.

The measures and sources of information which were used in respect of each of these criteria were as follows.

(a) *Occupation.* The measure taken was the proportion of occupied males in unskilled or semi-skilled jobs (Registrar General's socio-economic groups 7, 10, 11, 15, 16, 17). The 1961 Census was used as the source because the 1966 data were not available at that time.

(b) *Supplements in cash from the state.* The measure taken was the percentage of children in the school receiving free meals as recorded on the annual return in September 1966. This return is the basis of information supplied by local education authorities each year to the Department of Education and Science, so that this measure provides national comparability.

(c) *Overcrowding.* The measure was the percentage of households living at a density of more than $1\frac{1}{2}$ persons per room. Once again the source was the 1961 Census so that, although outdated, standard national comparisons could be made.

(d) *Lack of basic housing amenities.* The measure was the percentage of households lacking one or more of the four basic amenities. The source was the 1961 Census.

(e) *Poor attendance.* This was measured as the average absence during a sample week and was taken from the annual return in May 1967. On this measure there was no comparable data from other authorities.

(f) *Proportion of handicapped pupils.* The measure here was the percentage of children of low ability at the 11 + transfer stage in 1967. Low ability was defined as those placed in the bottom two of seven groups which contained 25 per cent of the children. The N.F.E.R. had standardised the test for the Authority on a national sample and therefore national comparability was assured.

(g) *Immigrant children.* This was measured as the proportion of immigrant children as recorded on the annual D.E.S. return in January 1967.

(h) *Teacher turnover.* The measure adopted was the proportion of full-time teachers in school in July 1967 who had taught there for less than three academic years. It provided national comparability. In the national survey reported in Volume II of the Plowden Report, figures were given of staff movement over a three-year period.

(i) *Pupil turnover*. The measure here was the percentage of pupils in the school who spent an incomplete year there. Unfortunately, the 1965–66 records had to be used and no national comparisons could be made apart from a crude approximation using the 1961 Census mobility tables.

Given the assembling of these measures, the next problem to be tackled was that of combining them into a single index for each school. The Plowden Report itself had evaded this question. The basic problem is, of course, what weight should be given to each factor since almost certainly they are not all equal. And a further complication is the possibility that important criteria have been omitted, for example, parental attitudes and family composition. In fact the London team, in the limited time available, decided to give each measure equal weight in the index. The final scores, Y, were obtained in the following way:—

$$
Y = \begin{cases} \dfrac{x-(\bar{x}-2s)}{4s} \times 100 \text{ if } \bar{x}-2s < x < \bar{x}+2s \\[2ex] 0 \text{ if } x < \bar{x}-2s \\[1ex] 100 \text{ if } x > \bar{x}+2s \end{cases}
$$

where x is the original score for a school

$\bar{x}$ is the mean for all I.L.E.A. schools

s is the standard deviation of the original scores.

After the general study had been completed and apart from decisions to improve the data where appropriate on the basis of the 1966 Census and to explore further the problem of weighting, progress was once again overtaken by events. This time it was the D.E.S. memorandum on increments for teachers in schools of exceptional difficulty which, as we have seen, specified the criteria to be used. The I.L.E.A. team accordingly recalculated the index which was the same as the one we have just described except for the following modifications. First the 1966 data were available and used. Second, a single measure (that of the percentage of households without an inside lavatory) was used instead of a composite measure of housing stress. Third, from the 1966 data it was possible to obtain a crude index of large families. The measure used was the percentage of children living in households containing six or more people. Fourth, information on pupil turnover was updated and improved as schools were asked to record the number of pupils who spent an incomplete year in their school in 1966–67. This revised index, then, was made up of ten items, each given equal weighting in the way that we have described.

The picture which emerged is shown in Table 4.1. This table records the percentage observations for the first, fiftieth, hundredth and 150th schools in order of degree of disadvantage as measured by the index. The final index consisted of approximately 600 schools, infant and junior schools on the same site being treated as one unit. Average percentages for England and Wales also provide the national norms on the same basis in the table.

Table 4.1

Index for E.P.A.: Percentages for each criterion

Criteria*

School	(a)	(b)	(c)	(d)	(e)	(f)	(g)	(h)	(i)	(j)
1st	47·8	43·4	15·9	35·6	29·5	14·7	68·1	75·0	83·3	55·5
50th	42·1	39·1	10·7	30·4	34·3	12·3	53·0	65·0	71·4	39·1
100th	39·3	36·6	9·1	26·2	13·5	10·8	35·0	49·4	66·7	28·5
150th	32·7	33·2	5·4	22·2	11·4	9·5	21·8	38·9	57·1	23·5
E+W Average	31·9[1]	26·7[1]	1·2	19·8	5·1	NA[2]	2·5	25·0	35·6[3]	9·5[1]

Notes

[1] National figures abstracted from 1961 Census as 1966 figures not available.
[2] National data not available.
[3] Not strictly comparable; figures used for E+W abstracted from Plowden Report.

*Criteria

(a) Social class composition
(b) Family size
(c) Overcrowding
(d) Housing stress
(e) Cash supplements
(f) Absenteeism
(g) Immigrants
(h) Retarded/handicapped pupils
(i) Teacher turnover
(j) Pupil turnover

In the school figuring first on the index nearly half of the employed men in the immediate area were in semi-skilled or unskilled jobs, half of the children in the area were in large families, one-eighth of the households in the area were technically overcrowded, and over one-third of them without inside lavatories. Nearly one-third of the children received free school dinners; an average of one-seventh of the children were absent in a selected week, two-thirds of the children were immigrants, three-quarters of them were placed in the lowest quartile on an ability test, over half of them had an incomplete year in the school and four out of five teachers in the school had been there for less than three years. Looking at the 150th school and comparing it with the "national average", there are only small differences in social class, family size and housing stress. However more than twice the national average receive free dinners; instead of one immigrant pupil for every 40 children it is one for every five. The incidence of teacher turnover is 50 per cent above the national average, and pupil turnover more than twice the national average. Whereas nationally a school class is defined as having ten out of 40 pupils of low ability and performance, this school has 16. For schools like this one the problem is not so much the area (housing stress, overcrowding, class composition) but much more the social pathologies which are reflected within the school (high rates of teacher turnover, large numbers of backward pupils).

Attempts were made to refine the index further by a weighting of the measure of each criterion. First correlation coefficients between the criteria measures were worked out for the Authority as a whole, for county and voluntary schools separately and for each of the ten administrative divisions.

The ten measures used were:

1. Occupation
2. Lack of inside w/c
3. Overcrowding
4. Free meals
5. Handicapped children

6. Immigrants
7. Teacher turnover
8. Pupil turnover
9. Absenteeism
10. Large families

The correlations were in general rather low and therefore when, as a second step, component analysis was carried out it was not possible to extract principal components accounting for a large proportion of the total variance. It was found that the first component accounted for 25·2 per cent of the variance over all the I.L.E.A. schools, with a range of 23·2 per cent to 38·4 per cent between divisions. The first four components accounted for 61·8 per cent of the variance over the Authority as a whole with a range between divisions of 60·9 per cent to 71·6 per cent. Across the divisions there was marked similarity in the weighting of the principal components. In nearly all cases variables 1, 3, 4, 5 and 6 had heavy weightings.

As a means of ranking schools this principal components analysis was unsatisfactory. It would, of course, have been possible to rank on the first component about which there was much similarity across divisions, but this method would have been unsatisfactory given that the first component accounted for only 25 per cent of the total variance. There are several possible reasons for the unsatisfactory result, but at all events it was decided that the analysis did not warrant weighting and ranking according to loadings of the principal component and, for the time being therefore, equal weighting of all ten items constitutes the index.

Dr. Little and Miss Mabey drew the following conclusions from their work on an E.P.A. index. "It is the logic of this index that is important, not its detail; in other words attempting to designate areas of special concern by objective, reproduceable criteria and measures which are agreed prior to the designation. In addition, the reason for giving equal weighting to these factors was not because we thought that a weighted index would not be more useful, it was simply because there is no theoretical or empirical justification for a differential weighting scheme. A further issue is whether any system of weighting (either intuitively defended or empirically evolved) would be satisfactory either for one local area or for the whole country. Put another way, are the same criteria satisfactory for the variety of local conditions that add up to the United Kingdom? We cannot give a definite answer to these questions: the only assertion we would make is that the attempt to obtain general agreement is worthwhile, and initially this should concentrate upon outlining relevant criteria, and after that developing adequate measures. The index described above is an example of what might be done; it is the first step in rational resource allocation but not a final answer.

"Essentially the index was an attempt to create an instrument that turned a policy objective into administrative practice. Its main limitations stem from the following:—

1. Lack of either clarity or specificity in the policy objective(s).
2. Lack of empirical-theoretical support for the policy objectives.

3. Lack of precision in criteria for determining policy.
4. Lack of adequate measures of agreed criteria.

In a sense they are limitations that stem from ignorance about the meaning and cause of multiple deprivation and lack of available data about the distribution of deprived areas. A final point is worth making about the index as an administrative tool; it was designed to help with determining both the volume of "need" in a large authority and the distribution of extra resources designed to help educational priority areas. It was not designed as a means of evaluating the effectiveness of any help that was to be given. Possibly it might enable a comparison to be made between degree of deprivation and amount of resources mobilised, but its very nature does not permit any measurement of the impact of resources allocated. To do this another, and different, index would be necessary (although some of the criteria might be common). The reason for this is that the Plowden Report recommended the use of the education system as a means of funnelling resources to disadvantaged areas to compensate children for these disadvantages. The Plowden strategy did not recommend operating on the socio-economic causes of deprivation, merely using the school as a means of compensating for these deprivations."

Part Two

Action and Research

Our preliminary definition of the problem came out of the context which we have described in Part I. The "terms of reference" which had been formally set out in our application for funds to the S.S.R.C. and the D.E.S. (and in the Dundee application to the S.S.R.C. and the Scottish Education Department) were to carry out and to evaluate an action programme with four objectives:

(a) to raise the educational performance of the children;

(b) to improve the morale of teachers;

(c) to increase the involvement of parents in their children's education; and

(d) to increase the "sense of responsibility" for their communities of the people living in them.

All these were aims directly derived from Plowden and, given their far-reaching character, it hardly needs to be explained why we also wrote a caveat into our application:—

"It is not, of course, expected that each objective will necessarily be achieved and certainly not to an equal extent. The function of research will be to discover, so far as possible, how far if at all they have been attained in practice."

Possible strategies were constrained by a budget which put severe limits on resources of material, energy and time. A balance had also to be struck between two aims. On the one hand there was the unitary principle of an action-research team based on Oxford having as its aim the production of a working policy for E.P.A. practice which would, at least in principle, be national in its scope. On the other hand there was the principle of local diagnosis and local autonomy which would take account of the variations in needs and possibilities arising from the peculiar characteristics of each of the four experimental districts. Guidelines emerged from our early Oxford conferences, in particular the decision to carry out an inter-project experiment to test a hypothesis about the content of pre-schooling. This is reported in Chapter 7. Agreement also emerged that the general focus of each individual project should be on the school in its community setting and that each element of a local project would be conceived primarily in relation to this theme. The outcomes are summarised in Chapters 9, 10, 11 and 12.

Within this framework however each local team was free to devise a programme adjusted to local needs and its own resources. Inevitably therefore different styles of both action and research developed in the four districts. As we show in Chapter 5, the conditions varied and in particular the West Riding district had sharply contrasted features compared with those of the other three districts which are all situated in the inner rings of conurbations. But even this is to oversimplify. Liverpool 8 is nearer to the textbook Bethnal Green than is Birmingham's Sparkbrook or London's Deptford. And the Birmingham district is more affected by the problems of immigration and population movement than Deptford or Liverpool.

Accordingly the Birmingham programme was slanted towards the literacy problems of immigrants and especially those for whom English was a second language. In Deptford there was considerable preoccupation with the central role of the teacher and this should be noted in relation to our survey finding that dissatisfaction was greatest among the Deptford teachers. As the Project Director Charles Betty put it, "It seemed logical, therefore, to realise our project's stated aims by working through the teachers" ... "it was considered esssential that local teachers were seen to be part of our team. The emphasis would be on strengthening and re-evaluating their role within the school environment and to influence them to become agents of social change in the neighbourhood community. All our efforts would be futile if our programme to sustain and nourish the community was dissipated when we withdrew. So the emphasis would be on support for the teachers with the underlying principle of self-propagation."[1]

All four projects were concerned to devise action programmes which would be effective in producing institutional change. But again differences emerged. The Liverpool team were energetic and inventive in the pursuit of extra private resources. The Birmingham team accepted more pessimistic assumptions concerning the long-term availability of both public and private resources. Thus there were different definitions of the possibilities of change. Moreover the concern with effective change had consequences for the balance between action and research. Eric Midwinter would make no claim on behalf of the Liverpool project that its results and recommendations are based on clinically experimental research. "One hopes the findings will be of value, but they are not the consequence of a pure and controlled laboratory investigation. They have been very carefully garnered and assessed, but the trap of offering half-baked superficial figures has, one hopes, been avoided." The West Riding presents a contrasting style and point of view. There was, as they wrote in their final report, "pressure from several sources, including some members of the team, for what others saw as 'instant action'; the pressure for this type of approach was probably less in the West Riding than in any of the other projects. Being more remote, it received less attention from individuals coming to find out what was 'going on', and there were no other projects in the immediate area which could be seen as in competition. The aim of this type of approach would have been to have got a large range of action schemes going as quickly as possible—the emphasis being on number and extent rather than on the content of such action. Getting the 'whole scene going' would have shown that there was a response from the community or schools or whoever else was approached. This type of project has its attractions and is a valid method of operation, particularly in schemes where the object is temporary 'mobilisation' of a range of resources and people. But it was generally rejected partly for the reasons given—the team's lack of experience about the area and of primary education. None of the team felt sufficiently 'charismatic' to work in this way, and there was certainly a fear that action set in train so quickly would not be sustained. The problems of the area seemed to be too deep rooted for a 'morale booster' of this type to have

---

[1] It will be seen in Volume V that the Dundee project worked basically through the local authority and other local educational institutions.

any long-term effect." Indeed the West Riding team followed the working principle of discouraging publicity about the project at least in its early stages so as not to be seen to be making extensive claims about what it might achieve. There was correspondingly greater concentration on achieving a stronger meaning for the word 'evaluation'.

Guidelines and working principles thus began to develop in each of the local projects with variations on the two main themes of pre-schooling and the community school. As projects were discussed in greater detail, it became clear that there were two main types of programme under consideration. First there were specific and obvious needs, recognised by most and acceptable to all. The obvious example here is the provision of pre-schooling and equally obvious were the reading problems of non-English speaking children.

Apart from this first type of project, however, there was a second type of action where the objectives were institutional. The resilience to change of traditional patterns of schooling has often been remarked. Institutional conservatism is characteristic of all types of school but perhaps particularly in E.P.A. schools because of the exceptional day-to-day pressure. A school with a considerable proportion of its pupils receiving free meals or free clothing is likely to spend more time dealing with "non-educational" aspects of school life than would be the case in a suburban school. No extra staffing provision is formally made for these purposes and in at least some of the E.P.A. schools the head teachers have responsibility for a class of children as well as for the extra administration generated by E.P.A. community conditions. Consequently there is likely to be resistance to changes which entail, at least temporarily, an increased work-load. Many studies, not only in E.P.A.s, have emphasised the slowness with which schools alter their organisation; they are often insulated against external changes. Attention has recently been focused on innovations in primary school methods—the so-called "Plowden revolution"—and on the re-organisation at secondary level. But these changes are rapid only by comparison with educational change at other periods and not by comparison with the rate of change in other social or economic institutions. After all, activity methods were certainly practised before the war. This is not to say that there cannot be a rapid transformation in an individual school, through the appointment of a new head teacher or through rebuilding or through the rapid turnover of pupils which we have seen occur in some of the Birmingham E.P.A. schools. But such changes are not changes in the educational system as such. Systematic change has to rely on the slower movement of the general educational climate and of gradual developments in the training, including in-service training, of teachers.

Innumerable reasons have been put forward to explain the slow rate of educational change. What the projects were concerned with was to develop and test forms of intervention which would not only induce rapid initial change but which would also leave a self-perpetuating innovatory habit in local school systems after the withdrawal of the project team itself.

CHAPTER 5

The E.P.A.s and their Schools[1]

We turn now to a description of the four English districts in which we have worked. Three of them—the London, Birmingham and Liverpool E.P.A.s —were located in the inner rings of large conurbations; the fourth comprised two small, isolated and economically depressed mining towns in the West Riding of Yorkshire. Three of the E.P.A.s were defined as geographical districts within whose boundaries all primary schools took part in the project. The Liverpool E.P.A. followed a different model, for there a number of schools located over a wider area were selected to take part, while other schools within the same area were not. Each E.P.A. has its own distinctive character. Here are the impressions formed by one of us out of early acquaintance with one of the project schools in Liverpool, which may serve as a first sketch of conditions in E.P.A.s in the inner ring of a conurbation:

"The other day I went to a district at the wrong end of Liverpool Cathedral. The 'catchment area' has been almost flattened by bulldozers in the name of civic planning leaving a Board School in gaunt black and beautiful gothic, the survivor of four 'great' Education Acts, standing in a sea of rubble. Three hundred yards away is the new planning— high rise flats teeming with anonymous migrant families: and on the other side the decaying remnants of a 19th century working class community, defeated and waiting for demolition. Nearby is a street of homelessness, drinkers of methylated spirits and brothels: there were dirty drawn curtains, broken windows patched with newspaper and two three-year-olds playing with a dustbin in the middle of the street. In the school there was a seven-year-old class of all the races and an old school mistress with grey hair in a bun and unfashionable clothes, yet eager and interested in the children who hummed about her in colourful activity. With what sociologists call 'inner direction' this woman also creates a civilised haven in the centre of chaotic urban degradation. Because of her in this multi-racial English slum . . . a few children have daily experience of civility, moral purpose and intellectual adventure which could and should be connoted by the very word 'city'. In these districts the school is often alone as a stable and stabilising institution while all around there is family breakdown and the rawest of community at the lowest common denominator of individuals thrown together with no common social inheritance. But institutions cannot permanently depend on the occasional gifted teacher *sui generis*."[2]

---

[1] This chapter is mainly the work of Joan Payne. Our description of the four English projects also applies in the main to the Scottish project in Dundee, but the latter is presented in detail in Volume V.

[2] A. H. Halsey, "Educational Priority Areas", *Encounter*, March 1969.

The West Riding mining town is very different. "From the crags one can look down on the town almost in plan, through a thin gauze of smoke. Here and there, a church or school stands out by its size, but the main impression is of rows of terraced houses; straight streets with small brick pavements, alternating with asphalted areas between two rows of houses. Some houses open straight on to the pavements: others have tiny front yards. At the back, each house has its own small bricked back yard, coal store and outside lavatory. Between this and the next row's back yards is a communal space—where washing can be hung across and cars parked, and children play. Often the streets where the houses face each other may be deserted, but the 'backs' humming with activity; many families rarely use their front doors.

"The houses themselves may vary in size slightly; but basically they are 'two up and two down': in some there is a small kitchen built at the back, with an extra bedroom on top; in others a small alcove in the back room serves as the kitchen. A few of the larger houses have a third storey with an attic bedroom, but even here the rooms are still very small. At intervals, there are corner shops, houses where the front room has been converted.

"Though there are patches of green—football pitches, allotments and a few trees—the over-riding impression is of greyness, emphasised particularly in winter by smoke and fog; the brickwork is darkened by grime, and the woodwork, though often well maintained, is almost uniformly painted green. Beyond the housing one can see the railway yards and river and pit—and beyond that open country. Still further away, one can see an exclusive stone village, perched on the hill opposite, and the buildings of a teacher training college, often picked out by the sun's rays, which may not penetrate to the valley below."

Visits, visual impressions and documentary sources on the social and demographic characteristics of possible areas helped in the choice of our four experimental districts; but having chosen them we had to build up a more comprehensive picture by systematic survey. This operation served several purposes: it provided the action teams with information to guide them in deciding which policies to pursue and how they should be implemented; it allowed a systematic comparison to be made between the four areas so that the effectiveness of differing strategies could be assessed in the light of differing local conditions; it gave a measure of the degree to which the selected areas satisfied the criteria proposed in the Plowden Report[1] for the identification of E.P.A.s; and it also suggested ways in which these criteria could be modified or supplemented.

During their first year in the field the project teams collected information, sometimes in considerable detail, on all but one of the Plowden criteria (incomplete families), as well as on a variety of other matters which were thought relevant to the problems of E.P.A.s. Existing sources were used where they were available, in particular the 1966 10 per cent Sample Census and the schools' own records. To fill the gaps where records did not exist three specially designed surveys were carried out. These were firstly, a survey of all teachers in the project schools via a postal questionnaire, which gathered information on their career histories, their attitudes

---

[1] Paragraph 153 (See also above, Chapter 3, p. 32.)

towards various aspects of teaching, and the degree of their job satisfaction; secondly, a study of a random sample of 800 mothers of children in the project schools conducted by means of interviews in the home; and thirdly, a survey of the ability and attainment of all the children in the project schools in which standardised tests of verbal ability and reading were administered. Details of these surveys and of all the analyses described in this chapter are reported in Volume II, which also contains some additional tables.

The 1966 Census[1] was already nearly three years out of date when the project began, a period which can bring considerable changes in areas undergoing rapid population movements and redevelopment. Nevertheless it provided the only source of information available to us about overall conditions in the areas, and some of the facts it revealed were striking.

The E.P.A. with the smallest population was the West Riding, with 17,600 inhabitants. London and Birmingham had 49,500 and 56,000 respectively, while the Liverpool E.P.A. covered a much larger district containing 85,000 people, though not working with all the schools in that district. The inner ring areas had all been receiving Irish and Commonwealth immigrants. This was especially true of the Birmingham E.P.A., where almost a third of residents had been born outside Great Britain, including over a fifth born outside the British Isles. In the London E.P.A. at Deptford the proportion of residents born outside Great Britain approached 10 per cent, and in the Liverpool district 6 per cent. In contrast, 99 per cent of the population of the West Riding mining towns were indigenous. These differences were reflected in the fact that 16 per cent of Birmingham and 17 per cent of Deptford E.P.A. residents had first come to live in the local authority area only within the previous five years, compared with 7 per cent in the West Riding E.P.A.

All four E.P.A.s were overwhelmingly working class, with disproportionately large numbers of unskilled and semi-skilled workers. In the three inner ring areas, one in five of all economically active and retired males were unskilled manual workers, though relatively few in the West Riding fell into this category because of the dominance of coal mining in local employment. The concomitant of this dominance was, however, that only 4·5 per cent of males were in non-routine white-collar jobs, a proportion which rose to only 8 per cent in Deptford and Birmingham, against 19 per cent in England as a whole.

Almost half the dwellings in England were owner-occupied in 1966. In three of the E.P.A.s this was true of fewer than one in five dwellings. In Birmingham the number was considerably higher, the difference being to some extent explained by the difficulty which Commonwealth immigrants have in obtaining any other form of accommodation.[2] Houses bought by immigrants are often given over to multi-occupation in order to meet mortgage

---

[1] Figures for the four E.P.A.s in this and the subsequent paragraphs were calculated from the *1966 10 per cent Sample Census—Special Tabulation of Basic Statistics*, and national figures were derived from the *1966 10 per cent Sample Census Great Britain Summary Tables*.

[2] See J. Rex and R. Moore, *Race, Community and Conflict*, Institute of Race Relations, 1967.

repayments; thus while 37 per cent of dwellings in our Birmingham district were owner occupied, only 28 per cent of households lived in dwellings which they owned themselves. Housing stress in Birmingham was further indicated by the 7 per cent of dwellings which were rented furnished, compared with 1 per cent in England as a whole.

Overcrowding was a serious problem in all except the West Riding. In Liverpool 21 per cent of households were sharing a dwelling, while in Deptford and Birmingham the figure was as high as 35 per cent, five times as many as in England as a whole. While 1 per cent of households in England were living at a density of more than $1\frac{1}{2}$ persons per room, 11 per cent in the Birmingham project area tolerated this degree of overcrowding. Not surprisingly, in these inner ring districts the large majority of households—from 64 per cent to 72 per cent—lacked exclusive use of at least one of the basic amenities of fixed bath, hot water tap and WC, and the situation for those households which were sharing a dwelling was considerably worse. Even in the West Riding, where there were virtually no shared dwellings, 45 per cent of households were in a similar position.

We were not able to obtain any direct information about income levels in the E.P.A.s, but some indication was gleaned from two sources. Firstly, the Census showed that while 46 per cent of households in England owned a car, only 33 per cent in our Deptford district and as low as 15 per cent in Liverpool possessed one. Secondly, we took from school records the number of children receiving free school dinners on one day in the summer term 1969. At this time eligibility for free meals was based solely on income and not family size, and yet 28 per cent of the Liverpool children were in

Table 5.1

Community links in four E.P.A. project areas

Percentage of respondents in various categories

	Deptford E.P.A. %	Birmingham E.P.A. %	Liverpool E.P.A. %	West Riding E.P.A. %
Child's mother was brought up in same area	28	10	60	65
Child's father was brought up in same area	27	4	57	69
Mother or father attended child's present school	9	2	25	25
Many of mother's relatives live nearby	44	45	51	66
Many of father's relatives live nearby	33	46	45	62
Many of mother's and father's friends live nearby	50	56	58	86
Child plays with local children after school	77	76	90	95
Total no. of respondents	(204)	(181)	(191)	(195)

Source: E.P.A. Project Parental Survey, 1969.

receipt of them. In Deptford and the West Riding the proportions were 24 per cent and 19 per cent respectively, and in Birmingham 14 per cent. It must be remembered that these figures represent families who have successfully claimed free meals and not the numbers entitled to them. Claim forms are very complex, and language difficulties might well lead to both ignorance of entitlement and failure to apply.

The contrast between the Birmingham inner ring district in which Commonwealth immigrants had congregated and the two West Riding mining towns, which were not attracting new workers and had an ethnically homogeneous population, was demonstrated markedly by answers to a number of questions in the survey of parents. These findings are shown in Table 5.1 from which it is clear both that the West Riding had a much more stable population and that there were closer links among members of the community. The pattern in Deptford was similar to that in Birmingham, though not as extreme, while Liverpool approximated more nearly to the West Riding. It is noticeable in this table that questions about how long parents have lived in the same area differentiate the four E.P.A.s to a much greater extent than do questions about the nearness of friends and relations. This probably reflects the natural tendency of immigrant families to move to areas where they already know people who can assist them, and shows how an area where the majority of residents are relative newcomers can nevertheless become a closely knit community.

The survey of parents gave much more information about the families of the children in the project primary schools. Perhaps the most startling fact which it revealed was the number of children who came from large families of five or more siblings. As may be seen from Table 5.2, in no district was this proportion smaller than 24 per cent, and in Birmingham the majority of children came from such large families. Practically all the mothers interviewed in the West Riding and Liverpool had left school at the age of 15 or before, though in Birmingham and Deptford a few (13 per cent and 20 per cent respectively) stayed until they were 16. Despite the prevalence of large families at least a third of mothers in all the areas went out to work, and in Deptford almost one half did.

Table 5.2

Size of families of primary school children, by E.P.A.

	Deptford E.P.A. %	Birmingham E.P.A. %	Liverpool E.P.A. %	West Riding E.P.A. %
No information	0	0	1	0
1–2 children	31	9	19	36
3–4 children	39	36	43	41
5 or more children	30	55	37	24
Total no. of respondents	(204)	(181)	(191)	(195)

Source: E.P.A. Project Parental Survey, 1969.

In Deptford and Birmingham there were sufficient numbers of immigrants to enable us to look separately at their characteristics: in Deptford 47 of the sampled children came from West Indian families, and in Birmingham 48 came from West Indian and 52 from Asian families.[1] In both Deptford and Birmingham the West Indian families were somewhat larger than the non-immigrant families in the same E.P.A., but there were more large families among non-immigrants in Birmingham than among West Indians in Deptford. The average size of Asian families was also larger than that of non-immigrant families in Birmingham. It is difficult to compare standards of education across different countries, for the age of starting school may vary and school attendance may not be full time. However, on the evidence of school leaving age the West Indian mothers in both Deptford and Birmingham were somewhat better educated than their non-immigrant counterparts, while over half of the Asian mothers had not been to school at all. Roughly half of both West Indian and non-immigrant mothers went out to work in Deptford; in Birmingham rather more West Indian mothers and rather fewer non-immigrants did so. In contrast, not one of the Asian mothers who were interviewed had a job. Clearly the Asian mothers formed a very distinct group, largely cut off from society outside their own family and friends.

We have given a picture of the districts and the families which the project schools served; now, we shall describe the schools themselves. Information was collected on 45 separate primary schools or departments,[2] comprising 12 in London, 7 in Birmingham, 16 in Liverpool and 10 in the West Riding. In this 45, infant, junior and junior mixed with infants schools were represented in exactly equal numbers. All of the Liverpool schools, and all but one of those in Birmingham, were in receipt of the £75 E.P.A. salary supplement, though five project schools in Deptford and five in the West Riding were not. In fact at the local level, as we noted in Chapter 4, the allocation of the £75 supplement can seem somewhat arbitrary, and the distinction is less important in research terms than might first appear. The seven Birmingham schools were on average rather larger than those in the other areas, the smallest having 251 pupils on the roll in January 1969 and the largest 739. The 16 Liverpool schools and departments were rather smaller, ranging from 114 to 266 pupils. The spread in London was between 137 and 468 pupils, and in the West Riding from 115 to 354. Though the majority of the schools were maintained by the local authority, a handful were denominational. Only two schools were not co-educational, and these were both Roman Catholic junior schools in Liverpool. When the project began all but five of the 45 were housed in buildings which had been put up before the First World War.

Within each E.P.A. the number of pupils on the school roll fluctuated considerably from year to year as demolition and redevelopment shifted population across the district. One school had less than half the number of pupils it had had five years previously; another had almost half as many again. School buildings could not be adapted rapidly enough to meet

---

[1] The term "Asian" refers here and in the rest of the chapter to people from the Indian sub-continent. In the Parental Survey a family was classified as West Indian or Asian if at least one of the parents was brought up in those regions. Families of Irish origin were included in the non-immigrant group.

[2] An infant or junior department which had a separate head is counted in what follows as a separate school.

the changed demands on them, and some schools had empty classrooms while in others desks were crowded into corridors and any odd corner that could be found. Thus at one extreme there was a school with 122 square feet of floor space (including non-teaching space) per pupil, while in another in the same E.P.A. each pupil had only 30 square feet to himself. Pupil-teacher ratios, including full-time equivalents of part-time teachers, similarly varied from the low twenties to the mid thirties. Pupil-teacher ratio is not however a reliable indicator of the size of teaching groups, as part-time teachers in subjects such as music may be used to relieve the class teacher entirely, while in some schools the ratio may be statistically improved by the existence of small remedial groups, without any general reduction in class size. It was often apparent from the number of pupils per purpose-built classroom that teaching groups could be considerably larger than the pupil-teacher ratio would lead one to expect. It would be misleading, however, to give an average figure for all the project schools because of the considerable variations in pressure on resources.

In the inner ring E.P.A.s there were also wide variations in the proportions of immigrant pupils on the school roll. According to the D.E.S. definition of an immigrant, 4 per cent of children in Liverpool, 24 per cent in Deptford and 46 per cent in Birmingham were immigrants—there were none in the West Riding. In Deptford and Liverpool these children were by no means evenly distributed among the E.P.A. schools: three of the Deptford schools had no more than one in ten immigrant pupils on their rolls, while four schools had more than 40 per cent, and in Liverpool eight schools had no immigrant pupils at all while two had almost one in five. In the Birmingham schools the proportions were more constant, ranging from 35 per cent to 57 per cent.

As might be expected from what has already been said about the instability of the population in the inner ring areas, pupil turnover presented a serious problem in all the E.P.A.s except the West Riding. As a measure of this we took the number of pupils transferring to and from the schools during the course of the school year 1968–69, excluding, of course, those entering or leaving at the normal points, and expressed this as a percentage of the total number on the roll in January of that year. The result was startling: in Deptford 25 per cent, in Liverpool 29 per cent and in Birmingham 37 per cent of all pupils had moved during the school year, compared with only 11 per cent in the West Riding. In one school in Birmingham there had been almost 50 per cent turnover in the course of only one year.

Absenteeism was also high. Taking the total number of absences as a percentage of the total number of possible attendances during 1968–69 we found 11 per cent absenteeism in the West Riding and Birmingham, 13 per cent in Liverpool and 14 per cent in Deptford. These figures may be compared with a count for all I.L.E.A. primary schools, based on a survey taken on one day in September 1968, of 8·5 per cent.[1] Again, there were variations among schools, but in only five of them (four in the West Riding) was absenteeism as low as the I.L.E.A. average. In ten schools it was greater than 15 per cent.

---

[1] I.L.E.A. Research Report No. 2A, p. 2 (mimeo), January 1972.

From our survey of teachers[1] we learned something about the staff of these schools. The survey had a good response in all except the Liverpool district, where it was unacceptable to many teachers; hence we must leave Liverpool out of the present discussion. The most striking fact which emerged from the survey was the youth and inexperience of the Birmingham and, more particularly, the Deptford teachers, and the short time they stayed in the E.P.A. schools. The West Riding schools had the opposite characteristics: Table 5.3 shows that while 32 per cent and 27 per cent of teachers in the Deptford and Birmingham E.P.A.s respectively were not yet 25 years of age, only 10 per cent in the West Riding were as young as this. At the other end of the age scale, almost half of the West Riding teachers were over 45, compared with 28 per cent and 20 per cent of the teachers in the other two areas. Table 5.3 also shows that the Deptford and Birmingham E.P.A. teachers were considerably younger than teachers in all maintained primary schools in England and Wales, while the West Riding teachers were rather older than the national average.

Table 5.3

Age of teachers in E.P.A. project schools, compared with all teachers in maintained primary schools in England and Wales at March 1969

	Deptford E.P.A. %	Birmingham E.P.A. %	West Riding E.P.A. %	Teachers in all maintained primary schools in England and Wales %
No information	1	0	0	0
Under 25 years	32	27	10	18
25–34 years	21	40	19	22
35–44 years	18	13	26	23
45 years and over	28	20	46	36
Total %	100	100	100	100
(N)	(145)	(70)	(59)	(153, 259)

Source: E.P.A. Teacher Survey, 1969. Table 26, Statistics of Education 1969, Vol. 4, Teachers.

Table 5.4 shows the number of years which the teachers had spent in the school in which they were teaching at the time of the survey. One half of the West Riding teachers had been there for five years or longer, but only a quarter of those in Deptford and Birmingham. For well over a third of teachers in the last two areas their present school was their first, and almost a half of the teachers in Deptford and a third in Birmingham were unmarried. It seems that the inner ring schools depended to a large extent on young newly qualified teachers without family ties, and that the departure of these teachers either on marriage, the arrival of a first baby, or promotion, lead to a constant turnover in staff.

---

[1] Head teachers took part in the survey and are included in the figures in this account.

Table 5.4

Number of years which teachers have stayed in project schools, by E.P.A.

	Deptford E.P.A. %	Birmingham E.P.A. %	West Riding E.P.A. %
No information	2	3	3
Less than 2 years	42	36	29
2 years to 4 years 11 months	32	37	19
5 years and over	24	25	50
Total %	100	100	100
(N)	(145)	(70)	(59)

Source: E.P.A. Teacher Survey, 1969.

This impression was confirmed by data which we gathered directly from the school records. In both Deptford and Birmingham there was only one school in which more than half of the staff had stayed for three years or more, whereas six of the ten West Riding schools were in this position.

It is sometimes remarked that teachers in E.P.A. schools come from middle class families and live well outside the district in which they teach. This seemed true of the inner ring E.P.A.s, and once more there was a contrast between them and the mining towns. The fathers of two-thirds of the teachers in Deptford and Birmingham had white collar jobs, but in the West Riding 59 per cent were the children of manual workers. Only a handful of teachers in the inner ring schools lived within half a mile of their place of work, but 22 per cent of the West Riding teachers lived as close as this.

The Teacher Survey contained four attitude scales which had been used by the N.F.E.R. in their study of streaming in primary schools[1] and on which the scores of two nationally representative samples of teachers in streamed and non-streamed primary schools were known. We were thus able to investigate how the attitudes of E.P.A. teachers differed from those of their colleagues elsewhere. The scales were as follows:

Permissiveness: permissiveness of attitudes towards the child as a person;

Physical punishment: approval or disapproval of the use of physical punishment in schools;

Noise: tolerance or intolerance of noise in the classroom; and

Less able children: attitudes towards the worthwhileness and interest of teaching less able children.

On each scale junior teachers in the E.P.A. sample were compared first with teachers in the N.F.E.R. sample of streamed junior schools, secondly with teachers in the N.F.E.R. sample of non-streamed junior schools, and thirdly with infant teachers in the E.P.A. sample. Not unexpectedly it was found that the scores of E.P.A. infant teachers indicated a greater degree of

---

[1] J. C. Barker Lunn, *Streaming in the Primary School*, N.F.E.R., 1970.

permissiveness and less approval of physical punishment than those of the E.P.A. junior teachers, though no statistically significant difference was found between these two groups on the scales "Noise" and "Less able children". In turn the E.P.A. junior teachers were more permissive, more disapproving of physical punishment, and more tolerant of noise in the classroom than were teachers in the N.F.E.R. sample of streamed junior schools, but, contrary to expectation, they were *less* interested in less able children. Differences between the E.P.A. junior teachers and teachers in the N.F.E.R. sample of non-streamed junior schools were not as large, but the E.P.A. teachers still appeared significantly more permissive, more tolerant of noise, and less interested in teaching less able children.

These findings should be interpreted cautiously. All schools in both N.F.E.R. samples had at least a two form entry, while several of the E.P.A. project schools had only one class in each year group. It might well be the case that big schools create more problems of discipline than small schools where each child is known personally to the head. Moreover, we found that, within the E.P.A. sample, the younger teachers were both more permissive and more tolerant of noise than their older colleagues. It has already been shown that in the inner ring E.P.A. schools there was a disproportionately large number of young and inexperienced teachers, and it is more than likely that this provides part of the explanation why the E.P.A. teachers as a whole appeared more permissive than a national sample.

The apparently lower interest of the E.P.A. teachers in less able children demands more attention, for, as we shall discuss below, the ability and attainment tests which we administered showed that there were very many more low attaining children in the E.P.A. schools than in the population as a whole. It may be that the attitudes of the E.P.A. teachers are based on a more realistic assessment than teachers could have in schools where very few children could properly be regarded as retarded; or they may simply be overwhelmed by the enormity of the problem. Alternatively, because standards of attainment are generally much lower in E.P.A. schools, the less able child might be interpreted by the E.P.A. teacher as being someone who has much more serious learning difficulties than teachers in other schools would conceive of as being shown by less able children. In either case, it is clear that many E.P.A. teachers do not enjoy this important aspect of their job.

The final section of the teacher survey examined job satisfaction directly. It fell into two parts: in the first teachers were invited to say of each of 14 features whether their job was better than, the same as, or worse than the jobs of friends of approximately the same age and with equivalent qualifications, and in the second they were asked to compare 13 aspects of their teaching situation with that of teachers they knew in other schools. The responses of the teachers in all three E.P.A.s taken together are shown in Figures 5.1 and 5.2.

When comparing their jobs with those of friends, more teachers thought they were better off than thought they were worse off in respect of security, intellectual stimulation, opportunities to improve qualifications, and general satisfaction. Among these aspects security gave the most satisfaction. More teachers thought they were worse off than thought they were better

Figure 5.1: E.P.A. teachers' comparisons of their jobs with the jobs of friends of approximately the same age and with equivalent qualifications

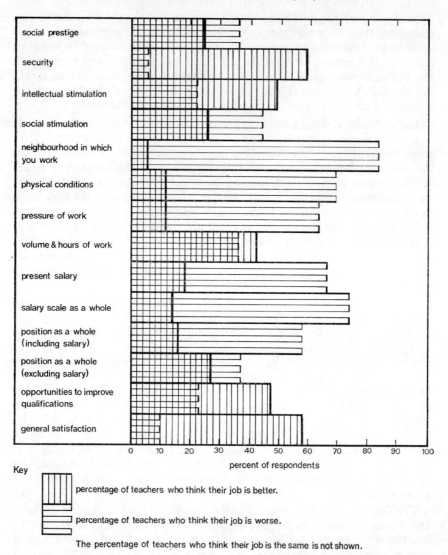

Key

percentage of teachers who think their job is better.

percentage of teachers who think their job is worse.

The percentage of teachers who think their job is the same is not shown.

off in regard to social prestige, social stimulation, the neighbourhood in which they worked, physical conditions, pressure of work, present salary, salary scale as a whole, position as a whole including salary, and position as a whole excluding salary. The neighbourhood was the cause of the most dissatisfaction, but salary levels were also a major focus for discontent. Although the teachers tended to regard themselves as better off in regard to volume and hours of work, most of them thought that the pressure of work while they were actually on the job was worse than in other occupations. What is more remarkable however is the fact that nearly 60 per cent of respondents felt that their job yielded more general satisfaction than did the jobs which their friends held. This contrasts with only 16 per cent who thought that they were better off in terms of their position as a whole including salary. It seems that for E.P.A. teachers psychological rewards are some compensation for low financial ones and poor working conditions.

The comparisons with teachers in other schools underlined this impression of a vocationally motivated teaching force. Only a small minority of E.P.A. teachers thought that their situation was better than that of teachers they knew in other schools in 11 of the aspects specified: intellectual and social stimulation, discipline, support from parents, pressure of work, volume and hours of work, physical conditions, neighbourhood, teaching facilities and equipment, recognition of work by the community, and ability of the children. On the other two items responses were totally reversed: these were the worthwhileness of the work and general satisfaction. As standards of attainment are generally lower in E.P.A. schools, this apparently high level of general satisfaction seems to conflict with the finding reported above, that the E.P.A. teachers were less interested in teaching less able children than were teachers in a national sample of schools. However we have found in conversation that they often mention the warmth and spontaneity of the children they teach, which certainly increases their satisfaction in their work. The features which E.P.A. teachers compared most unfavourably with other schools were support from parents, physical conditions, neighbourhood and the ability of the children—in effect the four features which have typically been used to characterise E.P.A. schools.

There are statistically significant differences between the three districts. The greatest discontent with salary was in Deptford, presumably because salaries were generally higher in London than in the other two regions and the difference was not fully compensated for by the London allowance. Teachers in both Deptford and Birmingham considered themselves worse off than teachers in the West Riding in respect both of the neighbourhood and physical conditions of work. The socially homogeneous and isolated small towns of the West Riding E.P.A. probably provided a more pleasant environment and at the same time afforded less opportunity for contrast than either of the inner ring areas, and indeed the average age of the schools was rather less in the West Riding. West Riding teachers were also more content with the social prestige of their job, and indeed in an area where only 4 per cent of males held non-routine white collar jobs it seems likely that teachers would be accorded more status than in the diversified occupational structure of large towns. The stability of the West Riding community probably explains why teachers there felt happier about the support they received from parents and the recognition of their work by the community. Their greater satisfaction with the level of discipline in the classroom could be interpreted as another aspect of the same factor.

The questions about job satisfaction were originally used in a study of probationary teachers carried out at the Bristol University Institute of Education, and we were hence able to compare the responses of the E.P.A.

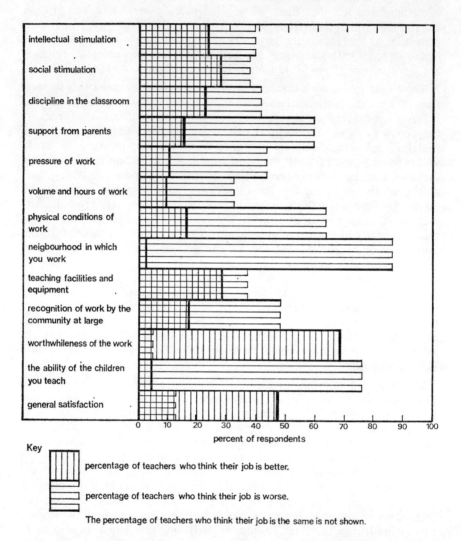

Figure 5.2: E.P.A. teachers' comparisons of their jobs with the jobs of teachers they know in other schools

Key

percentage of teachers who think their job is better.

percentage of teachers who think their job is worse.

The percentage of teachers who think their job is the same is not shown.

teachers with both a national sample[1] of teachers in their probationary year and two further samples in Southwark and Wolverhampton.[2] Our general finding was that E.P.A. teachers were generally more dissatisfied with aspects of their work than the non-E.P.A. teachers. A more detailed account of these comparisons is given in Volume II.

---

[1] J. K. Taylor and I. R. Dale, with M. A. Brimer, *A Survey of Teachers in their First Year of Service*, University of Bristol, 1971.

[2] R. Bolam, "Guidance for Probationer Teachers", *Trends in Education*, No. 21, 1970. Work on this second, regional survey is not yet complete.

Figure 5.3: Frequency distributions of scores of E.P.A. infant school children on Level 1 of the English Picture Vocabulary Test

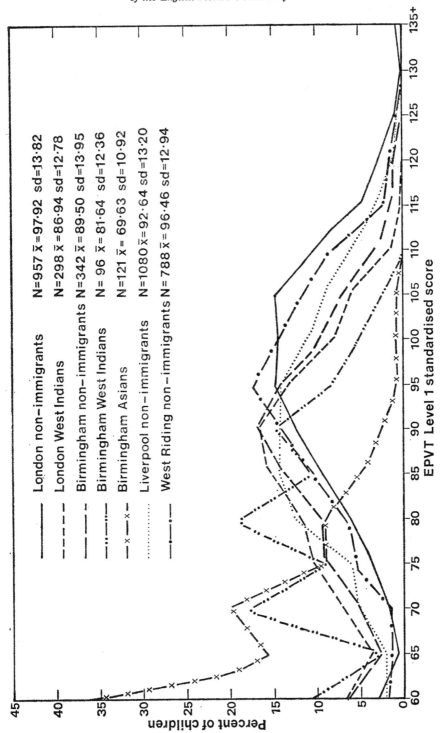

During the spring and summer terms of 1969 all children in the project schools were given the English Picture Vocabulary Test (E.P.V.T.), either Level 1 or Level 2 according to age, and in addition second, third and fourth year juniors completed the Reading Test Streaming Research A (S.R.A.). The E.P.V.T. is used as a test of listening vocabulary which is independent of reading skill and also of general verbal ability, the child's task being to identify one of four pictures which corresponds to a word spoken by the tester. Level 1 covers the age range 5 years to 8 years 11 months and is administered individually, while Level 2 is a group test which covers the ages 7 years to 11 years 11 months. The Reading Test S.R.A. is a group test which covers the junior school age range and which was specially developed by the N.F.E.R. for its study of streaming.[1] Children are asked to complete a given sentence with a word chosen from four or five alternatives, and have to read both the sentence and the options to perform the task.

It is to be expected that among the children who were absent when the tests were first administered would be a disproportionately large number of habitual poor attenders, and that the omission of these children would lead to estimates of mean scores that were too high. Thus every effort was made to follow up children who were absent at the first test session, though complete coverage was made impossible by the practical difficulties involved in repeated visits to the schools.[2]

In analysing the test scores it was obviously essential to distinguish between children who spoke English as their native tongue and those for whom it was a foreign language. Each January head teachers are required to return to the D.E.S. the number of children on their roll who have in their estimation language difficulties severe enough to impair their ability to benefit from ordinary class work. We collected this information from the school records, but it soon became obvious that variations in the heads' judgements of what constituted a serious language difficulty were so great as to make the classification useless for our purposes. Thus we felt that the best we could do was to use the D.E.S. definition of an immigrant child and to classify children by their country of origin. However, there were a number of children, especially in the Birmingham schools, who although not immigrants according to the D.E.S. definition because their parents had come to this country more than ten years previously, nevertheless spoke English as a second language with which they were only imperfectly familiar. This fact helps to explain the very low test scores which we obtained for non-immigrant children in Birmingham.

Figures 5.3 and 5.4 show the pattern of scores of non-immigrant and West Indian and Asian immigrant children in the four areas on Levels 1 and 2 of the E.P.V.T. On Level 1 the mean scores of non-immigrant children in all four areas fell well below the national mean of 100 points, varying from two points below in Deptford to over ten points below in Birmingham. In all of the areas a large number of children obtained scores which would

---

[1] J. C. Barker Lunn, *op. cit.*

[2] In the Birmingham E.P.A. it was necessary in order to complete the testing programme on time to test 50 per cent random samples of children in three of the project infant departments, and to forego the testing of fourth year juniors on the Reading Test S.R.A.

Figure 5.4: Frequency distributions of scores of E.P.A. junior school children on Level 2 of the English Picture Vocabulary Test

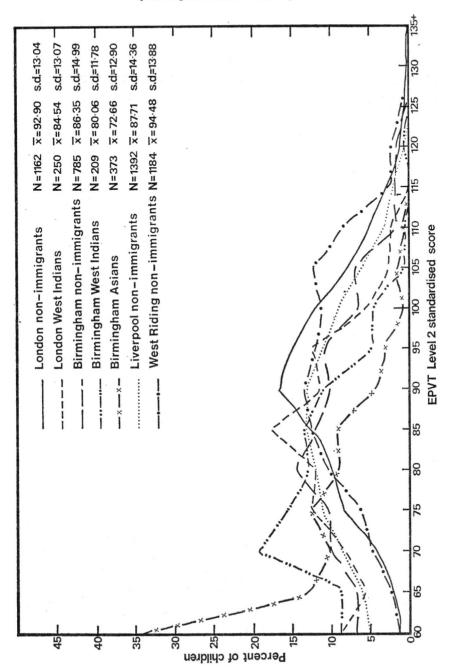

Figure 5.5: Frequency distributions of scores of E.P.A. junior school children on the Reading Test S.R.A.

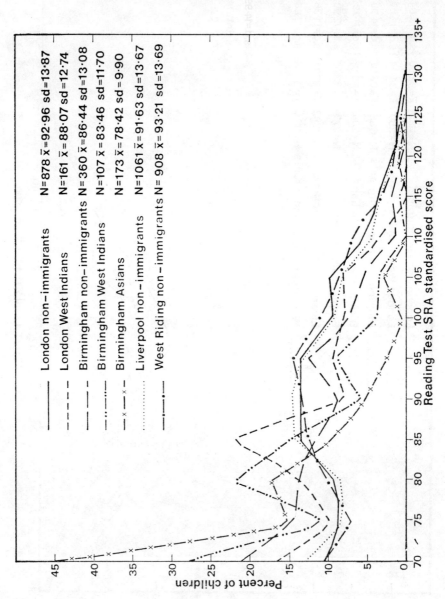

ordinarily be low enough to qualify them for places at schools for E.S.N. children. By Level 2 the mean score of non-immigrant children in all four areas had shifted downwards so that even the highest scoring area, the West Riding, was over five points below the national mean, while Birmingham lay almost 14 points below. The number of children barely managing to score at all on the test had increased.

In both Deptford and Birmingham on both levels of the E.P.V.T. the scores of the West Indian children were considerably below those of the non-immigrant group, the difference between the two means ranging from six to 11 points. Nevertheless the West Indian children, like the non-immigrants, did considerably better in Deptford than in Birmingham. The West Indian children's scores were also lower at Level 2 than at Level 1, though the lower limit of the test set bounds to the amount by which their score could fall.

About 35 per cent of the Asian children in Birmingham failed to obtain any score at all on either level of the E.P.V.T. We assume this to be a result of their difficulties with spoken English and hence regard the E.P.V.T. not as a measure of their general verbal ability but specifically as an indicator of their command of English. The test scores suggest the extent of the problem which the schools face in teaching English to these children.

The Reading Test S.R.A. scores (Figure 5.5) of non-immigrants were startlingly worse in Birmingham than in the other three areas. They suggested that over one-fifth of the children tested were complete non-readers while 45 per cent were virtual non-readers (scores of 80 or below). These scores are certainly affected by the "ten year rule" in the D.E.S. definition of an immigrant. This is not however the whole explanation, for the mean score of West Indian immigrant children was also four and a half points lower in Birmingham than in Deptford. Without further analysis or further data it is not possible to say whether the West Indian children in the two areas are drawn from comparable groups. Clearly within any ethnic group there will be similar variation in mean test scores, as there is within the non-immigrant population. It will also be recalled that there were more large families among all ethnic groups in Birmingham than in any other area.[1] The Birmingham scores may also be slightly depressed by the omission of fourth year juniors, though a breakdown of reading scores by age suggested that any such effect would be small.

In the remaining three areas the reading scores followed very similar curves, and the means all lay within one and a half points of each other at seven to eight points below the national mean. Complete non-readers formed between 10 per cent and 13 per cent of those tested, and virtual non-readers about 25 per cent. The youngest children to take the S.R.A. reading test were already in the second year of junior school, an

---

[1] Level 2 of the E.P.V.T. was administered in 1965 to a sample of 59 boys and 65 girls aged 10 years 9 months to 11 years 3 months attending Birmingham schools. The sample was representative of all Birmingham schoolchildren in respect of type of school, parental occupation and position in family, and mean scores were obtained of 97·98 for boys and 88·32 for girls. The study is reported in M. A. Brimer and L. M. Dunn, *Manual for the English Picture Vocabulary Tests*, Educational Evaluation Enterprises, 1962.

age at which it is usually assumed that all except the specially retarded have made considerable progress in reading. Thus the child with a reading age of eight years has mastered most of the basic reading skills and should be able to read the level of material found in the popular press.

In both Deptford and Birmingham there were six to seven per cent more non-readers among the West Indian children than among the non-immigrants. Forty-five per cent of the Asian children in Birmingham gained no score at all on the test, and a total of 75 per cent were virtual non-readers of the English language.

The national survey of achievement in schools conducted in the U.S.A. for the Coleman Report[1] produced evidence that poor children fall even further behind in relation to national norms as they progress through school. When we analysed the test scores of children in the E.P.A. schools by age we found that on average they also deteriorated over the course of the primary school career, but that the deterioration was reversed at two points. The first was in the months immediately following entry to school at five years, a phenomenon which was also observed in the American survey. It seems that the initial impact of schools on children from impoverished areas is in general favourable. The gains did not persist for long however, and by the time children reached six and a half years their scores were already beginning to fall. A second peak occurred in the last two years preceding secondary school selection. In many schools the best teachers are allocated to these age groups and teaching is especially intensive. Although the overall fall-off in the scores of E.P.A. children in relation to those of children in more favoured areas is extremely disturbing, it is encouraging to find that a greater input of teaching resources such as occurs during the final two years appears to be rewarded with a measurable improvement in the children's skills, for it implies that an increase in teaching resources throughout the school could offset the decline altogether.

In the West Riding, children in the first four years of the local secondary modern school were also tested on the appropriate level of the E.P.V.T. (Level 3). Again a pattern of progressive decline was found, with a sharp drop in the fourth, and for most children, final year.

These then are our four Plowden educational priority areas. They certainly suffer from multiple economic and social deprivations and their schools labour under difficulties brought into them by the characteristics of the surrounding neighbourhood. But there is no unique description of either the E.P.A. or the E.P.A. school. The West Riding represents a distinctive type of economic misfortune and community stability. The city E.P.A.s are variously complicated by urban redevelopment, migration and immigration and their schools by teacher and pupil turnover and by children from families with different cultural backgrounds. Even these children, however, are by no means identical copies of each other. The Liverpool E.P.A., and to a lesser extent Deptford, appear to have more of the residual characteristics of a settled working class community, with a considerable proportion of parents brought up in the same area, than Birmingham, with its high influx of newcomers. No doubt too there is a wide range of condi-

---

[1] J. S. Coleman, *et al.*, *op. cit.*

tions nationally which escapes the view presented in our four districts, for example in some rural areas and peripheral redevelopment housing estates. We therefore infer that the definition of E.P.A., the diagnosis of its ills and the prescriptions for its amelioration must always be based on detailed local study.

CHAPTER 6

Pre-Schooling—Provision

No one in the project teams doubted that pre-schooling had to occupy a large place in our programmes. The initial diagnoses revealed either inadequacy or, in the case of the West Riding, complete absence of pre-school provision. Action was therefore taken in all four districts to raise the level of provision. We also wanted to know what kind of pre-schooling would be most appropriate to the needs of E.P.A. children and set out to discover this in a national pre-school experiment and in the action-researches in Birmingham and the West Riding which are reported below in Chapters 7 and 8. Nothing in our experience or the national statistics suggests that anything approaching a satisfactory scale of provision has yet been achieved in the E.P.A.s. Certainly the plan to include a pre-school element in our activities was strongly if not unanimously supported by local teachers.

Pre-schooling in Britain

Pre-school provision includes L.E.A. nursery schools, nursery classes, independent nurseries, health authority day nurseries,[1] registered child minder groups, nurseries run by industry and a host of welfare organisations both statutory and voluntary, as well as the vast but indeterminate number of playgroups. The statistics on the number of pre-school places available in this country are unreliable except for those relating to local education authority nursery schools, and even these are complicated by the fact that the nursery school accommodates children from two to five years whereas the nursery class attached to an infant school normally caters for children from three to five years. Moreover, many nursery schools, with accommodation for say 40 children, admit half full-time and the rest half-time. It is important too to distinguish between the L.E.A. nursery unit and the day nursery run by the local health authority for children who need to be looked after for a full working day. The number of day nurseries fell between 1956 and 1967 though this was probably compensated by the growth of private provision. Table 6.1 shows the trends from 1956 to 1967, i.e. in the decade before we began our work.

Nursery classes attached to primary schools in fact account for nearly three times the number in separate nursery schools. But the overall provision is small.

On the basis of a careful analysis of the official data, Tessa Blackstone drew similar conclusions with regard to places in nursery schools and nursery classes provided both by the state and independently in 1965. "Although the contribution of the maintained sector is higher than that of the independent sector, the role of the latter is far higher than in the rest

---

[1] From April 1971 day nurseries became the responsibility of the social service departments.

of the educational system. This is most true of the administrative counties, and least true of Wales. Within the maintained sector the majority of the places are in nursery classes, not nursery schools, but the degree to which this is true varies according to the type of authority. Within the independent sector most places are in nurseries registered as 'premises' under the local health authorities. Most maintained places are full-time, but circumstantial evidence suggests that most independent places are part-time. Finally the proportion of the child population receiving pre-school education is small. The percentage of three to four-year-olds involved at any one time in either the maintained or the independent sector is approximately 10 per cent."[1]

There has been some increase in the state provision of nursery places during the period of our studies, mainly under the stimulus of the urban programme. Meanwhile the playgroup movement has gathered strength. The Save the Children Fund has concentrated some of its energies in establishing and underwriting playgroups in areas of great social need; but with limited funds at its disposal, it can only scratch the surface. In 1969 some 82 Save the Children Fund playgroups were operating in new housing estates, skyscraper flats and in overcrowded areas of industrial Britain. Other bodies are also active. The Advisory Centre for Education has its Association of Multi-Racial Playgroups and the Priority Area Playgroups Project in Birmingham. The Community Relations Commission is also showing some interest in cities with a large immigrant population. The activities of these bodies indicate the need for statutory help and initiative in educational priority areas, in sharp contrast to the self-help so evident in the playgroup movement as a whole.

The introduction of the urban programme gave weight to the idea that pre-school provision could be satisfied, particularly in E.P.A.s, by the provision of nursery schools and classes through the D.E.S. and day nurseries through the Ministry of Health. The programme did indeed hold out hopes but an analysis of its immediate provision showed that the problem would be only marginally ameliorated even in E.P.A.s—though it was stated that "the Home Secretary made it clear that the programme will necessarily be a continuing one".[2] A sum of £20 to £25 million was proposed over the four years 1969–73 for both current and capital expenditure based on a 75 per cent grant to local authorities, capital expenditure being limited to £3 million in the first year. This sum was only partially concerned with nursery provision including, as it did, provision of children's homes. No mention was made of aid to playgroups. But on 23rd May 1969 the Under-Secretary of State for Health and Social Security stated, "We welcome the valuable contribution which playgroups can make to the opportunities for the development of the under-fives . . . where there were insufficient groups to meet the needs of priority children, the Secretary of State hoped that authorities would encourage suitable people and organisations to start a nursery group . . . that aid to playgroups would be a particularly useful

[1] Tessa Blackstone, *A Fair Start: The Provision of Pre-School Education*, Allen Lane, 1971, p. 95. An attempt at estimating pre-school provision of all forms may be found in Van der Eyken, *The Pre-School Years*, 1969, Chapter 8.

[2] Joint Circular, Home Office, D.E.S. and Ministry of Health, 4th October 1968.

object of expenditure in the second phase of (the Government's) programme of aid to urban areas of social deprivation." The voluntary playgroup-nursery movement had received official recognition.

The urban programme phase two, dated 7th February 1969, acknowledged the part that playgroups might play in the expansion of pre-school provision; the circular widened its scope from phase one to include a mixed bag of projects ranging from teachers' centres, in-service courses for teachers, family advice centres, to "aid to voluntary societies, for example those providing playgroups, play spaces, adventure play-grounds; playgroup advisers". Up to £2 million was allocated for capital expenditure in the financial year. This was the first legislative acknowledge-ment that voluntary efforts in areas of dire social need might deserve assistance from Government sources.

The rapid development of the playgroup movement does however raise certain problems. At present there are a number of acts of Parliament which, in a rather devious way, allow aid to playgroups.[1] But there is an anomaly. Whereas nursery education is clearly the responsibility of the L.E.A., voluntary nurseries and playgroups fall under the Health Com-mittee or Children's Committee of a local authority and, after April 1971, under the new Social Services Committee. The Plowden Report recom-mended that "Voluntary groups . . . should be subject to inspection by local *education* authorities and H.M. Inspectorate" whereas the Seebohm Report stated that "the majority (8 out of 10) of us think that the social service department should be given the clear responsibility for providing,

Table 6.1

Health Authority Day Nurseries and Child Minders

	1956	1966	1967
1. Nurseries provided by local authorities and voluntary organisations under the 1946 Act	547 (26,109)	445 (21,157)	444 (21,169)
2. Number of nurseries registered under the 1948 Act	464 (12,018)	3,083 (75,132)	4,382 (109,141)
3. Number of child minders	881 (6,964)	3,887 (32,336)	5,039 (42,696)
(Figures in brackets refer to its number of places)			

(A proportion of registered child minders were in fact self-help groups or voluntary bodies providing playgroups)

Source: Report of the Committee on Local Authority and Allied Personal Social Services (1968) (Seebohm).

[1] The most important are:—
    Section 46(2) of the Children Act 1948.
    Section 1 of the Children and Young Persons Act 1963.
    Section 65 of the Health Services and Public Health Act 1968.
Such aid would be administered by local authorities either through the Children or Health Committees or as from April 1971 the Social Services Committee. The Housing Act (1957) and the Local Government Act (1948) have somewhat limited powers in respect of aid to playgroups which were, of course, not known when these Acts were passed. In a similar way it is vaguely possible to aid playgroups under the Physical Training and Recreation Act (1937) and this is the only act, at present, under which the education committee of a local authority might give aid—though clearly intentions in this respect were hardly applicable in 1937.

supporting or supervising playgroups for children under five, seeking relevant assistance from the education, health, housing and parks departments. They should also be able to subsidise, and in consequence inspect, voluntary non-profit making activities such as pre-school playgroups". Few educationists would fall in with the Seebohm view but clarification of this point is needed if the initiative shown by some voluntary associations in deprived areas is to bear fruit.

Meanwhile most playgroups are forced to operate in premises ill-designed for nursery work, with minimal toilet and washing facilities, inadequate storage space, low heating standards in winter and often with no outside play space. By contrast state nursery provision appears sumptuous. The Plowden Report suggested that the D.E.S. "should undertake a careful study of present requirements (for nursery education) which may be unnecessarily *lavish* in some respects".[1] Certainly the cost of an infant school place is considerably less than that of a nursery place.

Provision in the four E.P.A. districts

Among our four districts the most dramatic case from the point of view of increased provision is that of the West Riding project district where there was no formal provision at the beginning of the project, though there was a highly developed informal network of child minding by relatives. The schools and the project team put pre-school provision at the top of their list of priorities for the area and with the help of the L.E.A. and the second and third phases of the urban programme they created universal provision of one kind or another in one of the two towns.[2] In the three city districts the project teams also raised the level of provision. In the I.L.E.A. opportunities for pre-schooling were relatively good but the project financed a new playgroup as part of the design for a study of language development among pre-school children in collaboration with Rachel Macmillan College. Overall provision in Deptford approached 30 per cent. In Birmingham the pre-school conditions of the project district were less favourable. In January 1969 the size of the pre-school age group (i.e. three and four-year-olds on which the Plowden Report based its forecast of needs) was 3,250. For these children there was a nursery unit run by the L.E.A., three city day nurseries run by the health authorities and six voluntary playgroups. These together had 300 places or provision for about 10 per cent of the three and four-year-olds. But, as a result of the first and second phases of the urban programme, together with voluntary efforts, 200 new nursery places, 60 new day nursery places and 60 new playgroup places had been added by 1971. Plowden had suggested that provision should be made for 15 per cent of the three-year-olds full-time, 35 per cent of the three-year-olds part-time, 15 per cent of the four-year-olds full-time and 75 per cent of the four-year-olds part-time. On this basis approximately 2,250 places would have been needed in the Balsall Heath—Sparkbrook area: in fact there were 620 places in 1971 after two urban aid programmes.

---

[1] Plowden, paragraph 1097 (ii).

[2] A detailed account of pre-school action-research in the West Riding and Birmingham is given in Chapter 8 below.

The methods used in increasing pre-school provision by the project teams were limited by our resources. In all cases the setting up of new nursery places or playgroups depended on the co-operation of either statutory or voluntary bodies. In Birmingham the existence of the action-research programme gave impetus to two community associations which had interest in playgroups. The project initiated new playgroups, underwrote them, and tried to ensure that they were sponsored by an organisation which would still exist after the project ended. Apart from the aim of providing more pre-schooling in an area of deprivation, there was also the more proximate end of ensuring that there were sufficient playgroups in the area to satisfy our national research design. Of the eight playgroups ultimately included in the design, three were initiated or supported by the project financially.

The development of the Liverpool pre-school programme had a disappointing start. In the first six months no more than 60 children were newly involved in pre-school provision and despite the generous offer of the L.E.A. to pay for up to six half-time staff, only one suitable person had been found until, in the last year of the project, another assistant was appointed. It became obvious that a tiny project could not embark on a large-scale programme of provision while at the same time engaged in many other E.P.A. activities. Moreover, success in founding a new playgroup sometimes revealed an unsuspected danger. Where existing playgroups had been struggling on meagre resources, the sudden appearance of a well financed venture next door could be highly demoralising. Thus, combining virtue with necessity, the Liverpool team changed its tactic from provision to support. In co-operation with the area community warden it attempted to draw all the playgroups in the locality into a loose federation for mutual benefit—sharing ideas, fund-raising, equipment, bulk purchasing, training and friendship in what is too frequently an isolated situation.

From that point the project built up a successful record of pre-school action. It gave £1,000 to support the association, and with the help of the Liverpool Save the Children Fund supervisor undertook a survey of the twenty -odd groups in the area in order to learn their problems and methods of working. Some 50 sociology students from local colleges of education collaborated in a survey of parents of pre-school children to try to assess specific requirements. Meanwhile the Moores Family Charity foundation created a pre-school fellowship, initially for three years but now permanently: and a second appointment is about to be made under the aegis of the Liverpool Council of Social Service.

There was also the experiment with a mobile pre-school unit. The Corporation Transport Department sold the project a double-decker bus cheaply and agreed to garage, fuel and lubricate and service it at nominal charges. After some months' negotiation the licence fee was reduced from a prohibitive £200 to a reasonable £25 per annum. The task of conversion and decoration was taken on by the staff and pupils of the technical and art departments of the local comprehensive school. This was an early example of linking one stage of education and another, in this case the use of secondary school boys to help under-fives and at the same time enabling them to apply their technical knowledge. These children readily solved problems set to them concerning smaller children playing on a bus and senior girls proved to be highly successful assistants in the Playmobile. The bus was to visit key points, such as blocks of flats, for a session or so each week. Upstairs was to be the "quiet room" with Wendy house, sand tray and story corner. Downstairs were to be rope ladders, barrels and dummy steering wheels. There was a supply of busman's hats for the children and safety gates were added at strategic points.

The E.P.A. Playgroups Association and the Playmobile both flourished in the second year of the Liverpool project. There were regular meetings, a developing system of mutual financial support and education of the participating parents. The whole enterprise revolved around the crucial full-time organiser who also held major responsibility for the Playmobile. It should also be mentioned that Liverpool managed to link the world of private playgroups and statutory nursery provision by using a primary school for playgroup purposes together with its staff and student help. In effect what was created was a pre-reception unit for mothers and children which assembled two or three times a week, illustrating the general idea of voluntary effort within a framework of statutory provision.

In Deptford support for pre-school provision followed similar lines. Contact was also maintained with exploratory studies of pre-school language work at Goldsmiths' College and, as we have mentioned, there was a study of language development among pre-school children in co-operation with Rachel Macmillan College which will be reported separately in Volume III.

Our concern with pre-schooling led to an increased awareness of the need not just for expansion but for types of provision which would maximise the effectiveness of positive discrimination and lay the foundations for radical improvement of the partnership between the educational system and the community. Most especially we were impressed by the potential contribution and hitherto neglected use of the reserves of energy and enthusiasm among the parents of pre-school children in E.P.A. districts. Organised pre-schooling, we would now insist, must use and direct that energy to constructive educational purposes.[1]

---

[1] Though Scottish conditions differ in some ways from English, it will be seen in Volume V that the Dundee experience reinforces these conclusions.

CHAPTER 7

The National Pre-School Experiment[1]

We have discussed the extent of pre-school provision and the attempts of the four projects to increase the number of places in their areas. An increase is necessary for social reasons alone: children living in busy urban streets or new high rise flats often have no safe place to play and low family incomes could be supplemented if mothers were free to go out to work. But attendance at nursery or playgroup can also serve an educational purpose, and therefore we felt we should be concerned not only with the number of pre-school groups in the E.P.A.s, but also with the content of the pre-school curriculum.

Intelligence grows at a very fast rate during the pre-school years, and already on entry to the infant school there are substantial differences in the performance of children from different social classes. Our own programme of testing in primary schools which we reported in Chapter 5 revealed that E.P.A. five-year-olds were scoring well below national norms on a vocabulary test. This fact was brought home even more sharply when the scores on the same vocabulary test of children in pre-school groups in the Birmingham E.P.A. were compared with the scores of children in a playgroup in a middle class district. Even when immigrant children with language difficulties were excluded the mean standardised score of the E.P.A. children was 93 points—seven points below the national mean—while the middle class children recorded a mean score of 108. On this basis the E.P.A. children could be considered to be about a year behind the middle class children. Our testing programme, along with other studies, suggested that this gap between E.P.A. and middle class children widens as the children grow older. The pre-school years could therefore be vital to the E.P.A. child.

Five-year-olds from middle class homes settle down to school work much more easily on the whole than do E.P.A. children. In many cases they are already used to having books around the home, they have learned how to use a pencil and a brush, they have been provided with educational toys, and their parents have valued highly activities requiring quiet and concentration. It is unlikely that the E.P.A. child will have these advantages, but pre-school education can begin to develop the skills he will need for success in school later on.

The social handicap of E.P.A. children is also conspicuous in language development. This is a product of many factors, among which are large families and difficult living conditions which can mean that mothers do not have time to spend with individual children, and the unfamiliarity of some immigrant groups with the English language or with "standard" English. But the causes may go deeper than this. The Newsoms[2] have found

---

[1]This chapter was written by Joan Payne who was responsible for the analysis but who joined the project after the experiment had already been designed.

[2]J. and E. Newsom, *Four Years Old in an Urban Community*, George Allen and Unwin, 1968.

systematic differences between middle class and working class families in the role played by speech in everyday life. Working class children for example are less likely to be allowed to talk at meals and to be told a bedtime story. While the working class mother tends to tell her children to fight their own battles, the middle class mother will intervene in disputes, hear both sides, and arbitrate. Verbal explanations for disobedience are also much more likely to be accepted by middle class mothers, and they in turn tend to adopt verbal methods of control, taking care to explain the principles underlying their actions. The middle class child has therefore both greater opportunity and greater incentive to develop articulateness.

Skill with language lies at the very root of success in school, and we were anxious to explore ways by which pre-school education could be used to help the language development of E.P.A. children. The British nursery school tradition emphasises social and emotional development. This is extremely important, and for the middle class child whose home already provides adequate educational stimuli it may be right to concentrate efforts in this field. For the E.P.A. child, however, it is not enough by itself, for he will never be rid of the educational handicap he bears at five years of age.

At present, as we saw in Chapter 6, only a minority of E.P.A. children attend pre-school at all, and of these many go to voluntary playgroups rather than local authority nursery schools and classes. A local authority nursery must have at least one qualified teacher on its staff and meet certain standards of premises and equipment, but playgroups are often run on a shoe-string by unqualified or inexperienced leaders. We wanted to try out a programme aimed at language development which would be of use to playgroups working under difficult conditions, and it seemed to us that this purpose might be served by a programme which laid down clear procedures for the instructor to follow. There should be a logical sequence of lessons, and equipment provided with suggestions on how it should be used. There was obviously the danger that untrained teachers would interpret such material too rigidly, but we felt it was worthwhile experimenting to see how feasible the approach was. We felt moreover that such a programme might have some value as part of the nursery school day. Traditional nursery school methods in this country allow the child free choice of activities, but observation in a nursery in Birmingham suggested that the amount of individual communication between teacher and child could be surprisingly small, with much of it arising from practical details such as putting on hats and coats. Although a qualified nursery teacher has the training to conduct language work without the assistance of a specially devised programme, the introduction of such a programme might be useful in drawing her attention in a systematic way to the particular language problems of the children in her care.

When the E.P.A. project began no British pre-school language programme was available, although a good deal of work has been done since then, some of which we shall look at in the following chapter. We therefore selected an American programme, Level P of the Peabody Language

Development Kit (P.L.D.K.)[1] to try out in the E.P.A. context. The P.L.D.K. was originally designed for use with poor children aged three to five years in the Southern states of America, where it had shown some success. It is a structured programme in the sense that it sets specific learning goals which are reached by a series of lessons in a set sequence, the content of the lessons being laid down in considerable detail. The teaching methods are however by no means as formal as some other American programmes which have acquired a degree of notoriety among British educationalists;[2] they include stories, songs, games and rhymes as well as question and answer and repetition. Moreover, the kit had already been introduced into a non-E.P.A. nursery school in Slough by the N.F.E.R., where it had been well received by the staff and found to be popular among the children. For these reasons we hoped that it would be acceptable to E.P.A. nursery teachers and play-group leaders; even so, some aspects aroused antagonism.[3]

The aims of the P.L.D.K. are to increase children's command of grammar and vocabulary, to encourage verbal fluency and compreh sion, and to develop powers of auditory and visual discrimination. The materials include puppets, picture cards, posters, geometrical shapes, records of songs, stories and various noises, and other miscellaneous items such as a doll which can be dressed and a xylophone. A teacher's manual gives detailed instructions on how these materials should be used in each of 180 daily 20-minute lessons covering two years' work. The lessons are designed for groups of eight to ten children and are so organised that the teacher speaks individually to each child as well as conducting group activities.

The American origin of the kit inevitably brought drawbacks, partly because the text contained Americanisms and partly because there were cultural references unfamiliar to English children. In addition, some of the grammatical mistakes which the P.L.D.K. attempts to correct, though common among the Southern Negro children for whom it was intended, are not made by English children—for example, difficulty in forming plurals. Some of these defects were remedied by Brimer's modifications to the manual, but nothing could be done about others short of re-making the materials. As most children following the kit had already become acquainted with many aspects of American speech and culture through television, we hoped that the kit's failings would not prove too serious in practice.

The P.L.D.K. was introduced on an experimental one-year basis into seven nursery classes and playgroups in three of the four project areas. All the children in the nursery classes and playgroups which used the kit took part in the lessons, this being achieved by splitting the children into two groups and conducting the lesson first with one group and then with the other. Thus the teaching groups consisted of 12 to 15 children, but as there

---

[1]The P.L.D.K. was developed by L. M. Dunn, J. O. Smith and K. B. Horton at the Peabody College for Teachers, Nashville, Tennessee. It was selected on the advice of M. A. Brimer of the Research Unit at Bristol University Institute of Education, who acted as research consultant to the E.P.A. Project. Mr. Brimer also advised on the design of the national pre-school experiment and the selection of tests.

[2]See, for example, C. Bereiter and S. Engelmann, *Teaching Disadvantaged Children in the Pre-School*, Prentice-Hall, 1966.

[3]In Dundee antagonism was such that the project team devised a special programme to replace the P.L.D.K. (See Vol. V.)

THE NATIONAL PRE-SCHOOL EXPERIMENT

were usually one or two absentees actual group size was rather closer to the recommended maximum of ten. Lessons were given both by qualified nursery teachers and nursery assistants with N.N.E.B. training, eleven being involved in all.

Obviously, the experience of the nursery teachers and assistants was a crucial part of the evaluation of the P.L.D.K. At the end of the experimental year all eleven were interviewed to ascertain their opinion of the P.L.D.K., the ways in which they had used it in their groups, and the benefits, if any, they felt it had given the children. Interviews, which were tape-recorded, were free ranging and unstructured to give them the opportunity to raise all the points they thought were relevant, and the most important themes were extracted from the verbatim transcripts.[1]

The initial reaction of most people to the kit was that of being impressed and intrigued, although two were "panic-stricken at the thought of coping with all those materials". These two were reassured on reading the manual, when they realised how well-charted the course was. Unfortunately, one teacher had the reverse feeling: "I was impressed when I saw the materials, but then the manual really put me off—I said, 'My God, they must think I'm an absolute idiot to want all this stuff'. I've been qualified for several years now so it felt like a real insult." From that moment on this teacher was 'anti-Peabody'. Several other teachers mentioned that they resented the somewhat patronising tone of the manual with its minutely detailed instructions, but none of them objected quite so violently; by and large the first reaction was one of interest in the aims of the project, coupled with a favourable impression of the materials provided and a slight unease about the didactic nature of the manual.

The equipment was generally liked: "Very interesting equipment—very like what we already have"; "Excellent apparatus, sturdy enough to withstand even the treatment it gets here"; "A good selection of stuff—saves you slogging around making your own". Each piece of apparatus earned both credit and discredit. Criticisms were mainly on the grounds of poor quality, cultural unsuitability, aesthetic distaste, and lack of validity as a teaching aid. But on the positive side, many instructors were grateful for the chance to use bright, gay apparatus which had great child appeal and was also a source of new ideas to the ever-inventive nursery teacher.

Views on the manual varied with the extent to which the teachers felt themselves to be bound by the letter of the book. Those who stuck rigidly to it disliked its didactic and condescending tone: "My God—what sort of a twit do they think I *am*?" was one heartfelt cry. Teachers dislike being told exactly what to say and do, especially when they suspect that much of the material is not suitable for their children. The group of teachers that adapted the working to suit their own needs felt happier about the manual. However, from what was said it seems the amount of deviation was not great and concerned the wording of lessons (i.e. elimination of Americanisms), not the content. A number of the teachers encouraged lessons to

---

[1]Interviews and analysis were performed by Helen Quigley of the N.F.E.R., and all statements about the interviews are derived from her paper, "A Report on Interviews with Eleven E.P.A. Nursery Teachers and Assistants using the P.L.D.K. Level P", 1970 (unpublished).

develop naturally when the occasion arose, e.g. if a colour chip lesson developed into a counting session leading to a discussion of concepts such as big and small. They felt this made the session more interesting for all concerned.

The pacing of the lessons presented problems, for no programme is going to move at exactly the correct pace for all the children using it. One teacher admitted to skipping—but not actually omitting—topics she thought would be boring; another group of teachers felt they had to expand the material given at a couple of points and so "paused" for a few related unprogrammed activities before going on to the next lesson. The consensus of opinion seemed to be that the programme moved unduly slowly at first but that it suddenly became much more difficult around lesson 50. The arbitrary placing of some lessons was also queried.

The idea of having a specific daily language session was questioned by those who felt the nursery already catered adequately for the linguistic needs of the children. These teachers would have preferred to have the equipment available to use as they wished throughout the day rather than have a "language time". Some teachers commented that they hated the feeling of "having to" do the programme every day—especially if this meant inter-rupting the children's play to hold the sessions. By contrast, others felt that setting aside a small part of each day to concentrate on language was a good idea and had assimilated the session into the daily routine without any difficulty. As one said, "I know I ought to do language every day, but I've never been as systematic as this before. I'm definitely being kept on my toes." Nobody favoured a return to the dark days of Formal Lessons In The Nursery, but several teachers felt this was an efficient way of coping with a very large problem in the short time available.

The P.L.D.K. manual stresses that the sessions should be followed up wherever possible by classroom work as this leads to a reinforcement of the child's learning which should result in quicker and easier ways to success. However, the amount of follow-up work varied greatly. Three teachers tried to tell stories and lead discussions in the classroom on topics that had been covered in the programme as well as emphasising colour, shapes, etc. where appropriate; another primed her staff to concentrate on specific sentence constructions; a fifth played the xylophone or sang some of the songs in the classroom. Five of the others felt that the usual daily routine of the nursery provided sufficient reinforcement, and one, who acted as a visiting teacher, would have liked to have done more follow-up work but had to leave this to the discretion of the class teachers.

In Birmingham one full-time nursery class, one half-day nursery class and two playgroups used the kit. Children's progress in each of these groups was compared with that of children in a control group of the same type where no special programme was being run. In Liverpool a full-time nursery class and a playgroup using the P.L.D.K. were similarly compared with control groups, and a part-time P.L.D.K. nursery in the West Riding was compared with a control part-time nursery in Liverpool. For the purposes of analysis we have treated the Birmingham groups as a separate unit from the Liverpool and West Riding groups.[1]

---

[1]A fuller account of the statistical analysis will be found in Volume II.

In order to check that the P.L.D.K. and control groups were comparable we asked an H.M.I. to visit all of them and, with the help of L.E.A. nursery advisers, to make separate assessments of quality of premises, equipment, environment and work, as well as the qualifications and experience of the staff. An overall ranking was also made. Of the seven pairs of P.L.D.K. and control groups, three were given similar assessments, in two (one in Birmingham and the other in Liverpool) the P.L.D.K. group received the better rating, and in two (again, one in Birmingham and the other in Liverpool) the control group was ranked higher. Thus there was no overall tendency in either Birmingham or Liverpool and West Riding for the groups running the P.L.D.K. to be otherwise superior or inferior to the groups with which they were compared.

We also collected information on the home circumstances of the children. Because the resources needed to conduct a full-scale survey were not available this data had to be assembled from various sources, including school records, interviews with mothers, and the personal knowledge of the staff. There were also a number of children for whom we were unable to obtain any information at all. Hence we do not place any great reliance on our findings in this sphere. Nevertheless in both the Birmingham and the Liverpool and West Riding groups the P.L.D.K. children tended to have fathers of higher occupational status than the control children, they were less likely to be the children of immigrants, and their housing conditions were also rather better. In addition, P.L.D.K. children in the Birmingham groups came from smaller families and were more likely to be first or only children than the control children, and their parents had had, on the whole, more education. None of the differences were very great, but as these factors have been found by other studies to be associated with better language development we nevertheless have to bear them in mind in interpreting the results of our own experiment.

Two tests of language ability were chosen to measure the children's progress on the basis that they were at that time the only purely language tests for pre-school children for which English norms had been established. These were the Pre-School Version of the English Picture Vocabulary Test[1] and the Experimental Version of the Reynell Developmental Language Scales (R.D.L.S.). The E.P.V.T. has already been described in Chapter 5.[2] It directly measures listening vocabulary, but it is also claimed to be indicative of general verbal ability. However we found in a separate study[3] that its validity as a measure of general verbal ability was somewhat lower than its validity as a measure of listening vocabulary. The same study showed it to have a test-retest stability of ·81 over an interval of four weeks in a sample of children similar to those taking part in the P.L.D.K. experiment. The R.D.L.S. takes a good deal longer to administer than the E.P.V.T. It gives separate scores for verbal comprehension and expressive language, the latter being obtained by summing scores on three subtests: structure, which measures the child's ability to talk in sentences of increasing length and complexity, vocabulary, and content—the ability to put ideas into

---

[1] Level 1 was used at the post-test for children who were aged five years or older.
[2] P. 74.

[3] J. Stevenson and J. Payne, "Reliability and Validity of the Pre-School Version of the English Picture Vocabulary Test and the Experimental Version of the Reynell Developmental Scales for Four-Year-Olds in E.P.A. Nursery Schools", 1972 (unpublished).

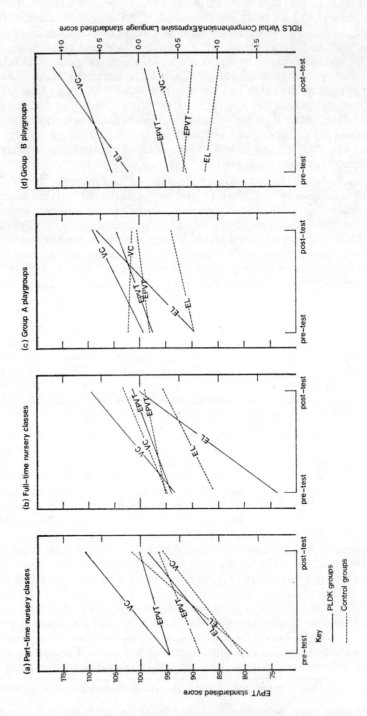

*Figure 7.1:   Pre-test and post-test scores of P.L.D.K.
and control groups in the Birmingham experiment.*

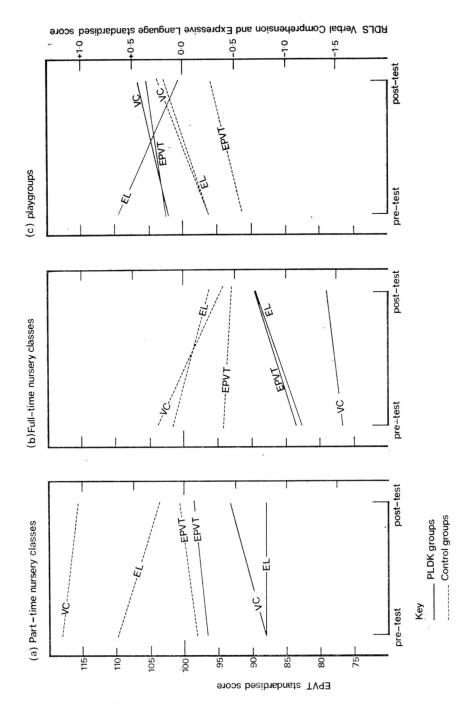

Figure 7.2:   Pre-test and post-test scores of P.L.D.K.
and control groups in the Liverpool and West Riding experiment.

words. In the study referred to above both the verbal comprehension and expressive language scales had good validities, but their test-retest stability was poor at ·58. All children including controls were tested before P.L.D.K. lessons began, as early as possible in the autumn term 1969, and again at the end of the programme during the summer term 1970. There was one exception to this procedure: the P.L.D.K. playgroup in Liverpool did not enter the experiment until after Christmas, so pre-testing there was carried out in January 1970.

The problem of turnover of children in the groups proved to be extremely serious. At the beginning of the experiment 20 to 30 children had been tested in each nursery class or playgroup; by the end of the year there remained of these on average only 15, with the numbers in the different groups ranging from 23 down to nine. The loss of numbers was greatest in Birmingham, and was due not only to families leaving the district but also to children entering school early, as the general exodus from the area meant that the schools had empty places to offer. This caused difficulties for the analysis, because the smaller two groups are, the larger any difference between them has generally to be in order to reach statistical significance.

The results of the tests in the Birmingham groups are shown in Figure 7.1 and in the Liverpool and West Riding groups in Figure 7.2. In each figure a separate graph for part-time nursery classes, full-time nursery classes and playgroups gives the pre-test and post-test scores on the E.P.V.T. and the Verbal Comprehension and Expressive Language Scales of the R.D.L.S. of both the P.L.D.K. group and the control group. A separate graph is given for each pair of P.L.D.K. and control playgroups in Birmingham, group A and group B.

Because of the problem of small numbers very few of the differences between P.L.D.K. and control groups in the amount of improvement between pre-test and post-test were statistically significant. We therefore must look instead at the overall trend of the results. The first thing to be noticed is that in almost every case the scores of the children in the P.L.D.K. groups were better at the end of the experimental year than they were at the beginning. In contrast the scores of the control groups show a much more varied pattern, sometimes rising and sometimes falling. When we compare specific P.L.D.K. groups and their controls we find that in general the P.L.D.K. groups improved more over the year on all three tests, thus supporting the view that the P.L.D.K. assists language development.

There are two exceptions to this generalisation. The first is the Liverpool playgroups, recorded in Figure 7.2(c), where the control group improved more on all three tests than the P.L.D.K. group, and indeed the score of the P.L.D.K. group on the Expressive Language Scale of the R.D.L.S. actually fell during the year. Although we cannot explain the deterioration on this one test, it will be remembered that the Liverpool P.L.D.K. group did not start the programme and were not tested until January 1970. Their progress over two terms is in fact being compared with the progress of the control children over three terms. The second exception concerns the part-time nursery classes in Birmingham (Figure 7.1(a)). Here the P.L.D.K. group improves a little more than the control on the Verbal Comprehension Scale, and the control group improves slightly more than the P.L.D.K. on the Expressive Language Scale and the E.P.V.T. The similarity of the progress made by children in these two groups is interesting, because both were given very high ratings by the H.M.I. who visited them and informal language work was part of the normal day in the control group. The evidence of these two groups suggests that in very good nursery schools the use of the P.L.D.K. makes no difference to the already excellent levels of progress.[1]

In the interviews at the end of the year we asked the P.L.D.K. teachers whether they felt the children had enjoyed the programme and whether they had progressed as a result of it. Few had any doubts about the first question. A typical comment was, "We only have to say 'P. Mooney time' and we get knocked over in the rush"—P. Mooney being a puppet who figures important-antly in the lessons. Another said, "They're fighting to come out each morning". A lot of this eagerness was attributed to the novelty of the situation and the children's great interest in P. Mooney—one teacher said she felt the group waited on tenterhooks throughout the session for P. Mooney to emerge.

There was one teacher who disagreed with this estimate of the children's enjoyment: "It's often a grind to get through it. I look at the lesson and know it's going to be boring and so, of course, when it comes to the lesson it *is* boring. The children don't enjoy it and neither do I." The other teachers complained about occasions when the children were bored, but no-one experienced it quite as constantly as this. Most teachers did find, however, that the brighter, older children seemed to be happiest and gained most from the sessions, the older but duller children seemed to become bored most quickly, and the younger children most often sat silently, appearing to be struck dumb with the novelty of the situation. Nevertheless a comment was made that several of the shyer children seemed particularly to enjoy the sessions.

None of the teachers felt that any child had suffered as a result of the programme and all agreed that the children had progressed during the year. The major difficulty was in deciding how much of the improvement was due to the programme and how much to the stimulating effect of the normal nursery environment. In making a decision of this sort obviously the teachers had to fall back on their own experience, and for this reason several said they wished there had been a control group within their own playgroup or nursery.

Eight of the eleven teachers had worked in their nursery for more than one year. All of these thought that the children had progressed, but they knew from experience that children progressed in their nurseries anyway, and three were convinced that the improvement was no more than they would normally have expected. The other five felt there probably had been some improvement which could not be attributed solely to the nursery. The teachers who were new to their nursery were unanimous in their belief that the children had improved—two cases were quoted of shy children who had whispered their first words in the peace of the small group and then grad-ually started to talk in the nursery.

---

[1]The Dundee results tend to confirm this finding. (See Vol. V.)

On the whole, then, the teachers' opinions confirm, though with reservations, the evidence of the test scores that the P.L.D.K. could be of benefit to the children. An important point in considering this improvement is whether it has been confined to the small groups in which the P.L.D.K. was taught, or, whether it has carried over into the children's other activities. Of the eleven teachers, one denied any improvement at all as a result of the P.L.D.K., and one felt nothing could be proved without a control group in the same nursery. Two others said that although the children had learned to speak in sentences in the room in which the programme was held, they forgot the moment they walked back into the nursery. The remaining seven felt that probably some of their hard work had rubbed off into the children's lives. Comments were made that the children would recognise animal pictures in books and say "That's in P. Mooney!" Use of colours and shapes was most frequently reported—the children in one nursery were said to mention the colour and shape of almost every object in a way they had not done before. Several teachers remarked that the children listened more keenly to the stories told in the nursery and that their memory of these had improved.

Throughout the accounts of the interviews one teacher stands out from the rest as disliking the P.L.D.K. from the start. She found that the children were bored by the lessons, and noticed no improvement which could be attributed to them. In fact Figure 7.2(a) shows that the children in her group did make some gains on the tests, but they were less than in any other P.L.D.K. group except the Liverpool playgroup which started late. This was almost certainly the result of her attitude to the programme. The way that new programmes depend for their success on the enthusiasm of the teachers using them is often thought by researchers to present problems for evaluation, for it is very difficult to control for differences in attitudes in the experimental design. In the design of the experiment we tried to take account of differences in enthusiasm by choosing randomly which nurseries or playgroups should use the P.L.D.K. and which should act as controls, and then persuading the groups to accept the outcome. This was to avoid the situation where the P.L.D.K. was tested out only in those groups which were most eager to innovate. In fact this attempt at randomisation proved fruitless because several of the groups which had been selected to use the P.L.D.K. but were unwilling to do so simply dropped out of the experiment. We now feel that our original conception of the issue was at fault. In a non-experimental situation it is highly unlikely that a programme would be imposed on a teacher against her will. To attempt to evaluate a programme which conflicts with the principles of the teacher using it is to give it an unfair trial.

When a new curriculum is brought into the classroom it is sometimes found that the benefit to the children comes not so much from the content of the material as from the stimulation of a novel experience and the heightened enthusiasm of the teacher. We thought that this might also happen with the P.L.D.K., and there was the further possibility that the children's language would improve simply because the programme provided an opportunity for more direct conversation between teacher and child than might otherwise have taken place. Hence a means was devised of testing this hypothesis. If children who had followed a new teaching programme

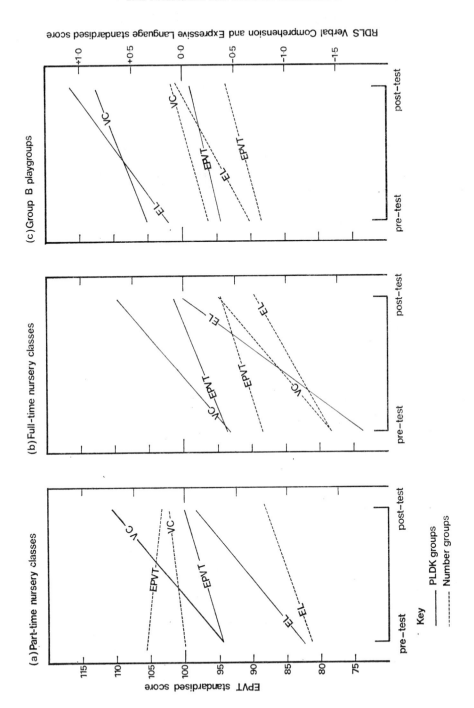

Figure 7.3: Pre-test and post-test scores of P.L.D.K. and Number groups in the Birmingham experiment.

with non-linguistic goals but methods involving individual conversation between child and teacher showed gains on tests of verbal ability as great as those made by the P.L.D.K. children, we would be forced to conclude that the specific language content of the P.L.D.K. lessons had little independent effect.

The programme we chose was mounted in the Birmingham E.P.A. and was designed to teach children number concepts. It is fully described in the following chapter where it is evaluated in its own right. At present we consider it only in relation to the light it sheds on the P.L.D.K.

The number programme was introduced into a playgroup in the Birmingham E.P.A. which was in fact given a slightly better overall assessment by the H.M.I. than the P.L.D.K. playgroup B with which it was compared. No differences were recorded between the home backgrounds of the children in the two groups. No L.E.A. nursery classes in the same district were free to use the programme, so two voluntary nursery groups were enlisted. These both had trained staff and children attending all day, but their standards of accommodation and equipment were not as good as the L.E.A. P.L.D.K. nurseries. However the home backgrounds of the children in these groups were very similar to those of the corresponding P.L.D.K. children. A group of part-timers in one of the voluntary nurseries formed the comparison with the part-time P.L.D.K. nursery children.

Children in the number groups were tested on the E.P.V.T. and the R.D.L.S. in exactly the same way as children in the P.L.D.K. groups, in the autumn term 1969 and at the end of the summer term 1970. Figure 7.3 shows the results. In the full-time nursery classes on the Verbal Comprehension Scale and in the playgroups on the E.P.V.T., P.L.D.K. and Number groups progressed equally. Otherwise the P.L.D.K. groups improved slightly more, but the differences were by no means as marked as they were between the P.L.D.K. and control groups. On only one test in one group (Figure 7.3(a)) did the language scores of the children following the number programme actually decline.

We conclude from these results that novelty and increased teacher–child communication formed part of the explanation of the gains we observed in the P.L.D.K. groups, but that the content of the P.L.D.K. itself made a contribution over and above this. This is said with the reservation that the nursery classes which followed the Number programme were not as well housed and equipped as the P.L.D.K. groups, and we cannot predict with certainty what the outcome would have been if they had been fully comparable. The teachers' comments make it clear that the P.L.D.K. is by no means ideal for pre-school groups in this country, but they also imply—and are supported in this by the test scores—that it would be worthwhile to develop British programmes. Such programmes should incorporate some of the ideas of the P.L.D.K. while leaving the teacher more scope to adapt the lessons to suit the particular needs of the children in her charge.

Teachers using the P.L.D.K. also noticed improvements which we did not measure in motivation and behaviour, and also a great deal of enjoyment in the learning process. We hope these gains will carry on into infant school, where they could prove to be even more important than the progress that was achieved in language skills.

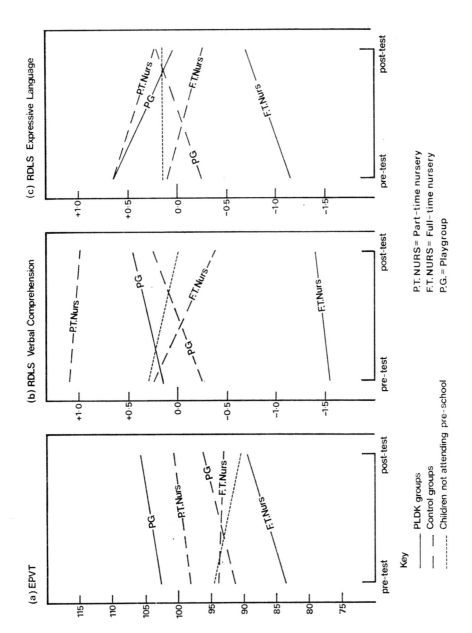

Figure 7.4: Pre-test and post-test scores of Liverpool children not attending pre-school compared with P.L.D.K. and control groups in Liverpool.

Children not attending playgroups and nurseries

We have examined the language development of children following different programmes in nurseries and playgroups, but ignored the majority of E.P.A. children who do not attend pre-school at all. How do they progress? American research suggests that they fall behind their peers in language skills as they grow older. A study which tried to find out what happens to our own E.P.A. children stands as post-script to the national pre-school experiment.

The subject is a very difficult one to investigate. Among the children who do not attend pre-school are some whose mothers prefer them to stay at home and who spend a lot of time talking and playing with them. We cannot assume that children who do not attend pre-school differ from those who do only in the lack of opportunity. To simplify the issue, therefore, we located a district in the Liverpool E.P.A. in which there was very little pre-school provision for any child, and from this district we hoped to select a random sample of children of pre-school age to compare with the children in the Liverpool nurseries and playgroups in the national pre-school experiment.

We then ran across another problem: we could find no suitable records from which to take the names and addresses of children in the right age group. There is typically so much population movement in inner-ring E.P.A.s that birth lists rapidly become out of date, and even health visitors' lists cannot keep pace. After many wasted calls we decided to knock on every door in a certain number of streets and simply ask whether a child of pre-school age lived there. Naturally under these circumstances a large number of parents refused to co-operate, and only 17 children were found who remained in the study for the whole of its duration. They appeared to live in poorer housing and to come from larger families than the children in the nurseries and playgroups.

The 17 were tested in their homes on the E.P.V.T. and the R.D.L.S. at the beginning of the study and again nine months later, and their scores are depicted in Figure 7.4 along with the scores of the other Liverpool groups. Because of the oddity of the sample we would not wish to make too much of the comparison, but on two of the tests the children not attending nurseries and playgroups deteriorated markedly, while on the third they showed no change. The evidence is slight, but it does suggest that E.P.A. children following a good pre-school programme make greater strides in language than those who must stay at home.

CHAPTER 8

Further Experiments in Pre-Schooling

Our evaluation of the American Peabody Language Development Kit suggested that language programmes have considerable potential in the pre-school. However Americanisms in the vocabulary and culturally unfamiliar items in the visual materials, together with methods alien to the traditional British approach to nursery school education, made the P.L.D.K. not entirely suitable for children in this country. Hence in all four projects work was undertaken to develop more appropriate programmes, three projects being interested in the development of language, and one in number concepts.

Liverpool

The project team in Liverpool experimented with designing a British pre-school kit which could be used in playgroups, as they were particularly conscious of the vague and unco-ordinated nature of much playgroup work, especially in language, and the lack of skilled organisers in many areas. Twenty-four stories were written, each accompanied by a large wall picture and a puppet presenter, Dr. Wotever. They were set in and around a block of flats and chiefly concerned two small boys, Red Herring and Fynan Haddock, an old widow in one of the flats, Mrs. Fluff-Fluff, and the caretaker, the irascible Mr. Pippin. Playgroup mothers and supervisors were encouraged to add as much local reference as possible. It was hoped too that infant reception classes might find some value in the kit. "Wotever Next", as it was called, was written using a basic vocabulary of 360 words drawn up on the basis of the local testing for the Peabody experiment carried out by the team, plus a new vocabulary of 360 words based on national norms: each story used the original 360 words and introduced 15 of the new ones. An introductory manual explained the method to be followed; it included the two full lists of words alphabetically and by category, and suggested how each story could be used and followed up in the groups over a week or a fortnight's work. It was too early by the end of the project to evaluate the benefits of "Wotever Next" since it came into operation only in the summer of 1971, but there was undoubtedly initial enthusiasm on the part of those using it.

London

During 1970–71 the Deptford project team worked together with a playgroup funded by the project and with the staff of a local nursery school to develop a pre-school language programme. The aim of this programme was not to produce a "kit" of materials and activities, but to promote the children's language development by directing the attention of the staff to "language-producing situations" in the normal pre-school class or group and increasing their awareness of language development. It was hoped that this would help staff to modify their own language interactions with the children, by concentrating more on one-to-one contacts and paying more attention to the stage reached by individual children.

Regular meetings were held throughout the year with the nursery staff involved, students working on the programme in the playgroup, and the project team. Staff were asked to make as many one-to-one language contacts as possible with the experimental children in their group. Records were kept of the activity during individual sessions, and analysed with a view to improving their effectiveness. Ten experimental children took part in each of three nursery classes and the morning session of the playgroup; controls were provided both within these groups by ten other children with whom the staff did not deliberately work, and by three other nursery classes and the playgroup afternoon session.

Children were tested at the beginning and end of the year on the Reynell Developmental Language Scales and the Pre-School version of the E.P.V.T., in order to assess language development. To gauge the programme's success in affecting the staff's behaviour in the pre-school group, an observation schedule was developed and samples of classroom behaviour were taken over a period of a month midway through the programme.

Results indicated no statistically significant improvement in language development for the experimental group over and above that made by either control group. The experimental groups (nursery and playgroup together) tended to improve, however, with respect to national norms. Differences in verbal behaviour were found between the experimental and control groups. The number of one-to-one verbal exchanges between staff and children was significantly higher in the experimental groups, possibly as a result of the nursery teacher reallocating duties within the classroom, and the special introduction of students into the playgroup.

The project team conclude that the programme at least indicates the way in which classroom behaviour of staff may be altered, and which of the typical pre-school activities may be most fruitfully exploited as "language-producing situations".

Birmingham

The number conservation programme in Birmingham, which was discussed in Chapter 7 in its role as a control in the national pre-school experiment, was also of interest in its own right. According to Piagetian theory, the child's concept of number and other mathematical concepts develops, on the whole, independently of adult intervention. When adults try to impose mathematical concepts on a child prematurely, the child's learning is merely verbal; true understanding comes only with mental growth. The concept of number conservation—that is, concepts such as "more" and "less" or "fewer", and the recognition that the number of objects in a row or a group remains constant however they are spaced— cannot be accelerated, but comes gradually through the child's own development. An increasing amount of research, however, on the one hand questions the order and the pace of the basic stages of cognitive growth postulated by Piaget, and on the other hand suggests the possibility of speeding up those stages by suitably structured programmes. The Birmingham work was based in particular on two previous studies[1] which indicated that it was possible to accelerate the course of conceptual development.

A second strand in Birmingham's decision to adopt this form of programme was the conclusion reached by the earlier studies quoted that non-verbal methods of learning concepts had proved superior to purely verbal methods, combined with the necessity of finding a programme which would contrast sufficiently with that of the P.L.D.K., with its strong reliance on language stimulus through constant teacher-child interaction and a mass of materials such as pictures, flash cards, stories, songs, records, and so on. The problem was two-fold. First there was the question of assessing changes in concept recognition by purely verbal means—a difficulty noted by many researchers. Secondly, there was the difficulty of using non-verbal techniques in promoting the child's conceptual development; these non-verbal techniques, it is argued, are less dependent on the child's level of vocabulary. Research indeed is inconclusive as to the role of language and verbal training in the development of number and other mathematical concepts in children. The decision to use non-verbal methods rested, however, on the need to design a programme sufficiently in contrast to the P.L.D.K.

The number programme was prepared for the Birmingham project by J. Mason and his colleague W. D. Clarke, and based on their previous experimental work and teaching experience. A detailed Teacher's Manual was written, setting out the rationale for the programme and giving details of the work to be followed in the "units". It stressed that research work already indicated that acceleration of number conservation was possible, given suitable programmes. This particular programme attempted to use the large amount of standard apparatus already found in nursery and infant classrooms but often used by teachers in an unstructured way. Beads of different shapes and colours, counters, matching cards, paper mosaic shapes, number recognition games, snap games, were amongst the materials used; there were also duplicated materials and filmstrips. Work included recognition of colours (necessary to the work in the later units), recognition of number symbols and ability to count up to nine, counting strategies, and structural apparatus. Details given in the Teacher's Manual for each "unit" specified objectives (e.g. Unit 1—"to help children to acquire the concepts of red and yellow"; Unit 54—"to see whether children are able to use the concepts of 'more' and 'same' using numbers 7 and 8"), materials to be used, and activities to follow. But this was only in the barest outline, as a good deal of freedom was allowed the teachers to develop their own techniques and materials. Teachers were issued with the materials, the Teacher's Manual, and individual record sheets for their pupils. The whole was approved by a specialist H.M.I. as "a very carefully prepared programme which would give teachers considerable encouragement".

---

[1] J. G. Wallace, "An inquiry into the development of concepts of number in young children involving a comparison of verbal and non-verbal methods of assessment and acceleration", Ph.D. thesis, Bristol University, 1967 (unpublished); J. Mason, M.A. thesis, Bristol University, 1969 (unpublished).

Figure 8.1: Comparison of number conservation groups with P.L.D.K. and control groups in Birmingham on the test for number concepts

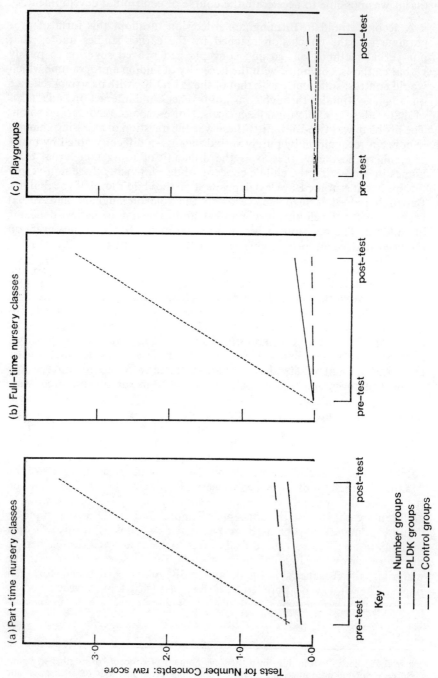

As explained in Chapter 7 the programme was used by three groups in Birmingham, namely a playgroup and two voluntary nurseries which had trained staff and full-day sessions, but whose premises and equipment were not of as high a standard as in L.E.A. nurseries. In one of these nurseries it was the part-timers who followed the lessons. The progress of the part-timers and full-timers in these nurseries was compared with members of part-time and full-time L.E.A. nurseries respectively, on the one hand with a group using the P.L.D.K., and on the other with a control group which was running no special programme. A similar comparison was made among playgroups.

The programme had to engage the children's attention over an entire school year, and some elements proved more successful than others. The films, once their novelty wore off, did not hold the children's attention especially well and many children continued to try to touch the objects on the screen. The programme tended to be repetitive and lacked variety despite its sixty-odd items. Nevertheless, staff in the groups managed to sustain the interest of their children even though the nursery schools normally allowed complete freedom in choice of activities and the number programme had to compete with all other interests. Staff were asked to concentrate the children's attention upon the materials, and to limit conversation to the tasks in hand; and many of the materials absorbed the children completely. The development in attention span was particularly striking in some children, notably in one group containing some of the most deprived children in the area with severe learning and behavioural problems. With such children, the project staff found that it was impossible to restrict conversation entirely during the programme, however convenient this would have been for the comparison with the Peabody programme. Nevertheless, the number groups felt very different in atmosphere from the Peabody groups—an austere regime on the surface, with no puppets, no songs, and no actions, yet apparently highly rewarding to some children.

As well as the two language tests used in the national pre-school experiment the children were tested at the beginning and the end of the year on a test for number concepts specially constructed by one of the programme's authors. It is generally recognised that there is extreme difficulty in assessing changes in concept recognition behaviour which is partly due to the difficulty of controlling the administration of the Piagetian-type tests most often used—for instance, whether the child is allowed to manipulate the test materials himself or merely observe the experimenter may influence the child's performance profoundly.[1] The test used in the Birmingham study attempted to meet these objections by making the procedure for administering the test uniform. Each test item consisted of questions on a set of materials in a particular arrangement (e.g. four blocks placed close together, and then spaced out in a longer row) and included a "suggestibility" question ("Can you tell me why?"). The test was not standardised, and so the scores do not contain a correction for age, and it is not possible to compare them with national norms.

The results are shown in Figure 8.1, which plots pre-test and post-test scores on the test for number concepts for each of the number conservation

---

[1] See for instance *Are Piagetian tests reliable?*, National Foundation for Educational Research, Slough, Bucks, 1969.

groups and the groups with which they were compared. It can be seen that at the beginning of the year all nine groups scored near to zero, and that while the P.L.D.K. and control groups made little or no progress during the year the nursery groups using the programme each gained over three points. The number conservation playgroup did not make progress, and this was because the playgroup staff found pressure of work too great to keep up the scheduled lessons throughout the year.

Looking at the progress of individual children in the number conservation groups we found that while some children improved enormously and could by the end of the year formulate clear and concise answers to the "suggestibility" item, others obtained no greater scores than they had at the beginning. Yet they had perhaps become more number conscious, and certainly their capacity to concentrate on a task had improved—an ability which was not measured directly by the tests used. It seems fair overall to conclude that for many children the programme was effective in accelerating the course of conceptual development in number.

West Riding

The West Riding individual language programme was intended, like the Birmingham number conservation programme, to be used as a comparison with the Peabody Language Development Kit. Unlike the Birmingham scheme, however, it was a language-oriented programme. As with the P.L.D.K., it was a structured language scheme, but employing a very different method, and was based on very different assumptions.

Pre-schooling constituted a major part of the total effort in the West Riding project and a full account will be found in Volume IV. The experiments with pre-school curriculum consisted of four stages. First there was a pilot scheme which began in the summer of 1969 catering for children from one of the two mining towns who were due to enter the local infant schools in September 1969. Second, there was a full year programme starting in September 1969 with larger numbers of children, separate from those who had participated in the pilot programme and entirely made up of children with no previous pre-school experience. Third, a study was made of a further pre-school group starting in September 1970. Fourth, the individual language programme, which had been developed with Red House pre-school groups, was extended to the reception classes of one of the infant schools.

The project team started from the assumption that the design of a pre-school programme must be preceded by diagnosis of the specific needs of the children for which the programme is designed. While pre-school education can meet a variety of needs—social mixing, physical skills, coordination, intellectual development, and so on—it is obvious that individual children have different needs: the only child from an isolated family may require more emphsis on social experience than the child from a large family in a densely populated urban environment. Similarly, one must ask whether groups differing in their environment and experience may require different group programmes.

The West Riding district had a stable, almost totally working class population, grouped round a single industry which in the past had not required a high level of education among its workers, and living at high density in close-packed terrace houses with communal playspace. A child's social experience, gained from playing in groups in the "backs" without adult supervision, almost from the time he could walk, ensured that his peers were a powerful socialising force well before the child entered school. Again, early independence from the family, and close involvement with the peer group, tended to encourage the physical skills and co-ordination needed for climbing walls or riding push carts. Few homes gave much scope for creative work such as painting, or small-scale activities such as handling scissors, paint brushes, or pencils; and teachers in the infant schools pointed out that many children entering school could not name colours correctly. Lack of concentration was another problem faced by the schools: children dashed from one activity to another and were easily distracted. It seemed that by the age of five many children had "switched off" in the learning situation; for them school was an alien and possibly irrelevant process, far less attractive than the already established peer group relationship with which the school was in competition. Skills needed for the learning situation in the school—concentration and motivation as well as fine manual skills like handling a pencil—could not easily be encouraged by peer group activities or cramped home conditions. By the time the child from a depressed area reaches school, he may already have established behaviour patterns and relationships that put him at a disadvantage in the learning situation. He may be more advanced than middle class children in social skills and certain physical skills, but in need of extra help with language, perceptual and conceptual skills. These however were group rather than individual characteristics: the local testing programme found children of all ability levels.

With this diagnosis, the project team argued that a programme was needed with a different content and methods from one assumed sufficient in better-endowed or more middle class areas.

Much research, especially in the United States, has gone into designing special programmes aimed at compensating for the "intellectual deficits" believed to exist. Closely structured programmes tend to reject traditional nursery methods of free play and self-chosen activities in favour of direct teaching and carefully sequenced materials. While these programmes vary in intensity from the one designed by Bereiter and Engelmann[1] to others which rely more on high staffing ratios to keep the children interested, the choice of materials and the pace of the programme tend to be controlled by the teacher rather than the child. The Peabody Language Development Kit used in the national pre-school experiment is an example of this type of programme, although considerably less intensive in pace than that designed by Bereiter and Engelmann. Children involved in such programmes often show large gains in measured intelligence, although follow-up studies suggest that the gains are not generally maintained—a fact which has led to criticism of elementary schooling in the States particularly in ghetto areas, to arguments in favour of earlier intervention still before age three, and to a reassessment of the assumptions underlying the design of the programmes in the first place. Many researchers have criticised the emphasis

---

[1] C. Bereiter and S. Engelmann, *op. cit.*

on rote learning based on behavioural learning theory in many of the programmes, and have stressed instead that gains may be due to improvement in the child's motivation—increased confidence in working with adults, greater confidence in test-taking—rather than basic cognitive gains.

The answer to these findings, however, should not be to revert to traditional free play methods based on a maturational view of development which allow free choice to the child. Children, like everybody else, will tend to choose to do what they are good at; and what may be a "deficiency" is hardly a "felt need". Thus a structured programme initiated by the teacher may still be required, but of a different type, concentrating rather on individual contact with the child designed to increase his concentration and stimulate enquiry rather than present him with information to be absorbed, and avoiding the typical reaction of "classroom behaviour" or "classroom skills" with which children in groups tend to mask their lack of comprehension of what is being taught.

The individual language programme developed by the project was based on the individual tutorial method used by Marion Blank in New York.[1] For 15 to 20 minutes each day individual children work with the teacher on a one-to-one basis separated from the group. This combines advantages from both the structured and the traditional child-centred approaches. The individual situation allows the materials to be geared to the child's level, and the method ensures that either the child understands what is being taught or the teacher learns more about the child's failure to understand. Blank argues that in normal nursery situations much of the interchange between adult and child passes by without the child needing to understand the content of what is being said, for the context and often the form of what is said indicate the required response. Teachers frequently provide the answers too easily and assume the child's ignorance from a vague response, when in fact the child if helped by further questions could have solved the problem himself. In the individual sessions the ideal is for the teacher to get the child to the solution of a problem by questioning him and encouraging him to use his own previous experience. This method, in contrast to teacher-initiated structured programmes, is based on a theory of "active" learning which fits well with the developments in primary education in this country. It was hoped to develop the individual programme as a stimulus or "catalyst" for the child's interest in the group work, and to link the individual sessions, although physically separate, closely to what was done in the group.

At the same time, a number of different emphases from traditional nursery techniques were incorporated into the group work. Children who already showed a considerable degree of independence of adults and even hostility to possible adult interference in their games had to be encouraged to see adults as positive sources of help; and they needed a great deal of intervention from adults to stimulate ideas and language. As well as the regular staff of the group, parents, local secondary school children, and other helpers were encouraged to take part, usually working with small groups of children

---

[1] M. Blank and F. Solomon, "A tutorial language program to develop abstract thinking in socially disadvantaged pre-school children", *Child Development*, 1968, 39(2), 379–389; "How shall the disadvantaged child be taught?", *Child Development*, 1969, 40(1), 47–61.

where the adult's role was to stimulate the child's language and help his concentration by furthering his own activities. To improve fine manual and perceptual skills there was more emphasis on work with scissors, painting, jigsaws, construction kits and so on, than large-scale apparatus such as climbing frames or bicycles. Role-play games were also encouraged as a context for language experimenting which can be readily understood by the child and which again arise from his own experience—firemen games or hospitals.

The group ran on a half-day basis for it seemed important not to reinforce the area's traditional view of schooling as taking over complete responsibility for the child's education. Half-day sessions would fit in more appropriately with a view of strengthening and reinforcing the work of the home rather than replacing it.

The 1969 pilot scheme helped to clarify method for both individual and group work. But perhaps more importantly, it developed a clearer conception of the relation between a pre-school programme and the child's experience outside the pre-school group. "Parental involvement" is conventionally taken to mean parents coming into the group and learning about the work being done in the group. Yet current research evidence all goes to show the relative impotence of the school in contrast to the home environment and the peer group. Clearly what is "learnt" at home is as much "education" as what goes on in school; and the effects of any pre-school programme must be marginal in relation to the child's total experience.

The pilot scheme suggests that there were in fact at least three levels of experience which could be affected by a pre-school programme. There were the individual sessions, short and closely structured. The second level was the group work, closely linked with the individual sessions on the one hand and with parents closely involved on the other. The third level was the child's experience outside the group. Obviously the ideal was to link all three levels and see each as a "priming" device for the others, and for the child to be able to see the interdependence—perhaps by transferring materials and ideas from one situation to another, perhaps by the involvement of his parents in the pre-school work and his "teacher" visiting and working in the home. One isolated example was the excitement of the mother who realised that her son's apparently odd remark about putting paint on her overalls stemmed from his experience of mixing paint in the group. No systematic work along these lines was done in the pre-school group during the main 1969–70 programme, although work with parents was extensively developed in the 1970–71 nursery group based on the education centre, Red House, and was continued with the 1971–72 group. Parents were encouraged to attend the nursery group regularly, where after a brief introduction from the teacher they worked with small groups of children, or accompanied the children on short trips in the neighbourhood. There was also discussion at the end of the session among the adults who had taken part, on their observations of children's behaviour. The nursery teacher made regular home visits to the families, and the mothers developed a regular evening session at the centre where there were cookery demonstrations, and discussions on education.

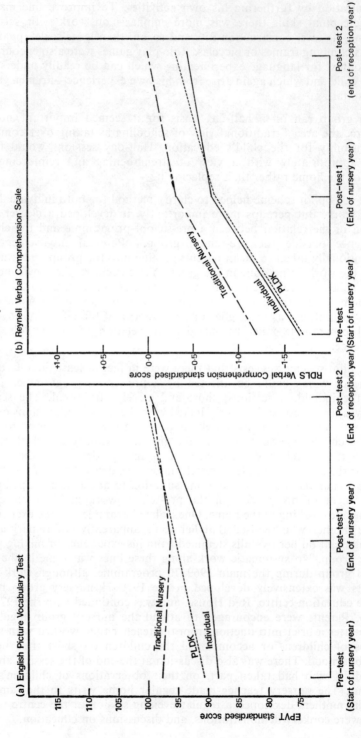

Figure 8.2: Pre-school Year and Follow-up Results—School A.

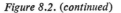

Figure 8.2. (continued)

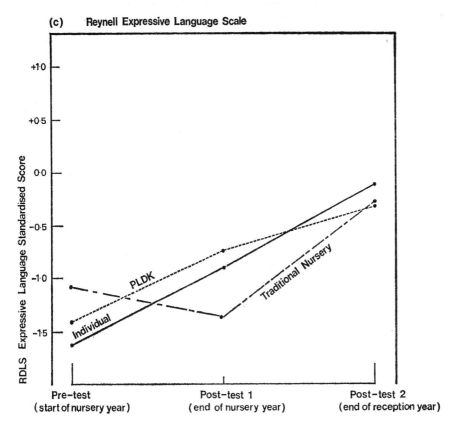

(c)   Reynell Expressive Language Scale

Though the children in the first stage (the pilot scheme in the summer of 1969) were followed through the first two years of infant school, no detailed assessment of their progress or comparison with non-nursery groups was undertaken. However, children in the second stage, the main scheme 1969–70, were tested at the beginning and end of their pre-school year on the Reynell Developmental Language Scales and the English Picture Vocabulary Test.[1] For this study the pre-school groups were drawn from two school catchment areas and contained virtually all children in the relevant age groups. In School A's catchment area, children were randomly assigned to three groups using the P.L.D.K., the individual language programme, and "traditional nursery" methods respectively; for School B there were two groups, one following the P.L.D.K. and the other "traditional nursery". Results at the end of this pre-school year are shown in Figures 8.2 and 8.3, together with results after the children's first year in infant school. We discuss these follow-up results below after dealing with results during the pre-school year.

---

[1] See Chapter 7 for details of these tests.

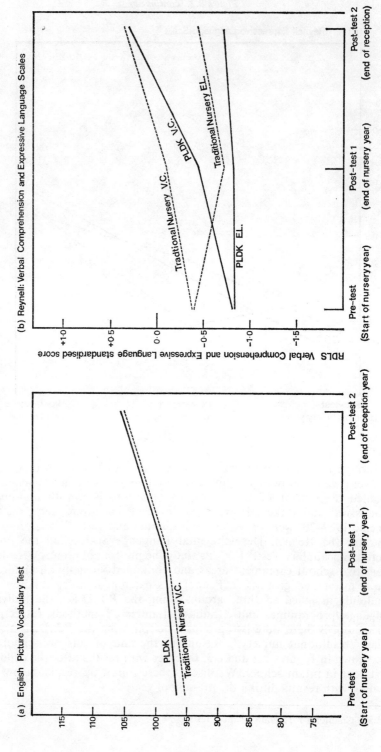

Figure 8.3: Pre-school Year and Follow-Up Results—School B.

In the third stage, 1970–71, the individual programme and the group programme within a single nursery group were compared to control for the effects of the group.

Though the results of the 1969–70 and 1970–71 pre-school schemes, like much research, may not have produced any clear-cut and unshakeable conclusions, the overall picture is remarkably consistent. Concentrating on the aspect of language skills and development it is clear that all groups on average start slightly below the "norm" for their age group, and in general make progress over the year—in a few cases reaching the "norm" level. It may be that some of this change is the result of "test familiarity" and greater confidence in adults, rather than any underlying change as a result of attendance at pre-school. But this explanation does not account for the variation in advance measured on the different tests. Thus in general children in all these groups made very similar and quite substantial progress on the verbal comprehension scale. And this change seems to relate to the type of experience that the child undergoes in the nursery class—he is expected to listen, and respond appropriately to verbal instruction. It seems, too, that a nursery class can have a "depressive effect" on the child's expressive skills, as these are measured by the Reynell scale; he perhaps tends to become more cautious and guarded particularly in his language in relation to adults. In the 1969–70 scheme it was in this aspect that the two language programmes (the Peabody and the individual language schemes) seemed to have the most positive effect in comparison to the "normal" nursery—counteracting the tendency of formal school organisation to check children's language flow. However, this was not repeated in the 1970–71 nursery group; expressive language skills improved in the non-individual group—perhaps because the number of adults, parents and secondary school children working in the education centre's group maintained the children's confidence and encouraged them to use their natural expressive skills.

No direct comparison was made with the progress of children not attending any form of pre-school, though research elsewhere has generally shown that such groups either remain the same or fall back slightly during the pre-school period.[1] Children who have not attended pre-school tend to make a spurt in their reception year—and many American studies of compensatory education, for example the "Westinghouse Report",[2] have shown that gains made by pre-school groups tend to disappear once children start school. The West Riding E.P.A. with a remarkably stable population provided a good setting for follow-up study as children joined the reception classes. Children from the 1969–70 scheme were followed for a further year, and tested again in the summer of 1971 (see Figures 8.2, 8.3).

The follow-up testing in summer 1971 assessed the longer-term effects of pre-school intervention after one year in the infant reception class. Two primary schools were involved, and results in both showed that instead of falling back at the end of the pre-school period the groups continued to make progress. In School A, the three groups who had followed

---

[1] See Chapter 7 for details of a study of this kind in Liverpool.
[2] Cicirelli *et al.*, 1969.

Figure 8.4: Results from the Individual Programme, Reception Classes, School A.

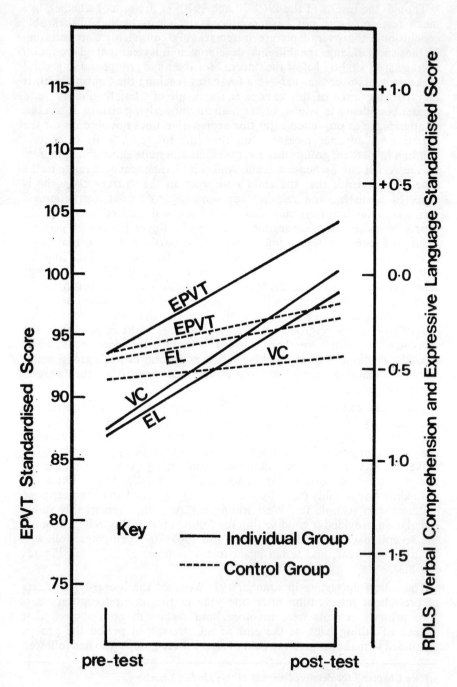

different programmes during the pre-school year (the P.L.D.K., the individual language programme, and the "traditional nursery" methods) showed strong convergence in the test results at the end of the reception year. This suggests that the different patterns of development revealed by the pre-school testing, and apparently related to the different pre-school programmes followed, were more or less ironed out by the common experience in school classes.

In this school, some of the children who had attended pre-school groups in the previous year were involved in the individual programme during their reception year, and this clearly influenced the general rate of advance. However, children in this school who were not involved in the individual programme also continued to make progress (Figure 8.4).

In this follow-up individual programme, half the children in two reception classes were randomly selected to take part and were given individual sessions by students and teachers in class time over the year. The results show that children who took part made significant gains on the E.P.V.T. and verbal comprehension scales, despite the fact that the majority had also made considerable gains during the pre-school year.

In School B, no special programmes were used in the reception classes, though children continued to make above average progress on all the measures used. These follow-up studies present an encouraging picture for the long-term effects of attendance at pre-school, though it should be stressed that there are a number of possible explanations for the pattern of results. Children by the third testing may have been increasingly familiar with test materials and methods; the children involved were the first in the area to pass through the nursery classes, and there was high interest and expectation from teachers about their progress. Virtually all children in the reception classes had experienced some form of nursery provision, making it possible for reception teachers to build on this rather than concentrate on children who had not been to pre-school. Despite these restrictions there is certainly no evidence to support the view that effects of pre-school work are quickly lost. Similarly the follow-up individual work in the reception classes demonstrated that further progress can be made by a second year of special work, and here comparison was made with children in the same classes, providing a control for most of the factors listed above.

The project team also conducted an informal survey with eight reception teachers and infant head teachers who received children from the pre-school groups. The results suggested the importance of achieving 100 per cent cover so that all children entering the reception classes had been to a nursery group. It also demonstrated the problems that can occur if the nursery group is organisationally separate from the infant class, though where there is a clash of principle, in this case over parental participation, it is not clear how this should best be resolved. Teachers generally stressed the contribution made by pre-schooling to the child's social development, despite the fact that the main intention in setting up the nursery groups, and mounting special programmes, was to accelerate the child's cognitive and linguistic development. Teachers mentioned cognitive development, and specific effects of the special programmes such as the Peabody Kit, but clearly placed more emphasis on social development. Many, too, clearly had a strongly "maturational" view of the children's cognitive development, again despite the fact that several of the assumptions under-lying the E.P.A. project, particularly its pre-school work, explicitly chal-lenged this stand-point. However, despite this emphasis on social develop-ment, the children in the 1969–70 pre-school groups continued to make substantial progress in linguistic skills. The results, here, apparently strongly support the teachers' assessment that children who had been to the nursery groups remained relatively more advanced than previous year groups, who had entered the school straight from home.

Conclusion

These four studies indicate various ways of approaching the task of producing materials and methods which are both applicable to the parti-cular problems of different localities and also acceptable to British teaching traditions. Much further work remains to be done. The West Riding study shows that, contrary to the American experience, gains made as a result of pre-school programmes can be maintained into the infant school. The high degree of pre-school cover, the continuity of approach from the pre-school groups (mostly attached to the infant schools) through into the schools, the exceptional stability of the area's population, and the considerable interest generated by the fact that the groups were the first to attend any form of pre-school, may all help to explain the progress shown by this particular study. The Birmingham work shows that number concepts can be considerably accelerated, and raises again the question of the relationship between verbal and non-verbal methods of learning. One would like to know more about which children benefited most from this type of programme and whether gains are maintained into school. The London project underlines the need to guide teachers' classroom behaviour in order to promote children's development. And finally the action in Liverpool highlights the need for more locally-oriented materials and methods at the pre-school level.

CHAPTER 9 ✓

The Community School and The Family

It is not wholly misleading to say that the E.P.A. problem reverses itself in the reception class of the primary school. What essentially we have argued about the pre-school years is the need to develop educationally informed families. After that, and with increasing difficulty among the higher age groups, the problem is to create socially informed schools. But to put the matter in its broadest perspective the problem at all stages is to integrate school and life. That is the concept of the community school. It comes to us directly from Plowden, though it can also be derived from the educational theories of John Dewey. In this and the following three chapters we review our work on this central element in the four projects and thereby hope to show that we have given the concept a more substantive and relevant meaning for E.P.A. circumstances than did our predecessors.

This chapter is arranged in five sections. First we consider the general problem of home and school links. Second we describe the strategy of a community education centre. Third we look at some experiments with home-school liaison teachers. Fourth we examine our experience of home visiting including an educational visitor service, and finally we consider the reverse traffic of school visiting.

1. *Home and School*

A child's performance in school is inseparably related to his experiences in his home; in the poor and socially disorganised districts which are commonly defined as E.P.A.s many parents have little conception of what the schools are trying to do and are not able therefore to give their children the support they need. The interest is there but there are social distances to be traversed if it is to be connected to effective learning. Accordingly the projects looked for ways to explain the schools' aims and methods, to encourage parents to recognise their own role in the educational process and so to develop understanding, skill and enthusiasm in the children's homes which would help them to get the maximum benefit from their schools.

But not only must parents understand schools, schools must also understand the families and environments in which the children live. Teachers have to know their pupils as persons and as products of the particular kin and community from which they come. Teaching and curricula must use and reflect the social and economic problems which surround the children in their daily lives. Only if education in the schools is relevant to the children's direct experiences will it engage their attention and interest. This argument may be couched in political as well as pedagogical terms. If we are concerned with the majority of children who will spend their lives in E.P.A.s, rather than only with the minority who will leave them for universities and colleges and middle class occupations elsewhere, then the schools must set out to equip their children to meet the grim reality of the social environment in which they live and to reform it in all its aspects, physical, organic, technical, cultural and moral. Only if they are armed with intimate familiarity with their immediate problems may they be expected to articulate the needs they feel and create the means for satisfying them. The obvious danger here is of creating a second-class education for second-class citizens through curricula restricted to local horizons. But what we intend is the opposite of a soporific: it is not to fit children for their station in life in an ascriptive sense. It is to accept that many children must live out their lives in deprived areas and to inspire them to think boldly about it rather than lapse into resigned apathy.

The partnership between home and school which we set out to establish through the community school may be expressed as the interacting effect of neighbourhood and school on the child. Where a middle class school tends to be a projection of the home, the E.P.A. school is more frequently alien to it. A possible policy under these circumstances is to wean the child completely away from the influence of the home, thus creating for him a divided world. But an alternative approach is to attempt complementary rather than compensatory education with the school trying to come to terms with the values of the community instead of implicitly opposing them. The lesson of the success of the middle class school is that it identifies with its environment; this could point the road for many an E.P.A. school. There are, of course, dangers in pushing this approach to its extremes where schools might come to reinforce and perpetuate values and attitudes which would widely be regarded as undesirable. Moral judgements have to be made about the ways of life that the schools should support and those they should try to change—even in E.P.A.s. But we set out in search of a constructive partnership between schools and parents even in the most deprived areas. The national survey of attitudes of E.P.A. parents had disposed, we were convinced, of the myth of unconcerned, feckless parents. Most parents are profoundly interested in their children's educational and social chances. They are often conscious of their inability to help their sons and daughters but are frequently hopeful that they will acquit themselves well. Most parents have a high regard and respect for schools, but however they admire the school they cannot always emulate it. Almost by definition, the E.P.A. parent is himself a school failure who perhaps neither enjoyed nor understood his own school. Today the whole process is even more confusing, with sophisticated and unfamiliar teaching methods, so that parents hesitate to interfere and are forced back to an implicit and uncomprehending trust. There are of course apathetic parents just as there are lethargic teachers. Again some take school for granted, as a chore, as a sort of junior national service that their children, like themselves, must undertake. Whatever they think there is a general tendency for educational matters to be left to the school. The object of home–school links is to increase the educational understanding of the parent and the social understanding of the teacher.

This linking process properly begins before the child goes to school, through parents becoming involved in pre-schooling. We began our programme by talking naively of parental involvement in vague terms— meaning the freedom of parents to take part in playgroups and home visiting by the project staffs. But experience soon taught us that it was, in a sense, misguided to talk in terms of parental involvement in pre-school work, however this term was to be defined. For it was clear that, measured by either time or learning, any pre-school programme, either full day or half day, has only a minor role in a child's life. An American research worker once calculated that his half-day one-year programme for pre-school children took up the equivalent of only 2 per cent of the child's waking life. The calculation illustrates the error and impertinence of thinking about parental involvement as if the school experience was the dominant educational influence on a child under five. It is more helpful to see school experience, at least initially, as peripheral to the wider experience of home and community. With this more realistic perspective it is then more likely that the potential of pre-school work may be brought to bear more effectively on the child's general educational development.

Consequently we do not see it as the function of pre-school work to try to develop "the whole child", if any meaning can be given to this phrase, but to add something to the normal experience of the child at home and with his peers, particularly where these experiences seem to be inadequate. The idea of developing the "whole child" seems to derive from a belief in the autonomy of the educational process in school. Where home and school values and methods overlap, as they may do in middle class areas, such a belief may be accurate and school experience may still be peripheral. Because both are pulling in the same direction, the relative effects of home and school are obscured. Where there is less overlap, it is critically important to recognise the relative influence of home and school, and to design intervention accordingly. The formal educational system cannot develop the "whole child". Unless some form of kibbutzim is introduced, this is clearly the preserve of the home. The function of pre-school should be complementary, concentrating on specific skills where it appears that the home experience is inadequate. Our attempts to translate this perspective into practical activity took various forms in the four projects and resulted in a wide range of experiments and innovations which we shall now try to describe.

2. *A Community Education Centre—West Riding's Red House*

The educational centre, Red House, which we met in Chapter 6, was unique among the various schemes introduced in the E.P.A.s. The centre had a resident warden with a family and also room for about eight other people to live in. The aim was to develop a centre which would work closely with the other educational institutions in the district—with schools, colleges and university departments, as well as with parents and with the community. The centre would overcome the rigid age-grouping which characterises most educational institutions, and try out schemes that involved children of all ages, and adults from different sources, schools, colleges or local families. It would be able to operate, too, outside the normal school day and term timetable, offering courses in the evenings, weekends and holiday periods.

Some community activities at the centre grew directly out of other schemes. Mothers of children coming to the pre-school formed a group of their own, holding regular meetings, discussion groups, cookery classes, organising trips and arranging children's and parents' parties. The intensive courses for junior schools regularly ended with parents' evenings attended by teachers and students involved in the courses—the number of parents present varying from eight to 45. Teachers and students who had worked with children in small groups for five or six weeks were able to discuss their work and progress with considerable knowledge and parents appreciated the detailed information.

One of the most important attributes of Red House is (it continued after the end of the project) that it provides a physical meeting place for all who are interested in education—a visible and easily recognisable expression of the concern to bring teachers and children, students and parents into a close and permanent relationship. As the day and evening courses developed, and as the centre and its staff became better known, so did contact with large numbers of children and their families. Parents were encouraged to take part in activities at the centre and this often brought to light difficulties at home that might influence the children's performance at school; it also led to social and community work in attempts to deal with family difficulties.

Holiday schemes run from the centre extended contacts to new children and families, though the main objective was to provide activities for children outside school time. It was from this type of contact that residential work began to develop. Though only a few children were taken into residence they came from the group of families whose contact with the centre had effectively developed from educational to social work. Many of these families came to know Red House through one of their children taking part in the educational programmes. Others had been referred by schools or social work agencies but even here it was often found that the centre was already in touch with one or other of the children involved. Without initial educational contact residential social work is both more difficult in itself and harder to justify.

Red House had to have multiple uses if it was to justify its cost and it had to be located in the community if its work was to be effective. Further, it had to be seen by local people as part of the normal educational resources of the area, not as a specialised institution for children from problem families. It was important that residential work should not be seen as a device for taking the child away from his family, even in a minority of cases. In any event, as a purely practical consideration, the centre had no statutory powers so that a residential stay required the full agreement of parents and child.

Experience with the community justified the multi-purpose approach. Certainly there were a number of children in the area who lived in circumstances which, judged by more affluent standards, might be considered intolerable; where housing conditions were extremely poor, the parents perhaps in debt, or separated, or ill and unable to provide adequate care. In these circumstances the effect of giving the children a short stay in relatively comfortable surroundings without altering the conditions to which they must return has to be carefully considered. It is a natural emotional response to try to get the child away even temporarily, but this overlooks the possible damage to the family of removing one or more of its members.

Residential work was deliberately developed slowly. The first resident came about four months after Red House opened, and in retrospect it was probably useful that she was not local though she attended the local secondary school during her three months' stay. Her presence showed that the centre was to be used residentially, but local people could not identify her as a girl with a particular need or from a known background. Subsequently, the numbers of children staying for social rather than educational reasons was never large. By the end of 1971 children from 33 different families had stayed, one or two on more than one occasion. Often it was a single child, at other times as many as five from the same family. The length of stay varied from one to twelve weeks, but generally it was short and arrangements were always made for children to go home or to a relative at the weekend.

In discussing a child's stay at the centre, it was made clear to parents that they had complete control over the decision. This is critically important since it helps to demonstrate the relationship between parents and the centre and to emphasise that it is not a statutory authority intervening between parents and children. Once this is understood, often rationalised as a "holiday stay" for the child, it is possible to gain the confidence of the family and parents may be willing to talk about their difficulties and accept advice about where they can go for guidance or material support. This sort of interchange usually developed soon after the residential stay, and after this in many cases support could gradually be reduced.

Experience with residential work underlined the need for closer home–school liaison. A number of children were referred to the centre with little or no information about their homes. In some cases information from schools was wrong or out of date but had coloured the teacher's impressions of a child's behaviour. Sometimes the impression left with the school had been the result of an aggressive visit from a parent. A general description such as "poor home background" may be a way of obscuring the real problems. It requires a detailed description of the child's actual living conditions to sharpen the focus of the teacher's attention. For this reason a brief account of the behaviour of children at the centre was sent to their teachers and full details of the family background given to the head of the school. In the junior schools it is mainly the head teachers who take on this "pastoral" role, and one or two visit the homes of their children when necessary. One head teacher claimed to spend about 50 per cent of his time on social work, particularly on counselling parents in his school and in their homes. In the secondary school year-tutors and a youth tutor do this kind of work, but teaching and other duties limit the time available for home contacts.

There can be a weakness in individual schools concentrating on the problems shown by their children. In many cases a single family problem may have repercussions in three different schools simultaneously, as individual children in the family react to the event. Contact between schools is therefore vital; without knowledge of what is happening to other family members each child's behaviour can easily be treated as an isolated problem, and misinterpreted as the outcome of individual personality.

The short residential stay can also be a useful diagnostic period. A number of children were referred by schools because of deviant behaviour.

In the residential context the child's behaviour can be examined and possibly discussed with parents or other family members. Although withdrawing a child from a difficult family situation may release him from quarrels between parents, or inadequate sleeping or living conditions, it may provoke other forms of stress. The evening meal at the centre was held *en famille* with everyone eating together. At times visitors joined the meal, and this invariably set up withdrawal symptoms in the children in residence. When other groups of children came to evening sessions at the centre and required attention, children in residence might respond by attention-seeking behaviour, often similar to that shown in school. However Red House provides a new environment where the child may be able to break away from previous behaviour patterns.

Many of the families whose children have stayed at the centre are living in or near poverty. The parents were quick to realise that they were receiving economic support. The centre acted in emergencies, buying shoes and clothing for example, and occasionally offering small loans. Though the local social services are technically able to help in these matters, they very rarely do so. The Supplementary Benefit Commission can make grants for specific purposes. But since it only responds to demands, the client must have knowledge of the grants available before he can apply. The social security staff do not appear to inform applicants of their rights and it was sometimes necessary to obtain information and then to help with filling in forms. The ability of Red House to provide immediate, but limited, economic support is extremely important. Such action can often prevent a much heavier burden on the social services later on.

A large number of children were involved in courses at the centre— roughly 1,000 children a year—some coming for only a single visit, others regularly throughout the year, but only a small proportion received intensive attention. Including the home visiting project (described below) and the home visiting associated with the pre-school work, few families were visited regularly. Table 9.1 shows the position in 1971, but the figures are inflated as some families may have been involved in different projects. The amount of attention given to residential and social work varied greatly; in general the aim was to wean the family away from the centre as quickly as possible but to keep in touch in case a crisis occurred. Long-term support might mean that a member of the family called at the centre when the situation became desperate at home, or it might mean that a child was invited to join in the evening activities once a week so that contact could be maintained.

Table 9.1

Frequency of Contact with Families

Programme	No. of families	Frequency of home visits
Home Visiting project	20	Weekly
Pre-school 1970	24	Every 2–3 weeks
Pre-school 1971	26	Every 2–3 weeks
Residential or social work	33	Daily at first; decreasing to every 4–12 weeks approximately.

The number of children staying at Red House increased steadily throughout 1971. But this has its negative side as the centre inevitably becomes linked to the more difficult families, who may be rejected by other members of the community. Possibly as more "normal" families with more limited or temporary problems begin to use the residential facilities the balance will be restored; and the centre's involvement with a cross-section of families and children in other parts of its programme helps to maintain this balance.

A number of families referred to the centre did not require residential treatment, but simply immediate support followed perhaps by referral to the relevant agency, and pressure for the case to receive attention. Sometimes the main need was the time and sympathy of another adult to listen to family or individual troubles; to remove children from their families in these circumstances would be a grave error.

Though some children came from outside the area, the most successful work was done with local children on the basis of a short "holiday" stay followed by continued support. It is vitally important that children in residence continue to attend their normal school and maintain social links with family and friends, and this is not possible with children from far away.

Holiday programmes are another Red House activity. In 1970–71 a small holiday scheme was set up using college students and a tutor who all had experience of similar programmes. Red House made the general arrangements with the local school for the holiday programme and served as the residential base for the students who, with their tutor, were responsible for planning the activities of the course.

To stabilise the numbers of children involved, invitations were sent out to 60 children through the junior schools, and plans were made for a three-day scheme. Seven different types of activity were offered and children could choose which they preferred. The aim was creative work—with music, puppet making, dragon making, the construction of a cavern from polystyrene, and "chariot" construction and making—and to encourage children to complete some particular piece of work by the end of the scheme. This was essential to prevent the drifting that had made previous schemes of this type difficult to sustain. After some initial demonstrations of basic construction the cavern began to grow in size and was still growing after two days. Tunnels of polystyrene were built and various "creatures" suspended inside the system. Twenty children at a time were able to crawl through the caves and tunnels and explore its mysteries. The chariots were made from Triwall slabs with pieces of carpet felt to act as runners. A simple box formed the sides. A group including some of the most difficult children were attracted to this activity and enjoyed the races around the large school hall which took place on the second day. The number of children attending increased as brothers, sisters and friends joined. The dragon grew in size as sections of old cartons were painted and fitted to children. When it finally emerged from its lair, to the chanting and dancing of the creative music group, the dragon was thirty feet long, with an enormous plaster-on-wire-mesh head. The puppet group made their own props and gave two performances in a makeshift theatre. On the final day over 100 children took part.

This scheme demonstrated the importance of tutor support for the student team. The method of "inviting" children also guaranteed an initial attendance, and the method of arranging specific small group activities lasting for three days ensured that children attended regularly and completed a single piece of work.

The following summer, a longer and more ambitious holiday programme was attempted. There is an obvious need for such a scheme during the summer holidays when schools and youth clubs are closed. Very few local families go away during this period, as the official pit week falls earlier in the year or during the Doncaster race week in September. The scheme was planned to last for three weeks during August and three paid leaders were appointed to run it. Two of them were former students who had taken part in the Christmas holiday programme and knew the area well, and the third, a teacher from a local junior school, had also been involved in running an evening course. Permission was obtained to use an open space belonging to the Council, and the Youth Service agreed to the use of the nearby youth club for indoor activities. A number of volunteers were recruited from a private boarding school which had developed links with the local secondary school, and had recently opened a hostel for its students in the district. The response was encouraging, as many of those who volunteered had originally been at the local secondary school, and had recently transferred to the private school as part of an exchange scheme.

A flexible programme was adopted which allowed team leaders and volunteers to develop activities where they had particular skills. Those familiar with teaching tended to concentrate on the more structured indoor activities or organised games outside. It was harder to maintain interest in the less structured situation on a large scale construction site nearby. Group activities in the centre were similar to those described in the first holiday programmes together with a series of special events such as coach trips to parks, films, a dog show and a hare and hounds race, to provide a focus for group activities each week. Parents also took part, organising rounders sessions, making costumes for a carnival, and finally joining in a parade through the streets which again drew the attention of the local community to what was going on. The project showed that it was possible to retain the interest and enthusiasm of large numbers of children over a considerable period of time and that volunteers could be drawn from older children in the community. But it was essential to have experienced leaders who were paid to take part and a centre which could look after administrative details and materials. The total cost amounted to £250 for the three-week programme. The local council agreed to meet part of the cost for a similar scheme in 1972, and have applied to the Urban Programme for further funds.

3. *The Home-School Liaison Teacher*

The many purposes pursued by Red House—community work, attempts to involve parents in school activities and ventures into social work—were taken up by other projects in different ways. In Birmingham and Deptford home-school liaison teachers were appointed and in Deptford the project also employed a school-based social worker.

The proposed role of the home–school liaison teacher is well described in a note sent by the Birmingham team to the project schools.

"Basically the reason for instituting this innovation is the nature of the E.P.A. schools. E.P.A.s are such because the neighbourhood is culturally deprived and suffers from all the socio-economic factors which we associate with slums. In general, all teachers are expected to develop good home–school links and this is a fairly easy task in a good area where parents come to the teacher. In E.P.A.s the school can be overwhelmed by the social problems to the neglect of educational problems and one cannot expect all members of the staff to have the time, or indeed the motivation, to attempt to find out about the background of every child. Nevertheless, it must be clear that to make any headway educationally in E.P.A.s a real understanding of the home problems a child faces is quite vital. To this end it is fairly obvious that if parents are to feel associated with a school—feel that the school cares—then contact with them on a personal basis is essential. How can one expect the individual class teacher to find the time to develop home–school relations and establish an understanding with parents of deprived children when such children are in the majority in an E.P.A. school? Hence the idea that if a member of staff has major duties in the home–school field then he can act as a liaison between class-based teacher and home. His timetable can be such as to allow home visits at times normally inconvenient to staff; he can substitute for a class teacher if a parent calls during school hours and wishes to speak to the class teacher. Finally, the home-school teacher is in a position to foster and organise various activities both during and after school hours which can involve groups of parents and occasionally parents with children."

Similar points were made in the particulars of the posts handed out to the applicants.

"The home-school liaison teacher will be regarded as a full member of the staff of the school and will have a part-time teaching programme— to be arranged to suit his interest and experience and the needs of the school. He or she will also visit parents in their homes both in school time and outside it—for which compensatory free time during the school day will be allowed.

"At this stage within the development of what the Plowden Report calls a community school it would not be helpful to try to define narrowly what the home–school liaison teacher's function should be but the objective is clear: to enlarge mutual understanding between the school and families and neighbourhood which it serves and to strengthen the help which they can give to each other, bearing in mind especially those children who need most help, and whose parents sometimes seek it least.

"The essential qualities are a vocation for this kind of work, willingness to experiment, and the capacity for establishing good personal relations both within the school and, outside it, with parents and with other social agencies."

In at least one case the appointment of the home–school liaison teacher was reckoned an outstanding success. This man decided at the beginning to concentrate on four activities: improving home–school relations, attempting to tackle special problems of individual need, establishing comprehensive records for children and their families, and giving extra attention to especially deprived children. The liaison work proceeded along these lines and it is significant that in the case of a particular school outing a simple plan to translate letters of invitation from the school to Asian parents into three Asian languages, and care to explain details of the arrangements, more than doubled the response rate.

Table 9.2
Parent Contacts with a Birmingham School:
Returns for 12 of the 15 term-time weeks January to May 1970

Total staff nos. 18 (for first 6 weeks); 17 (for second 6 weeks)

Forms returned over 12 weeks:	14	13	11	3	13	9	12	10	13	13	14	11
Parents seen (including those seen more than once)	48	37	25	11	12	20	33	9	14	22	16	27

The 7 members of the Infant staff each returned the following

number of forms for 12 weeks	11	11	3	5	4	11	8
Respective contacts made	57	49	3	12	0	31	46

The 11 members of the Junior staff each returned the following

number of forms for 12 weeks	9	9	4	9	10	9	7	2	10	7	7
Respective contacts made	12	8	1	9	6	3	2	0	1	10	24

Causes of contacts, as per categories on return form:

50 Dinner money	5 Clothing loss	27 Absenteeism	42 Medical	45 Educational	73 Social chat	26 Complaint	13 Referred

An enquiry was also made to discover the reasons why parents came to the school to see their child's teacher (Table 9.2). The response to medical examinations is not surprising, but it is perhaps salutary that teachers of small children be reminded of the worry attached to money transactions—in this instance over school dinners. The educational enquiries seem satisfactory though capable of further refinement, but the "social chat" figure is startling; here is the initial reason for thinking in terms of a community school in E.P.A.s. Some parents living in deprived and depressed circumstances are greatly in need of reassurance and turn perhaps to the representative of the establishment who is the least committed and the most objective—the teacher. In other words the school has the advantage of being the most detached of all the social agencies. The particularly large number of contacts made by infant as compared with junior teachers supports the argument that home-school relations are best begun at the infant or pre-school stage.

Before the end of a year the liaison teacher was firmly established. Among other schemes he was involved in various summer holiday plans which, in the case of some immigrants, meant intensive home visiting. The first steps were taken to form a home–school committee on which parents were to be strongly represented and at the same time an editorial board was formed to work on the production of a school magazine. After less than two years it was clear that the impact of the home–school liaison teacher on the school had been of major importance. Most of the proposals outlined at the beginning of the experiment were well established and nearly all the staff were fully behind the work, though teachers may need to be convinced that something effective can be done in E.P.A. schools beyond the conventional kindness given to deprived children.

Recent legislation withdrawing free milk from the primary sector, with the exception of children granted milk on medical grounds, led to further activity. Public notices were posted and followed by a letter to parents from the Chief Education Officer indicating that a child could be referred for a medical examination if a parent felt the need for free school milk. The home–school liaison teacher had already, before the beginning of term, checked with ten families in the area to see if they had read the public notices. Not one knew of the clinics which were being held. He persuaded teachers to co-operate in filling in a ten-point scale to recommend children to the medical officer. The staff agreed and the home–school teacher co-ordinated the work and supplemented returns with details from medical records and case notes. One morning session had been allocated by the medical officer to the school but three were eventually necessary, due no doubt to the relatively large numbers of children presented as a result of the exercise initiated by the home–school teacher.

A second appointment of a home–school liaison teacher in the same E.P.A. district was, however, less successful. This was a school where there already existed a number of activities to which parents were invited and where the head was especially interested in parents and their problems. Perhaps partly because of the head's interest in contacts with parents, the liaison teacher was not able to establish an independent role for himself and was never fully accepted by the other teachers. Some innovations were made, however, including a language class for immigrant mothers and occasional evenings where parents were invited to see how their children were taught. Although this school had many elements of the community school idea it seemed unable, or unwilling, to find a use for a specially appointed home–school teacher. A special post may not always be appropriate but this does not preclude the development of a community school with purposeful aims.

Two home–school liaison teachers were also appointed in Deptford. In both cases they were teachers already employed in the school who shed some of their teaching duties to free themselves for home–school work. The aim of the work, as defined by the Project Director, was to enlarge mutual understanding between school and family and to strengthen the help which they can give to each other, bearing in mind especially those children who need most help and whose parents sometimes seek it least. It was suggested that the liaison teacher should be experienced, that he should be additional to the normal school staff and that he should not assume the role of professional social worker or education welfare officer even though he might need to visit homes. His role within the school and the neighbourhood should be determined jointly by the head teacher and the Project Director. The liaison teachers were to be responsible for explaining the school's educational policy to parents and encouraging them to help their children in organising such activities as P.T.A.s, enabling parents with special skills to help in the school and in working in any way with parents which head teachers and staff felt desirable.

As in Birmingham, the Deptford liaison teachers felt their way slowly and experimentally. Exhibitions of educational equipment and children's books were mounted and valued as much for what the teachers learnt about the parents as vice versa. Although head teachers and the Project Director were very anxious to distinguish educational from social work, one liaison teacher especially found it impossible to separate the two aspects of his job. He emphasised the need to work closely with the various welfare agencies and also advocated training for his own job. He had himself attended a course in counselling which he had found very useful. The second liaison teacher had a slightly different conception of his role, seeing it as "selling education to parents". As he put it, his responsibility was not to improve the social lot of the parents so that they could improve the educational capacity of the children. Teachers are not trained to tackle social and community problems and even if they were there are already professionals doing this work. Liaison teachers, he thought, could influence a child's educational performance by creating and encouraging greater interest from his parents and greater understanding from his teachers. This liaison teacher saw himself partly as a public relations officer. Training would be valuable and if the job involved meeting parents at home, then social welfare training including self analysis, personal assessment, case study methods and knowledge of the legal rights of parents and children would be desirable.

Thus there is some uncertainty about the degree to which the home–school liaison teacher should or need become involved in social work. It is peculiarly likely that in an E.P.A. a high proportion of families will need services from one or other of the social work agencies. For the most part the liaison teachers recognised that their job was an educational one and believed that social problems should be passed on to professional social workers. This ideally is what the situation should be. Liaison teaching, like any other device for bringing the community into closer touch with the schools, is primarily concerned with interpreting the aims and methods of education to parents, with awakening their enthusiasm and encouraging them to recognise and to play their own part. To this extent the liaison teacher is involved with all parents. By contrast the social worker is properly concerned with breakdown; with cases where special problems put families in need of help from the social services. In practice a liaison teacher in an E.P.A. is likely to be in touch with many such families, but the aim should still be to refer them where possible to the specialised departments concerned. Of course sometimes the social services are inadequate and the liaison teacher will try to deal with emergencies. As we have seen Red House sometimes found itself offering psychological and economic support to families in emergency. And sometimes the statutory services are so incomprehensible or difficult of access that poorer families need help in applying to them. Nevertheless the liaison teacher's job should be clearly distinguished from social work and his relation to social workers thereby clarified.

In Deptford this relation was tackled experimentally through the appointment of a social worker based at the project office and working with two infant and one junior school. Within the broad aim of helping children to take full advantage of their educational opportunities, the project social worker's job was defined as:—

"experimental and designed partly to clarify the contribution an educational social worker might make to good relations between schools and homes. After much discussion the aims of the social worker were broadly defined as helping children to take full advantage of their educational opportunities and in particular to increase home–school contact and understanding, to examine further the relationship between (education) social work and the school, and to illustrate ways in which a social worker could assist in assessing and solving problems experienced in E.P.A. schools".

This sounds very similar to the work that might be undertaken by home-school liaison teachers, but in practice the activities of the social worker were concentrated on "problem" cases. During an 18-month period 177 children were referred to the social worker from the three schools which had a total school population of 666. Seventy-six per cent of the referrals came from the school staff, 16 per cent from other sources and the remainder were directly observed by the social worker. An analysis of the reasons given for referral showed 29 per cent as social problems, the same proportion as behaviour problems, 19 per cent as educational problems where children were making poor progress at school, 13 per cent as medical problems and 10 per cent as attendance problems. The social worker herself distinguished 80 selected families as follows. Twenty-six per cent educational problems, 21 per cent family problems, 21 per cent financial problems, 18 per cent housing problems, 14 per cent medical problems. A detailed description of the activities of the social worker will appear in Volume III. Her conclusions emphasise what would be widely agreed—that welfare work in relation to schools is more appropriately performed by social workers than by teachers and also that the major responsibility for taking the initiative in fostering good home–school relations should remain with teachers.[1]

4. *Home Visiting*

In some cases, visits to homes were arranged in connection with some special project. The West Riding, for example, had a home visiting programme for pre-school children over the age of 18 months. The main programme began in January 1971 and covered 20 children. All the families with children in the right age group agreed to take part. Mothers were interviewed about their child's development and ability, but an independent assessment was also made. In order to be able to test the effect of the programme on the child's development and particularly on the relationship between mother and child, a control group of children, matched on such factors as age, sex and father's occupation were drawn from a similar mining community. Certain features of the home environment were rated, for example the availability of toys and books, safety, noise and organisation, the relationship between mother and child and the mother's reaction

---

[1]The Dundee Report (Vol. V) echoes the emphasis on home visiting but argues for a school–connected educational social worker rather than a teacher.

to the child's initiative. The mothers were also asked if they would be willing to have their child tested by a psychologist and most agreed. Tests in both groups were carried out by the local child guidance educational psychologist using the Merrill-Palmer scale of mental tests, which measures both mental and motor development, covering the child's comprehension and ability to follow instructions, as well as his "approachability" and persistence. Both tests and rating scales were repeated at the end of the year and the details will appear in Volume IV.

Both groups were initially very similar in home background, relationship between mother and child, and the child's measured ability, though within each group there were wide differences. Some of the children were clearly receiving ample attention, play, learning and educational encouragement from their mothers and did not appear to need any further educational help. But none were omitted because it was felt that it would be possible to learn more about the child's development by examining a wide range of mothers and children rather than only those with specific needs. The children in the experimental group were visited for one or two hours every week. On each occasion the child was presented with a series of toys and their function was explained to the mother. The child had to finish one activity and put it away before he could have the next. Children were sometimes too eager to see "what came next" and would rush through everything without getting really involved. Sometimes they wanted to combine two activities to make a game and this was encouraged. All the children soon grasped the idea of "putting away" and there were rarely tears or angry scenes. Books were usually presented at the end of the session when the children had used up their energy and were more willing to sit quietly.

The visitor always tried to involve the mother in what the child was doing, partly so that she could enjoy her child's discovery and could encourage him—and partly to reassure her that the child was not being subject to pressures to do well but was being encouraged to go at his own pace. The children tended to do more when the mothers were working with them, and this underlined the dependence of the young child on his mother for guidance in the early stages.

As the parents saw that their children were able to learn they began to offer various suggestions. Fathers particularly were fascinated by the idea that they could teach their children from such an early age. One man who had done badly himself at school, remarked that while they were young, "all you can do is play with them". He had bought and encouraged his son to do jigsaws from an early age as this was one of his own hobbies, yet he had never realised that "playing" was "learning". He was a "natural" teacher for his children and, by realising the importance of his role, he was even more encouraged to carry on.

It was an important aim of the scheme to persuade the parents of their own capacity to educate their children and to arouse their interest in doing so; not only to benefit a particular child at a given time, but also to create an atmosphere within the home which would be a lasting support to other children throughout their education. Various methods were used to help mothers to appreciate their own importance for their child's development; lessons were modified to include the interests of parents; initiatives taken by parents were extended and discussed by the home teacher; activities were left in the home for the mother to share with the child and mothers were involved in decisions about the most appropriate toys to use.

As well as involving the mother it is important to support her skill in dealing with the child by reinforcing and extending her "natural" teaching role. Getting the mother and child ready to learn is often more important than what is actually done. The visitor must have the ideas and expertise to support the mother and child in the learning situation and this is very different from simply providing a family with a series of exercises to complete each week. A family may also need practical help in filling in forms and applying to the appropriate welfare agency for money or services that they may need. In a programme to promote the development of young children it is impossible to neglect this aspect of family life, for it is such economic and social factors which often influence the relationships between mother and child. A programme which ignores these problems and concentrates on strictly educational activities may have little long-term effect.

The programme was a success in immediately involving parents and bringing together home and school learning. Although some parents, and most of the fathers, were initially suspicious of the motives and effect of the project, they gradually became more interested and eventually were very reluctant for it to stop. When the visitor who started the project left all the parents were anxious for the scheme to continue. The mothers specified certain traits they hoped the new visitor would have. They did not want anyone who "looked around for dust" or who criticised their home or standard of housekeeping; they wanted someone they could "sit down and talk to", without worrying that they would be "told off" or that their conversation would find its way to neighbours or people in authority.

These reactions of the parents are important in defining the necessary characteristics of the home visitor. She must be unbiased, non-judgemental, able to work under any sort of conditions, knowledgeable without being dictatorial, helpful without being patronising, able to listen and sensitive to people's needs without appearing to probe into their private affairs. Such qualities are not necessarily acquired by training. The visitor needs knowledge of children and their learning patterns and a good understanding of human relationships, but it is not always a social scientist or highly qualified teacher who will make a good home visitor. A real interest in people and a desire to listen to and help them is more important than a degree, and respect for what most mothers have achieved already without any help is worth more than criticism based on a theory of what mothers ought to do.

Birmingham Midlands Arts Centre

A different and smaller scale home visiting scheme was developed in Birmingham in conjunction with the Midlands Arts Centre where groups of children from E.P.A. schools had attended for six-week periods as we explain in Chapter 12. There was a poor response from parents to invitations to come and see the children's work and home visiting was started to try and encourage parents to take an interest after ten groups had already had their courses at the Centre. Making contact with families was difficult, often involving repeated visits, especially in the case of immigrants; there were severe language problems—out of 40 Asian mothers interviewed, often with husbands, 35 either had no English at all or needed an interpreter. Nevertheless, as may be seen from Tables 9.3 and 9.4, many Asian families welcomed the visits and both children and adults expressed interest in the Centre.

Table 9.3

Keenness of Children to continue attending the Midlands Arts Centre

	White (incl. mixed)	West Indian	Asian	Total
Children who had already expressed a definite wish to attend M.A.C. again (subjects of experiment only: siblings excluded)	13	6	2	21
Children who expressed wish to attend when consulted after visit (siblings excluded)	19	17	12	48
TOTAL INTERESTED	32	23	14	69
Children whose opinion was unknown by parents	2	4	22*	28
Children who (for a variety of reasons) were not interested	10	2	4	16
TOTAL NOT INTERESTED	12	6	26	44
GRAND TOTAL	44	29	40	113

* Note the extremely high number of Asian parents who did not know their children's opinions. Many of these did not even know that their children were attending! (Partly language difficulty; partly lack of discussion between generations; and partly fear on the children's part that parents would not approve of them "enjoying themselves"!)

Table 9.4

Keenness of Mothers to attend the Midlands Arts Centre

	White (incl. mixed)	West Indian	Asian	Total
Mothers (or Mother-substitutes) who did express a wish to attend M.A.C. if their circumstances permitted	19	16	6	41
Mothers who instantly recognised the impossibility, or who did not wish to attend	25	13	34	72
TOTAL	44	29	40	113

Reasons for not attending the Centre were difficult to analyse; not all explanations could be taken as wholly genuine and multiple reasons for not attending inflate the figures beyond the actual numbers of families interviewed (Table 9.5).

Table 9.5

Main reasons given by mothers for finding difficulty in attending the Midlands Arts Centre

	White (incl. mixed)	West Indian	Asian	Total
INSUFFICENT TIME. Long or irregular working hours and/or large family	20	22	4	46
CAN'T AFFORD FEES.* Poor family, Social Security, or unsupported mother	7	5	1	13
NO BABY MINDER. Babies or pre-school children in family	8	3	3	14
NOT OUR CUSTOM. Women do not go out socially, and/or husband would not permit it	—	—	21	21
INSUFFICENT ENGLISH. Language difficulty would naturally limit social mixing	—	—	17	17
DUE TO BE RE-HOUSED. Hoping to move outside E.P.A. area!	9	1	—	10
POOR HEALTH. Likely to limit social life	2	2	—	4
TOO MANY OTHER LEISURE ACTIVITIES. Weekends filled already	6	—	—	6
TOTAL REASONS FELT TO BE TRULY GENUINE	52	33	46	131

* There were definitely many more families in this rather "touchy" category than wished to mention it or to admit it as a reason!

It appears that parents who did not consider joining the Midlands Arts Centre usually had good reasons, many of which were beyond their control. It is clear that indigenous and West Indian mothers go out to work as a normal part of life, and Asian mothers do not go out to work either because of custom or inability to speak English. The tendency for mothers in deprived areas to go out to work (other than in the special case of the Asians) emphasises the need for more day nurseries to cater for pre-school children and to offset the large number of unofficial child minders known to exist.

The results of the visiting scheme were meagre. Only five out of 24 mothers who filled in the form for family membership in the presence of the interviewer actually went to the centre and joined. All five seemed to be economically better off than the average: four of them came from the fringe of the E.P.A. and all but one were of immigrant origin.

Third-year students from a local college of education helped with the home visiting which, from their point of view, afforded experience of the circumstances in which the children they worked with in the schools and in the Midlands Arts Centre lived.

In London too, college students were involved in home visiting in con-nection with a scheme to develop relations between colleges and schools. Thirty students in a project school with a large proportion of immigrants helped in various ways in the classrooms especially with reading and mathe-matics and followed this up by visits to children's homes. The parents of all the children in one class were visited to try to convey the school's interest in their children and to explain what the students were doing in the school. In some cases students took children on local outings. Similar work was also attempted with coloured children, students approaching immigrant families to discover adults who might have difficulty in reading or speaking English. No attempt was made to assess the effectiveness of these efforts, but at least greater communication, understanding and co-operation now exist between a number of immigrant homes and some of the students, and at most some of the immigrants can speak English more fluently and read it more easily.

5. *School Visiting*

We have been discussing activities whereby schools and teachers may seek to explain themselves to, and come to know, the parents of the children they teach—the educational centre and the various home visiting programmes. We could also point to the educational shop or market store and the exhibitions which we describe in Chapter 12. These are all examples of a school venturing out into the neighbourhood to win support for its methods and its aims. The other side of the coin is the attempt to bring the parents into the schools. This is essential to the idea of the community school which we have developed in the course of our three years' work in E.P.A.s and it extends beyond the literal meaning of bringing parents into school buildings to meet teachers or for evening social or educational gatherings, to the idea of parents joining in the actual educational experiences and processes through which their children pass.

The Plowden Report makes only slight reference to this concept and clearly interprets the idea of the community school in the literal sense. "By this (community school) we mean a school which is open beyond the ordinary school hours for the use of children, their parents and, exceptionally, for other members of the community".[1] The Committee go on to talk about Cambridgeshire village colleges and about schools which organise a range of evening, weekend and holiday activities often for children, sometimes for parents.

It was London and Liverpool that devoted most attention to developing the community school. London concentrated its efforts on three schools where the staff was interested in the idea and ready to experiment and in all cases the organisation and programmes were very similar. In one school responsibility rested with the teacher who had taken on the liaison work and who had a special interest in developing relationships between the school and the neighbourhood. Aiming eventually to persuade teachers to base some of their teaching on the local environment, in the meantime he saw it as part of his job to help to educate both teachers and parents in general matters of concern to the community. It was decided that a committee of teachers and parents should be set up to organise evening activities and although it was originally planned to include only the fourth year junior children, in the end all ages were involved. Often over 150 parents, friends and children joined in the evening gatherings once a week and problems of organisation were settled by the organising committee. The first six or

---

[1]Plowden, paragraph 117.

nine months were devoted to developing a range of leisure activities so that the school "had something of the appearance of a youth club", but in the second and third years activities were extended to other evenings and to weekends and included visits to local entertainments and places of interest. An attempt to open the community school regularly for two nights a week failed after the chairman of the school managers learned that activities were to be extended to old people's visiting. This he did not approve, believing that such visiting should be carried out by the Church and for this, and other organisational reasons, he decided that the school should open for only one night each week. This is a droll comment on the original proposal to organise evening activities democratically through a committee of parents and teachers.

The other two community schools followed similar lines. They opened for at least one evening a week for a range of leisure time activities including drama, dressmaking, pottery, table tennis and outdoor games and organised visits to local sporting events and other entertainments. The emphasis was clearly on recreation, though hopes were expressed of developing educational activities as well. About 80 children and 20 or 30 adults were involved at one of the schools and 60 or 80 children at the other. In one school, however, the venture eventually failed because of lack of response from parents, a failure attributed by the Project Director to frequent changes in the staff of the school. Parents also took part in the rural studies programme, described in Chapter 10, accompanying their children to their country school and joining in classroom activities.

The more complicated matter of bringing parents into the classroom to join in the actual experience of learning and teaching was particularly emphasised in Liverpool. The first step was to arrange coffee mornings during which parents and other relatives visited the classroom and watched the children at work. But this was preparatory to parent-child projects in which the parent could both see and also contribute to the child's activity. The class was deemed to be a better focus than the school for this kind of gathering and the response was immediate.

Parents cannot help with the education of their children unless they understand it. The first step is observation, but to go from observation to participation presents problems. It is at this point that teachers may begin to worry that they will be supplanted, or their professional quality diluted, by the active presence of parents. There is no single answer for every E.P.A. teacher to the problem of how to come to know and to involve the parents of his children. It is wise to allow the relationship to develop naturally from informal contacts. Nor is it realistic, certainly in E.P.A.s, to think of the parent immediately adopting a teacher role. The parent's participation in school work is to acquaint him with the educational process through which the child is being guided by the teachers. And the best way of getting parents to understand it is to let them go through the same process. In fact the parent's role in the classroom is more like the child's than the teacher's. This is the chief reassurance for the teacher's fears. Another objection is that some parents will not be able to attend such sessions so that their children will suffer an added deprivation. This is a sad fact but an inescapable one. A valuable experiment should not be abandoned because some children do not receive the full benefit from it. Response to the class focus was, in the event, very enthusiastic; sometimes every child had a relative in attendance. Their interest was encouraging and there was little disruption of classroom discipline.

Thus there are good grounds for experiment with direct involvement. This can be by way of tutorial groups for parents, with a number of parents of slow readers, for example. Another approach, which also helps to mask the non-attendance of some parents, is to invite perhaps two parents to spend a day with the class, entertaining them to lunch and giving them the opportunity to engage in a normal school day's activity. Another method is the child–parent project. Here there is the mutual benefit of parents learning how children learn and simultaneously making a positive contribution to the education of the class. The parent observes and experiences the process instead of, as is more usual, seeing only the end product at open days and end-of-term entertainments.

Liverpool provided several examples of such projects. In each instance the street was taken as the theme, a reminder that the locality-based syllabus is well fitted to interest parents. One school had a scheme running over four consecutive Tuesday evenings. A class of 27 children and their parents set out to produce a 15-minute tape of the street as well as other kinds of work. Music making, creative writing, reminiscence and dramatisation of street scenes were included. The class teacher supervised the operation, completed a full series of home visits before and during the week, and two or three other teachers helped with aspects of the production and with refreshments. In the first week 27 children and 35 adults joined in, partly perhaps because a local car workers' strike enabled some shift working fathers to attend. Football matches kept the numbers of parents down on the following two evenings, but on the last night numbers jumped again and the whole sequence ended well. At another school a group of mothers, armed with tape recorders, interviewed local street dwellers in an attempt to build up a picture of the street culture. They worked so enthusiastically that the organising teacher's main difficulty was in controlling the flow of information.

The overall judgement of the Liverpool team on their attempts to involve parents in school work was highly optimistic. Completely satisfactory relations between home and school mean that parents must observe and participate in the educational process. The project has shown that the class is the most profitable focus for this exercise, with parents working together in groups with their children. The success of the evening efforts suggested that weekends too might be a viable time for schooling and this could be extended to holiday programmes of the kind we have mentioned in the Birmingham and West Riding districts. But the closest relationship between home and school develops in parent-child projects. Only four were attempted; success varied; but many lessons were learned. Evenings were used as well as afternoons and, predictably, creative and local studies seemed most suitable. It would be a significant advance if schools could be encouraged to run child–parent projects attempting to make sure that every parent has at least one chance of such an experience during the child's time at school. Though it could take a generation or more to persuade teachers and parents to co-operate at this level, it is the final step in the partnership.

CHAPTER 10

Curriculum Development in the E.P.A. Primary Schools

In all four areas curriculum development was regarded as one of the essential elements in the action-research programme. It was clearly linked with the first general aim of the E.P.A. programme, to raise educational standards, and the last, to encourage a sense of community responsibility. Naturally each project team developed its own ideas and emphasised different aspects of primary work but three main aims can be distinguished which guided the experiments in all the areas. The first is the improvement of skills which may be attempted by treating the traditional primary subjects in new ways, by introducing new subjects such as oral linguistic work or by integrating subjects through environmental studies or project work. The second is to provide a more enjoyable, that is intrinsically satisfying, curriculum and the third is to develop a more "relevant" education to give children a critical understanding of their environment. The last two aims are diffuse and can be pursued in various ways—through environmental studies or by encouraging self expression in artistic and leisure activities. Both these approaches allow parents to be involved in the child's education and also establish links between the school and the community. The three aims are not mutually exclusive. A more relevant curriculum based on the child's immediate surroundings and experience could stimulate learning and therefore improve skills as well as being enjoyable in itself and increasing his knowledge of and involvement in the community. Indeed almost all the team workers saw environmental studies as an ideal way of combining these three aims.

Nevertheless the emphasis on different activities varied in the four projects. Birmingham in particular and the West Riding to a lesser degree concentrated on improving reading, Liverpool paid special attention to developing an education which would be socially relevant and Deptford divided its efforts between environmental studies, language enrichment and extra teaching of mathematics.

In Birmingham low reading standards were tackled in two ways. First by a comprehensive programme using special materials and equipment and second by providing extra specialist teachers for remedial work. Only the first approach is relevant to this discussion as the remedial teaching was directed more to problems which hindered children reading than to developing curriculum.

The experiment was concentrated on two schools where the heads were specially interested in the material to be used. This consisted of S.R.A. *Reading Laboratories,* a box of finely graded selections of reading, printed on folded cards and colour coded according to difficulty, *Pilot Libraries,* a series of four boxes of graded books and *Word Games,* activities intended to develop phonic skills. The project team assessed the reading ages of the children and supplied appropriate S.R.A. material. Both schools made full use of the equipment and most teachers were enthusiastic. The children seemed keen about the higher level of *Reading Laboratories* and *Pilot*

Libraries but were less interested in the *Word Games*. Of course the material worked best with the best teachers who had the organisation and control necessary for using complex material and breaking the class down into smaller units. Both schools were well enough pleased with the apparatus to wish to try out other S.R.A. material such as the *Arithmetic Fact Kit*.

One of the schools already used audio-visual aids to reading and these were extended and introduced into the other school. There were taped stories and other material which the children could simply follow on the printed page or else use to follow instructions in their work book, and both schools used the Bell and Howell *Language Master*. At one school a full-time remedial teacher introduced the *Break Through to Literacy* material to the infants and first year juniors and supervised the audio-visual and S.R.A. material and the introduction of a new programme to develop perceptual skills provided by the remedial teaching service. He also set up a resources centre which organised, labelled and made available all the reading material in the school. At the other school an extra remedial teacher worked with groups of Asian children and others with reading disabilities.

An attempt to quantify the results of the year's reading drive with junior children suggested that literacy could be increased by remedial work at junior level. Gains of seven and ten points were recorded for the eight year olds in one school and for the nine year olds in the other, the older children showing the greatest improvement. The complete absence of progress in one group of eight year olds and one group of seven year olds in each school indicates that success or failure in learning to read is closely related to the performance of the teacher. No attempt was made to quantify the result of the *Break Through to Literacy* material in the infant school but the teachers were fully convinced of its value.

The West Riding project team devoted a large part of their effort in the field of curriculum development to the setting up of an audio-visual reading scheme which included language development for children who had reached the end of their primary education and were still unable to read or were functional non-readers. It was originally developed mainly for immigrant secondary school pupils but it was adapted for use in the West Riding by its author, Mrs. Caroline Moseley, who was attached to York University and also employed part time by the local authority to introduce this scheme to the schools. Tape recorders, head sets, microphones and Language Masters were all used as well as specially prepared programmed booklets, reading games and supplementary material. As in other projects it was found that the use of this equipment itself helped to motivate slow learners. The scheme assumes that older children with a history of reading failure should not be asked to perform tasks dependent on the printed word, and that reading should be presented in a structured way as a technical skill with an adult vocabulary and demanding concentration for not more than forty minutes a day. Thus early in the scheme the children are introduced to concepts such as "vowel" and "consonant". Both general language development work based on oral/aural methods, for example using and preparing tape slide programmes, and the structured phonic programme designed to improve reading skills, are included in the programme.

Four schools were asked to select the ten poorest readers in either the third or final year of junior school, giving forty children for the experimental group. All the teachers remained enthusiastic about the scheme throughout the year, and continued to use it during the following year, sometimes introducing their own modifications. One or two of the teachers found the complete programme too extensive to introduce into their class work at one go, and here they tended to concentrate on the phonic reading aspect and spent less time on language development work.

A similar sized group of children was drawn from six junior schools in different parts of the county with similar catchment areas to form a control group, matched on characteristics such as background, age, sex and initial reading ability. Both groups were given a series of tests in Autumn 1970 and after the end of the programme in Summer 1971; these included reading tests, one phonically graded, a vocabulary test, a test of attitudes to school and short term memory tests. On the non phonic reading test, the experimental group made better progress, significantly so in terms of reading age, making on average nine months progress over the year as against four months for the control. In standardised terms these changes were not significant. On the phonic test, most closely related to the programme, the experimental group gained significantly in both reading age, gaining more than a year, and also in standardised terms. The experimental groups ended up with a higher score on the phonic test than on the non phonic test, whereas the control groups continued to do better on the non phonic test. On vocabulary tests, however, the control made significantly greater progress during the year, so that the hope that the general language work would be reflected in improved vocabulary was not realised. In fact little of the work with tape slide programmes was carried out with the children in the reading scheme as the reading component alone was enough for many teachers to cope with.

There appeared to be no changes on the attitude scale that could be related to the reading programme, though the control group expressed themselves more satisfied with school both before and after the course. On the test of short term memory there were also no apparent changes related to the reading scheme. Teachers involved in the programme felt that the children had made good progress in the year and children who had had difficulty in concentrating were now encouraged to try more advanced work. In some cases this increased confidence affected other aspects of their school work.

In addition to the reading scheme the West Riding team initiated several pre-school projects and these two types of activity took about half the available resources. The other main development was the setting up of Red House (described in chapter 9), which was intended partly as a centre where heads, teachers and parents could see groups of their children working away from the usual structure of the school. Curriculum development was not the main aim of the activities at the centre but it was nevertheless an element in the children's work. Intensive courses were organised for eighteen children at a time who attended for half a day throughout half one term. The children were second year juniors from three different schools and each course was staffed by four students backed up by the E.P.A. team. Some changes were made in the second year when the idea of forming groups of children drawn from different schools was abandoned and instead complete classes went to the centre with their class teacher.

It was hoped that this would mean that ideas developed at the centre might be more easily transferred to schools. And in practice this seemed to happen. The second year courses were much more successful in relating work in the centre to ordinary school work—primarily because both class teachers and also students worked in both contexts.

The courses were too short and their content, deliberately, too imprecisely defined to allow any formal evaluation of their success. But they demonstrated that students could do very valuable work with small groups of children and that teachers and students could learn new ideas and techniques from one another. The children too benefited from the extra adult attention and the more varied experience during school time. Over the two years there were roughly twelve courses, each with eighteen children, during the first year but nearly twice as many in the second year when whole classes attended. About 150 students in all took part in the work.

The number of children involved in the courses was never large but the purpose of the centre was to show what could be done with existing resources and to develop new ideas. By standing outside the normal school situation it could organise courses that cut across the boundaries of other institutions. Though there were some points of conflict with the schools there was also close cooperation and several schools have taken over ideas developed at the centre such as using students with small groups of children. This spreading of ideas is an important measure of success.

In Deptford an ambitious and large scale environmental studies programme was an attempt to combine the three themes of E.P.A. curriculum development, the improvement of skills and the development of a more relevant and more enjoyable curriculum. Ideally the study of the environment would be enjoyable, interesting and relevant for the children and would thus stimulate learning.

The programme involved four hundred fourth year juniors from seven schools, fifteen teachers and a variable number of students and parents who spent one day a week throughout the school year at the environmental studies centre in Kent about fifteen miles from Deptford. The curriculum was kept flexible to allow each group to develop its own particular interests, but the general idea was that the normal primary school subjects, creative writing, number work, science, art and craft, should be directed to examining the immediate surroundings of the centre and to comparing this environment with that of Deptford. Appropriate teaching material was developed and a teacher's manual was produced which included a general account of the aims of the environmental studies, a description with maps of walks in the neighbourhoods and suggestions about how to study various topics.

Attempts to assess the scheme by testing the children's academic progress and changes in their attitudes to school and motivation to do well gave disappointing results. There were no significant differences in the changes in performance over a period in English and Maths between the children taking part in the scheme and a control group. There were no significantly different changes in attitude to school between the two groups. In study skills—a type of school activity related to the intended content of the environmental scheme—the children going into the country were performing less well than those who did not by the end of the year. The project director, however, questioned the relevance of quantitative evaluation for such a programme and whether the original aim of improving the children's educational performance was appropriate, especially in view of the comparatively short time available. Most of the teachers thought that the scheme had improved their pupils' motivation and the quality and quantity of their work in spite of the test evidence. There was wide agreement that the visits had provided enjoyable and stimulating experiences though there were reservations about the length and time taken on the bus journeys and the cramped nature of the centre's premises.

The social relevance of the programme seems to have received little emphasis though the director hoped that the project might foster a sense of social responsibility as the children became aware of the differences between the country environment in Kent and their own neighbourhood. A comparison of the two areas was part of the curriculum though it seems possible that less stress was laid on this than on investigating the immediate surroundings in Kent. Perhaps the country centre was too detached and remote from the children's background. A number of parents accompanied the children on their visits but it seems that, however enjoyable and fruitful in terms of home–school relationships, the trip was not seen as an extension of their experience in their own community.

Further attempts to develop a community based curriculum were linked to the plans for community schools in Deptford which were described in chapter 9. All the schools involved in the project made some attempt to foster links with children's homes, but three made special efforts to develop the Plowden conception of the community school. This, as the director saw it, would involve first the organisation of joint activities for parents, children and other members of the community based on the school premises, second, an analysis and examination of the local environment by the community school members and third, the working out of a school curriculum based on the immediate locality. Evening activities became quickly established at least in two of the schools as we have seen, but studies of the local environment and the development of curricula based upon it did not seem to advance very far.

The mathematics project, another curricular experiment, was designed to improve the children's number work, but it concentrated on the teachers in the hope that their increased knowledge and understanding would mean better teaching and hence more successful learning for the children. Local colleges of education provided facilities for the investigation and explanation of the language of modern mathematics.

Finally, a language programme for eight year olds adopted a rather more novel approach; it involved introducing a new type of activity or even a new subject into the classrooms. The immediate aims were to increase fluency, enlarge vocabulary and encourage children to use more complex linguistic structures. The project was developed jointly by the project team, the local district inspector and the teachers taking part. The teaching programme was described as based on Bernstein's linguistic theories and various "teaching packages" were produced to structure work in the classroom. In the second year the emphasis of the programme shifted from improving children's performance to improving the theoretical and practical competence of the teachers. This raised the problem of how to evaluate the work which was done. It was decided to interview the teachers taking part to find out what they thought about the project and to test the children's verbal behaviour to see whether there were any changes. In general the teachers felt that it had been successful and had improved the children's linguistic capabilities, though two teachers had reservations about its value for children of lower intelligence. But the results of the evaluation of the children's spoken language were disappointing; those taking part showed no significant improvement over a control group of children.

The Liverpool team quickly decided that its brief was to develop a "community" rather than a compensatory type of education for its E.P.A. The ultimate goal was the community school and the core of this concept was held to be a "community syllabus". It would be necessary to improve children's skills but this would be subordinate to developing a relevant and enjoyable curriculum. Relevant here meant not simply in touch with the child's own experience but also relevant to the community in which he lives and designed to promote a sense of community spirit and responsibility. This was seen as an urgent task and a number of small scale curricular innovations were introduced during the first and second years, all intended to develop a community based curriculum.

In one school with the help of various firms and the children's own collections an empty classroom was turned into a supermarket. This became the hub of mathematical work for a whole year and also led to varied social and creative studies, so linking a number of separate subjects and providing a picturesque illustration of a community oriented curriculum. The supermarket suggested other possibilities such as a bank, surgery or municipal agency all of which could be used to equip children to meet everyday situations comfortably and critically.

A second experiment was designed to increase the child's awareness of his environment, his social awareness, his interest in reading, number work and motor skills and to use environmental features as a basis for creative work. Small groups of students and children—twelve students to thirty eight year olds—investigated their neighbourhoods, making models of local factories and garages, examining the architecture of local buildings and so on. Both students and teachers considered the children had benefited educationally as well as socially.

In another case local institutions such as school, church, street and home were studied and a further project aimed to increase the children's range of leisure activities, hoping to benefit them both immediately and in their future lives. One day a week was devoted to creative expression with two groups of thirty children over nine, two class teachers and eight students. It was hoped that children in difficulties with one mode of expression, say language, might succeed in another, say movement, and the local environment was to provide the stimulus for activity. One school initiated an animal and plant life project which was an intensification of what has often been attempted in other schools and produced enjoyable and interesting work, but a cultural enrichment project with junior school children which intended to examine the physical riches of the environment and also to draw out the "literary legacy" of the children did not develop chiefly because of organisational difficulties.

There were two separate ventures in infant mathematics. In one a specialist college maths tutor and students helped in the classroom and also began to develop an individual maths kit for infants. In the other three tutors and a number of students acted as extra classroom helpers. This project did not do anything new but teachers felt it worth while as they were able to do things which were difficult without extra help. Some of those taking part, however, thought that the aims and methods of the project should have been more carefully defined. Possibly this would have been useful in a subject like infant maths which is not likely to differ much in approach from school to school.

Social and creative studies for infants was the ninth curricular experiment. In one school in addition to the class teacher a tutor and eight students were involved with sixty infant children. Well known festivals throughout the year were used as a focus of curricular work—harvest festival, Guy Fawkes and so on. All the strands of infant work—number, music, drama, language, and movement were gathered together in the preparation for a celebration of the festivals. Parents were invited to take part and the festivals proved a very successful way of encouraging the shy ones.

By the third year of the project in Liverpool, curricular work was being undertaken in some thirty schools, normally with the assistance of students. The value of creative work was now becoming apparent. Children who were behind the norms in literary and number work could perhaps communicate in other ways, through dramatic and artistic expression and these creative ventures were ideal for attracting parents. The team also recruited the Liverpool Everyman Theatre team to assist. This was done most effectively in "The Day of the Disaster", a stylised improvisation on the interrelated themes of immigration, housing and unemployment. Performed in over twenty schools with the active participation of nine-to-eleven year olds, it gave something like fifteen hundred children the opportunity to play out and examine the roles associated with such predicaments and it ended with a tribunal before which the leading actor, personifying "the system", was examined by the children. It should be stressed that it was the *social* environment and not just the *local* environment that was in question; television, which is scarcely a localised topic, is of great import in the child's environmental experience and, as such, worthy of investigation. It could, of course, be argued that it is futile to consider material outside the ambit of the child's social experience, on the grounds that children can only relate with understanding to concepts which are comprehensible within their own grasp of reality. This was a strong argument with many teachers. Not only could it be argued that a community-based or environmentally-oriented curriculum was, on moral and social grounds, the most suitable, it could also be pressed that children should not be presented with extra-environmental (in this broader sense) material. Here the child-centredness of the progressive educationist and the social precepts of the community educator meet.

In promoting a study of the social environment as an all-embracing exercise, including the inculcation of basic skills, the projects were exposing a major fallacy of English community schooling. However "open" the school may become in relation to parents, residents and other members of the community, it cannot validly claim the title of a fully developed community school until it has a community curriculum. There is much work to be done in this field. We are still at a rather primitive stage, but these pioneer curricular explorations give promise of important progress yet to be made.

The effects of a community based syllabus aiming at critical and constructive understanding of the environment are long term and cannot easily be measured by the conventional methods of educational research. But there was general agreement among the teachers that children had made some educational gains, particularly in terms of social relationships, language and communications. The improvement of the child-adult ratio with the use of students and the introduction of fresh stimuli and equipment seemed to have been the major causes. These innovations do not seem to have led to problems of discipline or time wasting or to a decline in academic standards.

The Liverpool team drew four major conclusions from their various experiments. First, the balance of the curriculum should change from "academic" to "social" and should be based on the realities of the immediate environment. Language programmes and reading and writing should be concerned with subjects within children's direct experience. Second, it would be appropriate for schools to increase the time devoted to creative pursuits in order to entertain and involve parents and community. Parents have shown their interest in music, drama and art, and work with a local reference is more likely to engage their attention. Third, social environmental studies should concentrate on skills rather than on information. Social studies should not be a collection of irrelevant facts, used perhaps for practising reading and writing but rather an exploration of the world which itself is served by reading, writing and number work. Fourth, teaching attitudes and the atmosphere of the school must change. E.P.A. community education presumes that the E.P.A. should be radically reformed and that the children should be "forewarned and forearmed for the struggle". This does not mean that the teacher should form a revolutionary cell in the classroom but that both teachers and children should develop a critical but tolerant attitude to a range of social institutions, ideas and aspirations. Beyond the long term hope for a higher level of social participation, the community oriented curriculum has other advantages. It is likely that the children will do as well or better in traditional subjects because they will be linked to their own experience. In realising that education is about himself and his community just as much as about a more remote middle class world the child will gain a sense of his worth and parents will more readily give their interest and support.

CHAPTER 11

The Community School and the Teacher

It emerges from Chapters 9 to 10 that an effective partnership between school and home and an effective curriculum for the E.P.A. children were essential elements of our developing conception of the community school. But the lynch-pin of that school is, and must remain, the teacher. The quality of teaching is the fundamental basis for success in the community school as in any other school. Our task in this chapter is to look directly at the E.P.A. teacher in the light of the action taken in the four projects to strengthen the links between teachers and their communities. We have seen something of the characteristics of teachers in the project schools in Chapter 5 where we underlined the characteristic youth and inexperience of E.P.A. teachers in Deptford, Birmingham and presumably Liverpool, and the contrasting stability and rootedness of the teaching staff in the West Riding mining towns. Here we can concentrate on the efforts made in all four districts to link the schools to colleges of education and on the implications of the community school idea for teacher training both in college and in service.

We have noted too, in Chapter 3, that an early response of government to the Plowden Report was to finance a £75 per annum (later £83)[1] increment for teachers in E.P.A. schools. We may therefore begin with an evaluation made by the London research team of the impact of the new allowance.

The £75 Allowance

One of the objects of the £75 allowance was to encourage teachers to stay in schools in difficult areas in order to give a more stable classroom environment for the pupils. The impact of the allowance was measured by comparing the mobility rates of teachers in the 78 I.L.E.A. schools receiving it with the rates in the 79 schools ranked immediately below them on the E.P.A. index. Both groups of schools were similar, varying marginally in the severity of certain problems. More evidence was collected by asking head teachers and a sample of assistant teachers in schools in E.P.A. areas about their views on the extra allowance.

Between 1967–68 and 1968–69 full-time staff in schools receiving the award increased from 713 to 765 and numbers resigning fell from 170 to 142 (Table 11.1). Using 1967–68 as a base year (index 100), the resignation index for 1968–69 in the schools receiving the £75 was 83·5. Thus, there was a fall in resignations of 16·5 index points from the schools benefiting from the £75 during the first full school year of its operation. The index of full-time staff in these schools rose at the same time by 7·3 index points. The resignation index for 1969–70, however, was 106·5 (an increase of

---

[1] The new Burnham agreement has increased the E.P.A. teachers' allowance again to £105 (*Guardian*, *Times*, 23rd May 1972).

Table 11.1

Schools receiving £75 allowance compared with those not receiving it: full-time staff and resigners 1967–68, 1968–69 and 1969–70

School	1967–68 Full-time staff	Re-signers	1968–69 Full-time staff	Resigners	1969–70 Full-time staff	Resigners
£75	713	170	765	142	825	191
Non £75	746	215	783	219	855	224
Index value						
£75	100	100	107·3	83·5	115·5	106·5
Non £75	100	100	105·0	101·4	114·6	104·2

6·5 index points from the base year). This contrasts with the position in the schools not receiving the £75 allowance. Following its introduction there was a slight increase in resignations (from 215 to 219: index to 101·4) from the schools not receiving it. During 1969–70, however, the resignation index continued to rise only slightly (to 104·2) in contrast to the larger rise in that year to 106·5 from the schools receiving the allowance.

The proportionate rate of change can be seen more readily in Table 11.2 which gives the mean number of resignations per school.

Table 11.2

Average number of resigners and full-time staff in schools receiving and not receiving £75: by year

	Mean no. of resigners Receiving £75	Not receiving £75	Mean no. of full-time staff Receiving £75	Not receiving £75
1967–68	2·18	2·72	9·14	9·44
1968–69	1·82	2·77	9·81	9·91
1969–70	2·45	2·84	10·58	10·76

Schools receiving the £75 had a slightly lower mean resignation rate than the comparison group in the first year (2·18 per school: 2·72 per school). Over the first year the mean resignation rate fell (to 1·82 per school) in the schools receiving the £75, and remained fairly constant in the schools not receiving the allowance. In the second year of the scheme's operation there was a slight decrease in the mean resignation rate in the comparison schools, and an increase to above the previous level of resignations in the schools included in the scheme (i.e., to a mean resignation rate of 2·45 in 1969–70 compared to 2·18 in 1968–69).

In discussions with head teachers about the salary increment we tried to find out what they thought the Department of Education and Science intended to achieve and what effect they thought the award actually had on the staff of schools receiving it and also on those in schools not receiving it.

We also tried to discover their view about the principle and practice of supplementing the salary of teachers working in E.P.A. schools. We spoke to twelve Deptford head teachers all of whom thought their school was in an educational priority area and presumed therefore that it should have received the £75 allowance for its staff. In fact five schools did not receive it.

All the Deptford heads except two thought the purpose of the scheme was to attract teachers to education priority area schools. One thought the object was to improve morale and another thought that the Department was unclear about why it allocated the money.

None of the seven Deptford head teachers in schools receiving the increment had noticed any effect on their staffing position and this they attributed to three main reasons. First, all thought the allowance was too small; at the time it represented an additional gross salary of between four and six per cent. Second, the heads believed there were more fundamental matters affecting mobility; marriage and pregnancy were significant for young women while the heads themselves could have an important influence on movement among their staff. Third, the duration of the allowance was uncertain; particular schools might cease to qualify when the awards were reassessed.

Among head teachers in the five schools not qualifying for awards there was some resentment at their own exclusion, though the majority felt that the £75 would make little difference in the long run.

Only one of the heads objected to any differential salary for staff in E.P.A. schools, arguing that it would be better to spend the money on recruiting more teachers. The others supported the awards for various reasons, to compensate for, and in recognition of, the special difficulties of the job as well as to increase the number of teachers entering this kind of work. Two of the heads favoured extra allowances only for teachers who showed special capacities and another feared higher salaries might attract the wrong kind of staff and would have preferred to have more posts of special responsibility, a suggestion supported by one of her colleagues who thought this would be a powerful means of keeping good teachers in E.P.A.s.

We extended our enquiry into teachers' attitudes to four groups of I.L.E.A. schools away from the Deptford area where we interviewed 20 heads of schools receiving the allowance and 27 heads of nearby schools not receiving it. Half the heads of schools qualifying for the award thought that it had no effect on their own schools and half believed there was some resentment in schools not receiving it. In fact opinion in the schools not having the £75 was evenly divided between heads noticing no effects and those who reported disappointment among their staff. Two-thirds of the head teachers thought the allowance had no effect on the schools which did receive it.

Thus head teachers were in general unenthusiastic about the special allowance. It seemed to give displeasure to many who did not receive it, but to afford no significant advantage to those who did. It was the amount that was at issue rather than the principle. Most heads, whether or not their schools received the award, agreed that there should be one, and the most popular amount suggested was £120. Eighteen heads would like to have seen selective payments to specially capable teachers, but the majority agreed with the present system.

Discussions with assistant teachers in I.L.E.A. schools showed the great majority in favour of universal allowances at a flat rate. Only five out of 147 teachers approached objected to an E.P.A. increment of any kind; among the others criticism was directed at the small amount involved. No teachers who received awards, however, thought the extra money affected their willingness to work in E.P.A. schools and none of those without the extra allowance admitted that they would go to a school in order to receive it. In general the views of the assistant teachers were very similar to those of the heads; there was wide-spread doubt that the present system of awards was having any significant influence on any of the schools.

Our enquiry suggests then that the £75 award scheme was largely ineffectual. The initial drop in resignations from qualifying schools was reversed after only a year, perhaps because small salary increases may have an immediate impact on morale but no long-term effect. Head teachers' views were mixed, most approving of the idea in principle but considering the amount too small. The majority saw no effect in the qualifying schools and a rather smaller majority believed there to be some resentment in similar schools which had not been recognised by the D.E.S. Assistant teachers also approved the scheme in principle but thought the awards too small and did not believe the existing scheme had any effect on the movements of staff.

Although in the main the heads favoured some form of salary differential for teachers in E.P.A. schools, they recognised certain problems in implementing them. Should E.P.A. schools be defined in terms of the amount of money available for salary differentials or in terms of independent criteria? Should the salary allowance go to all teachers working in such schools or should it be selective? Should the allowance go to individuals who work in a particular school or to the school itself to be allocated by the head teacher? There was some disagreement about the proper amount for the award and about who should receive it. Head teachers, of course, are on a higher salary than the majority of teachers affected by the allowance and this may colour their views on the impact of so small a sum. It seems worthwhile, if the policy of an E.P.A. teachers' allowance is to be seriously debated, to consider the views of those most affected—the assistant teachers —and such objective data as exists on recruitment and turnover. Our own small enquiry suggested that assistant teachers found the £75 quite inadequate.

Links to Colleges of Education

The three city districts all had several colleges of education nearby and all made efforts to enlist their co-operation with the E.P.A. action-reasearch programme. In the West Riding all the colleges except one were further away but Red House provided a convenient centre for college students.

At the beginning of our programme the links were somewhat tenuous. After his initial explorations in Deptford the London action director reported that a patchwork of communication existed between some of the project schools and the local colleges of education: a few of the schools had excellent arrangements with colleges; others had only intermittent contact and in one case a project school had had no students from local colleges for over two years though Goldsmiths' College was only a quarter of a mile away and there were three others within a six-mile radius. The Birmingham team similarly made a systematic approach to all the colleges in the area with disappointing results.

Nevertheless, by dint of continued effort, the links began to strengthen. In Birmingham a successful arrangement was made with St. Peter's College, Saltley, for all 16 members of an option course in the college to be linked to a particular school in the Birmingham project for one day a week, teaching groups of children in a "micro-teaching" situation. Or to take an example from London, arrangements were made with Rachel Macmillan College for the "adoption" of a class of second-year children by about 40 students. This pilot venture in one-to-one relationships between students and children was enthusiastically received at both ends and was developed later in the programme to cover four schools and most of the second-year students at the college during the summer term. At the end of the second year of the project over 100 students were involved either in the one-to-one relationship or in an alternative infant mathematics enrichment programme. In the third year the link was still further extended to include a third project concerned with English for immigrants.

Meanwhile, in the West Riding, students were closely involved in many of the programmes which developed at Red House; in the intensive courses where, as we saw in the last chapter, something like 150 students taught children in small groups, and in the holiday programmes organised in local schools. The experiments in group work were reckoned to be to the advantage of all concerned; children benefiting from close contact with interested adults; teachers and students each learning from one another's experience; and parents learning about their children's progress from people who had had opportunities to observe them closely. That the idea of using students to work with small groups of children spread to some of the local schools is a fair reflection of the success of the experiment.

In Liverpool what the Plowden Report called "a continuing link" between colleges and E.P.A. schools became a larger element in the project than had originally been planned and developed throughout the three years with the help of a college tutor liaison group.

Teacher education was a major item in the Liverpool activities and great importance was attached to the development of E.P.A. option courses for college students both as a significant aspect of E.P.A. reform and as a possible influence on teacher education generally.

The Liverpool colleges of education became particularly involved in the project in its second year. Six colleges organised 14 student teams to work regularly in the project schools and also in the three "control" schools included in the team's work. Two other colleges arranged attachments for shorter periods and the result, as in Deptford, was that nearly 200 students might be in the field in a given week, supporting the project work in the schools in a variety of ways and also gaining experience useful to themselves in their professional training. They were led by 17 tutors who constituted the college tutor liaison committee for the project.

Where tutors were efficient, committed and stimulating—and the majority were—there were no problems. But, failing tutors with these qualities, problems could be overwhelming. E.P.A. teacher education cannot be left to chance. If the E.P.A. option course is to become an integral part of the college curriculum, steps must be taken to guarantee adequate tutorial support. There is a pressing need for in-service training not only for tutors but for advisers, inspectors, teacher centre wardens and heads and, indeed, for anyone dealing with teacher trainees or young teachers in E.P.A.s. The Project Director was invited to help to plan a one-year in-service course on the teaching of socially disadvantaged children which included a major component under the heading of "E.P.A. Thought and Practice". Such a development is an important step towards better education in deprived areas.

The success of students following the E.P.A. option course varied, predictably enough, according to the attitude of the school and the commitment of the college. During the first year of the project most schools were won over to the idea, although one in particular was worried by the constant attachment, seeing it as a loss of curricular time rather than an advantage. But in only two cases were the teams unwelcome; in general they were received far more kindly than they had a right to expect in the stress of E.P.A. schooling. The commitment of the college was highly significant and a correlation quickly showed itself between the success of the students and the quality of the principals. Where the college principal and authorities gave high priority to E.P.A.s difficulties were overcome. Most of the obstacles were administrative, concerning timetabling, travel, the desires of other college departments or groupings and so on. No college ever said openly that it did not regard E.P.A. problems as urgent. Nonetheless by the same token, organisational barriers should have been less difficult to surmount than philosophic ones.

The variation in college support was one of the chief points to emerge at the E.P.A. students' conference in the spring of 1970. The main aim of the conference was to give the students a better understanding of the whole E.P.A. programme so that they might see their own efforts in the context of the national design. The intercollegiate discussions were regarded as crucial and were seen as the most rewarding element of the conference, students becoming increasingly critical or appreciative of their own colleges as they learnt about the kinds of support offered in others.

All these college courses have been nurtured from the beginning in conjunction with the schools, but with no national brief. This explains both their success and their varied nature. The three essentials requested by the project—a tutor led team, a regular attachment and intramural aid— seemed justified but there was great variety in the activities. If the movement continues to grow and if some such course became a prescribed qualification for the salary increment in E.P.A. schools, the area training organisation might have to look more closely at the situation. This is the more necessary as so much E.P.A. work has become part of the students' certificate requirements through new forms of school practice and special studies of groups of children and of special aspects of the attachment. But although some standardisation may be required it is to be hoped that it would not inhibit the kind of vitality evident in the Liverpool experiment.

A question arises, given the variety of approach, as to whether all or only some of the colleges should bear the brunt of E.P.A. work. There are difficulties in concentration even though it would be more economical of tutors; students cannot be expected to choose the E.P.A. course until their second or third year and might then find themselves in the wrong college, and some institutions might be completely cut off from E.P.A. problems.

Head teachers, teachers, tutors and students were all asked their opinion of the special courses. The tutors were enthusiastic and wanted the courses to continue, believing them to provide a valuable opportunity for students to develop a firm relationship with schools and children. The class teachers were rather less emphatic in their support. Ten out of 13 wanted the scheme to go on and several felt that a half-day attachment was too short and suggested one whole day a week would be better, but three did not want the courses to continue. The main reaction, however, was favourable, emphasising the benefit to the children of the attention of the students. This appreciative response was welcome for it was, of course, the class teachers who had borne the brunt of what could have been regarded as a gross invasion of the classroom. Head teachers were also divided; nine out of eleven voted unreservedly for continuation, but there was a strong and determined negative voice. Criticism, however, was directed at the organisation rather than the principle. By and large the special courses were reckoned the most useful aspect of the whole project and a progressive step in the field of teacher education. For head teachers as well as teachers (rarely the first to applaud colleges of education) to agree on this, with even so small a sample, was a significant result.

Some of the most interesting evidence came from the representative sample of 80 students who completed a report of their school attachment. Sixty of them were using these attachments directly for their certificate courses either in lieu of a school practice or as the basis for some special study, thus demonstrating the feasibility of linking the courses to the main body of college work. The great majority of students were convinced that children benefited greatly from the extra individual attention they received, but were less certain about the benefits of the course to themselves.[1] In general, the students were favourably disposed, valuing the regular contact with the schools as a way of bringing theory and practice together and because they could observe the school situation over a longer period. Others preferred a block placement and found the weekly scheme an unsatisfactory way of developing good communications with the schools and also difficult to fit in with their other college work.

It was hardly surprising that the great majority of students said that the course was a valuable introduction for E.P.A. work, claiming a greater understanding of the characteristic problems of educating children in depressed areas. A question about future intentions showed over one third

---

[1] With Scottish modesty, the Dundee students reported the opposite (Vol. V).

of the students intending to teach in E.P.A.s and eleven who expected to do so after some other experience elsewhere. On the other hand there were 13 who definitely did not want to go to E.P.A. schools. The value of the special courses may be seen partly as enabling certain students to decide against E.P.A. work as well as encouraging others to enter it.

There is no doubt that teachers and head teachers considered the teacher education programme the most valuable aspect of the project. Practically every school is anxious to retain the college link permanently and there are signs in one or two colleges that some of the findings may be influencing general teaching and not just the E.P.A. courses. The Liverpool University Settlement has also started three-week part-time residential E.P.A. courses. Students negotiate close contacts with a variety of local community institutions so that teachers in training have direct experience of the special characteristics of social and educational problems in poor areas.

As the project enlarged to embrace more schools so did its teacher education schedule grow. At various times the project fielded as many as 30 teams. In all, something approaching 300 students were given practical experience of E.P.A. work, much of it in connection with the project extension programme. A second student conference was held in 1971 which devoted itself to E.P.A. problems and it seems that this will become an annual event and tutors and many college authorities are as determined as the schools that the continuing link shall persist.

Looking back over the experience of all four projects, it is fair to conclude that what Plowden called "the continuing link" between E.P.A. schools and colleges of education has been firmly established in a sufficient number of cases to prove its viability as a national arrangement. An enquiry covering the whole country and exploring further the problems of both training courses and practical arrangements between colleges and schools is now needed. For our own part we are sufficiently confident of our local experience to include national recommendations on this aspect of the quality of teaching in E.P.A. schools in our final chapter.[1]

---

[1] The Dundee Report (Vol. V) confirms this conclusion.

CHAPTER 12

The Community School and the Community

We can now try to close the circle of the community school. In the preceding chapters we have illustrated it from various points on the circumference—the family, the college of education, the social services, the retail market and so on. We have not, it must be conceded, stopped to look closely from all possible vantage points. Two in particular must be mentioned—the Town Hall and the industrial enterprise. Apart from a brief reference to the government of the community school we have scarcely touched on the administrative implications of our conception of community schooling. Nevertheless they exist and they affect the work of all local authority departments, not only that of education. The viability of the community school rests in part on policies for housing and civic redevelopment. The registers and staff records of many E.P.A. schools in the inner rings of the cities betray all too obviously the absence of community. The organisation of the personal social services needs to be integrated with community school catchment areas. And, where circumstances permit, the architects and planners can create the bricks and mortar of a community school by intelligent grouping of health clinics, shopping centres and recreational facilities with school buildings.

Industry too has a perspective on the community school which we have largely neglected in our action-research. In part and implicitly we tend to identify the community interest in education with the mother and housewife. In our account of the projects there is evidence here and there of efforts to recruit fathers and mild surprise when a response has been forthcoming. Again the school visit to the factory is taken for granted while the reverse is practically never contemplated. Industry appears in the picture almost exclusively as either a possible source of charitable gift or as the vague fate of children after secondary school. All this is unrealistic and unsatisfactory. In any further action-research on the community school and especially a project extended to secondary schooling, the workplace, the father and the working mother ought to find a more prominent place.

Meanwhile, to complete our own story, we have to refer to three aspects of community school development which have been inadequately treated in the last three chapters. They are the publicising of education in the community at large, the use of cultural facilities in the community, and finally, the potential contribution of adult education.

Apart from direct contact with children's families—either through some kind of home visiting or by getting the parents to come to the schools—attempts were also made to arouse the interest of the community through publications, exhibitions, educational shops and site improvement work.

Liverpool paid a lot of attention to a variety of school publications—a prospectus describing the life and work of the school and produced with the help of the art college; newsletters with articles on the work of the school, including one on the I.T.A. with a transcribed piece from the *Liverpool Echo* for parents to try out; and a school magazine consisting of children's contributions with articles from parents promised for later editions. These were well received, each in its way trying to explain the aims and methods of the school to parents so that they might better help their children. The publications were deliberately designed to be as professional as possible so that they might compete with commercial productions in their style and presentation. They were an exercise in public relations to establish communications between teachers and parents.

The three publications had mixed success. The newsletter seemed to have little impact and there was in fact no second edition. On the other hand teachers thought that the prospectus achieved its aim and was a good advertisement for the school. Although the written response was not large, comments generally indicated that readers were impressed. The magazine was popular and successful with successive editions carrying contributions from parents and others.

As the E.P.A. programme in Liverpool expanded it became harder to publish individually, though eight schools in fact continued to do so. So the project team decided to publish a general magazine once a term. Each of the first three editions had a main theme—home and school, curriculum in the community, and school and community—and the special advantage of "Back Home", as the journal was named, was that it could be used independently or as a backing or folder for school, class, or individual material. All but one of 34 schools distributed the publication and the project team looked ahead to a tripartite journal—a national cover, a local contribution and a school insertion.

Exhibitions were also an important part of the E.P.A. work in Liverpool. The initial experiment was confined to one school which provided examples of children's work to display in one or two local shops. Success was immediate and the displays were extended to a dozen or more shops with the shopkeepers surprised and delighted because it helped to keep their establishments busy. The small exhibitions started appositely enough with work on fish in the fishmonger's and so on but, with the help of students, there began a weekly change of display. Soon exhibitions were extended to two local pubs and the local doctor's surgery waiting room. Another venture was a travelling exhibition organised by one of the secondary schools supported by the school band and the schools choir who sang a specially written song to introduce the audiences to the performance. The children danced and mimed and produced improvised drama. The show visited local firms and was also seen by parents, old age pensioners and groups of primary teachers, by all of whom it was well received.

The success of the displays in local shops led to a much more ambitious attempt at a large departmental store, T. J. Hughes. All the project schools joined in and the firm provided space, which was more conventionally to be found housing Father Christmas, his Toy Fair and the Fairy Grotto, for a fortnight's exhibition. The title was "Child in the City" and the aim was to demonstrate to parents and others the goals and methods of the local schools. An art lecturer from a local college was responsible for the design and for selecting a representative range of classroom work. This he managed with the help of six of his students and with a collection of enlarged photographs of the area produced by a local photographer.

Each project school had a small stand displaying work which had often been carried out in connection with the project curricular experiments with the help of students and which reflected the local environment. In addition there were stalls advertising the playgroup federation and adult education and the Liverpool C.A.S.E. organised an Education Shop. This offered postal replies for queries that could not be answered immediately and there was a heavy demand for a series of eleven leaflets written by local specialists on various aspects of school activities like maths or reading. A final and important feature was a daily series of "live" demonstrations covering practically every branch of the school curriculum in a simulated classroom in the theatre area of the firm's exhibition space.

During the fortnight about ten thousand visitors, including some fifty truants, came to the exhibition and store executives thought that it was the most successful they had had in recent years.

The "live" demonstrations were the most salutary part of the proceedings. The items to which parents have traditionally been invited—drama, music and dancing—drew large crowds usually over 150, in two or three cases over 200 and, on one Saturday afternoon, 300. When it was modern maths or social studies or even an art workshop, and when the audience were expected to move around, inspecting and questioning, numbers sank sometimes to under 20. This suggests that if we are to inform parents about less "theatrical" subjects we must think of a more theatrical form of presentation, such as a "modern maths musical" or a social studies documentary drama. And if parental engagement is thought to be fundamentally important perhaps the curriculum should be planned to encourage it with an emphasis on music, drama and dancing.

An attempt was made to discover public reactions to the exhibition by handing out questionnaires to some three per cent of the visitors. Two thirds had come to the store especially to see the exhibition but a large minority—130 people—had seen it in the course of ordinary shopping and this shows how using a shop may involve people who might not otherwise come. The infant displays were the most popular among the women though men preferred the exhibitions of junior work. Only five people commented unfavourably out of 342 who were interviewed. Among the critics were a child care officer who was not convinced that an exhibition of this kind got through to parents and children, and a woman social welfare worker who said that the material was out of context in a shop and that parents could visit the schools if they were interested.

A rather different kind of exhibition materialised almost by chance after the Liverpool University Arts Festival, for which children's work had been requested, collapsed and the project team decided to organise a festival of its own. It had three themes—"destruction", "city-selling" and "street folk"—and there were live performances and local radio broadcasts as well as displays of work. The performances were supported by the school band and the children constructed a giant pop singer as a centre piece. There were seven separate sketches—each with evocative titles: "Folks who live in our Street", "Street Dances and Games", "The Great Fire of Liverpool", and "Everton Sound", "Harmony and Understanding", "Looking at Liverpool" and "Liverpool Through the Seasons".

Another feature of publicity work was the development of the education kiosk, along the lines of the normal education shop, but visualised as a packable, mobile kit. It had a free-standing three-part screen with racks for literature, copies of specially prepared single-sheet leaflets on both curricular and administrative aspects of education and a uniform for the assistant. The colours and pattern of the kiosk, literature and uniform were constant, providing a unified kit which could quickly be erected at any key point, bingo hall, railway station, factory canteen, department store or football ground. The kiosk was used experimentally at the Liverpool Show, which has an audience of thousands, and it is hoped to produce it on a larger scale in the coming years as a quick and simple way of providing educational information to the public.

Rather similar was the market stall established in the West Riding, to extend the experiments with displays of children's work and with information and advice centres which had been tried in other areas. Besides acting as an advice and display centre, the stall carried a range of children's books and toys which were not available locally. The stock carried by the stall consisted of toys and books that could generally be regarded as "educational", not in order to restrict choice to this kind of toy but to supplement what already existed. Besides the newsagents selling toys and books, there were usually two or three other toy stalls in the market and more at Christmas time. On the whole, the schools were eager to co-operate, and circulated information to families, so that most parents in the area knew about the stall when it opened. Several schools prepared displays and teachers came down in the lunch hour to look at the stock and to buy items for themselves. Sales varied widely from week to week—affected by holidays, rival attractions like November 5th and strikes or short working in the pit. But the stall built up a regular and increasing sale and particularly at Christmas. The small things were most popular—crayons, pencils, paint, brushes, paper, sticky paper shapes, plasticine, chalks, and so on and the actual number of sales was fairly high. The buyers were mainly mothers with young children. At this age the mother buys for the child and is interested in getting him used to educational materials. Later, children are given pocket money and choose for themselves but the stall sold very little to older children. By this age the books available are almost all solid print, which both parents and children clearly find formidable. But there is resistance to developments which aim to combat this problem; parents tend to select what they know—for example Ladybird books. The stall stocked books for teenage children but again was unsuccessful, and these sales were mainly to young mothers.

The growth of pre-school activities obviously had an impact on buying, mothers frequently asking for a particular item they were familiar with at the nursery group, and then discussing the merits of the various items available. Later, the stall was used increasingly by the playgroups in the area, both as a source of ideas for equipment and how it could be used, and as a means of stimulating parents in the groups to try out equipment and activities in the home. Arrangements were made on a dozen or more occasions for the stall to visit playgroup coffee mornings and evenings and local clinics. In this way, one can see the reinforcing effect that a project like the market stall may have on pre-school work. This effect was also noticed in the home visiting project; families who had been introduced to toys and books in the home and had accepted the fact that their child was ready for them, came round to the stall to see what was available.

For the first year the stall operated almost entirely in one of the two towns, the aim being to see whether such a venture would work. In fact there were enough sales for the operation almost to cover its costs—the profits meeting rent and pay for someone to man the stall. In addition to people who bought from the stall a large number came to look and ask about toys and books or talk about education in general. Many came specially to see the display which was changed each week. Although the "advice" aspect of the stall was not particularly prominent, it developed as an important function, particularly when an educational change was imminent such as the early entry to school that occurred in September 1970. The stall also kept stocks of welfare forms and offered advice on how to apply for benefits such as free meals, clothing, welfare milk, family income supplement and supplementary benefits. The fact that people could come and "browse" at the stall and that advice could be asked and given during discussion of the suitability of a particular book or toy, made it easier for those who might otherwise be cautious of asking for help.

The stall also became a focal point for details about project work. "Condensation", the Red House magazine, was issued from the stall; and announcements made about the holiday schemes run by the project. Following the Summer Project there were special displays of the children's constructions and paintings—and one week a second stall had to be hired to house the display. Coloured slides of the holiday scheme were shown continuously on a daylight screen. Throughout the afternoons when there were slide shows perhaps 20 people collected to watch, comment and ask questions: with ten to 15 shows each afternoon, several hundred people must have seen the slides and talked to some of the organisers of the Summer Project. As a method of presentation this compared favourably to a formal meeting with slides where attendance of over 100 people would be unusual. As a final stage, a full colour 8mm movie film of the Summer Project was shown in the same way.

It is important not to separate the function of selling from that of advice and information. The market stall project demonstrated the need for both activities in E.P.A.s. The steady sale indicates that there is a need for the type of material the stall provides, and that changes in educational provision —the opening of nursery classes or home visiting projects—can stimulate demand.

Although the stall project roughly "broke even" this does not take into account the time put in by E.P.A. team members. Thus a district with a total population of 17,000 and a primary school population of 2,000 is unlikely ever to support enough sales to make the stall a genuinely paying proposition. Yet an approach to publishers with a request for direct sales discount and for sample display and other material that could be used on the stall and demonstrated in Red House, playgroups, and clinics, brought a surprisingly interested and helpful response. This suggests that once a small-scale venture of this kind has been demonstrated as feasible and valuable, suppliers may be prepared to create special terms.

Another community project which seemed to arouse great interest was the site improvement scheme developed in Liverpool. Schools cultivated gardens and children painted murals on their playground walls, including a dramatic waterfront scene, and decorated them with hanging baskets and large bowls of flowers. Fears of vandalism proved groundless, perhaps because the children and others felt it was their own creation and invested considerable pride in their work.

By declaring war on their own site teachers and children can demonstrate to the community their intentions to look critically and positively at their surroundings. Ideally such activities draw curricular and community concerns together. Each piece of work grows from part of the syllabus so that the adult observer, as well as noticing the social value for the children and the community, is also informed of what the school is attempting in a curricular sense. There is great scope for improvement schemes of this kind and they are beginning to be extended beyond the school boundaries to, for example, Christmas decorations for a shopping precinct and a waste land junk sculpture enterprise.

The bus fitted out as a mobile playschool was a unique experiment but an idea which was later adopted in other areas. Its pilot runs were chiefly to the playgroups in the federation and it soon showed itself to be a viable playspace and became very popular. Fifteen was the optimal number of children, but 20 could be managed in reasonable comfort. The bus has attracted considerable interest elsewhere in the city and country and over two years it has appeared ten times on television.

A different kind of experiment was that based on the Midlands Arts Centre in Birmingham. It was an attempt to bridge a cultural gap by introducing E.P.A. children to some aspects of the culture of the larger community beyond the boundaries of their own immediate experience and it aimed at providing enjoyment and also encouraging links between school and home and community. Children used the resources of the centre for creative work and artistic self-expression but, according to the teacher/ leader based at the centre, much of the activity started from experience based on the local environment and involved visits to places of local interest.

Certain problems arose in using the centre, however, as an independent organisation depending on voluntary subscriptions, assistance from the Arts Council and the Local Authority and fees. Although there was much sympathy for the needs of the E.P.A. and a readiness to place the centre's facilities at the disposal of the project, its organisation could not be entirely geared to the needs of the E.P.A. children and their families. It had been hoped for example after the children's short experience of the centre to encourage the parents to join and attend with their children as a family unit. But, as we saw in Chapter 9, only a handful of families eventually came. In so far as the reasons for this disappointing result may have been the middle class image of the centre and the fees it charged, it demonstrates the problems of trying to break down cultural barriers through institutions which may be seen to reflect alien values.

The scheme began on a comparatively small scale but grew to involve about 300 children. In the first year 15 nine to ten year olds were chosen from one school and attended the centre for one whole day a week throughout one school year. In the second year two other schools joined in and all children aged nine to ten in the three schools attended for one whole day for six consecutive weeks. This short period did of course have considerable drawbacks but the aim was stimulation and enjoyment rather than academic gains. The children enjoyed their experience and wanted to go on with it, while the schools continued to express enthusiasm for the scheme, without however enlisting the support of the local education authority.

Adult Education

We end this chapter, and the four chapters on various aspects of the community school, with a note about adult education. At the beginning of the academic year 1969–70 Tom Lovett joined the Liverpool team as W.E.A. tutor-organiser and in the following two years he and his colleagues made a novel contribution to adult education in working-class communities. A wide variety of activities were initiated involving local residents, children, teachers and school managers. Some were successful, others will demand further research and development. All have shown that there is a real need and a potential demand for adult education in E.P.A.s especially if interpreted with flexibility and imagination.[1]

Adult education in the E.P.A. can be seen as a number of separate but related activities. It offers educational advice and assistance to local residents' groups and community councils, it caters for the spare-time interests of local parents and it encourages discussion among residents of the numerous problems they face as parents, married couples and citizens.

All these various activities contribute to the process of community development and change. A community school in an E.P.A. which seeks only the limited, though important, role of helping parents to understand and encourage the educational development of their children will not be the dynamic centre for community re-generation and growth which is an essential element in the whole concept, unless it is deeply involved in the whole variety of the problems facing such communities. A brief description of the numerous adult educational activities in the Liverpool E.P.A. may illustrate the possible nature and purpose of such a community school.

Of great importance are the links the tutor-organiser has established with a number of residents' groups and community councils. Such groups are concerned with the whole range of problems facing the population in the E.P.A., including bad housing, lack of recreational facilities for children and vandalism—in essence the breakdown of established neighbourhoods and communities. They are, in fact, a practical illustration of the Plowden recommendation that residents in an E.P.A. should be encouraged to develop a sense of community awareness and responsibility.

These groups are actually "learning through doing", picking up practical skills and knowledge in their efforts to solve some of their more pressing problems. The tutor-organiser has offered his services as an educationalist in a variety of ways; by helping residents to establish a group and community centre for their neighbourhood, in running a summer play scheme

---

[1] What follows is largely Mr. Lovett's own account of his activities which was reported in the Liverpool project's *Projectile*, Summer 1971.

involving local residents, their children and students from a local college of education, through helping, in co-operation with local teachers, a local community council to examine education facilities and problems in its area, in working with and advising local residents on a housing scheme, and by helping a community council to "interpret" a local government publication designed to encourage community participation in local affairs.

In many parts of the Liverpool E.P.A. classes have been arranged in home management, hairdressing, keep-fit, art and pottery for local women. In one area these activities were arranged after an informal house to house survey. Links were established with the local community council and the activities centred on a building which, it is hoped, may become a community centre for the area. In one community centre, run by local residents, over 40 mothers are attending a course in home management.

Such activities are not just a means of catering for recreational interests and needs, important though that is. In encouraging self confidence they are a vital factor in helping to overcome the many problems that the local population face as parents and residents. There is a vital link between such activities and the whole process of community development and regeneration.

At another level the tutor-organiser has set up a number of informal discussion groups in schools, community centres, private homes and pubs. Such groups offer local residents an opportunity to discuss a whole range of issues to do with the family, neighbourhood, school, church and local authority as well as more private and personal problems such as birth control, abortion, divorce and drugs. These have proved extremely successful especially when linked to a local radio series written by the tutor-organiser. Their success indicates the need for a forum where parents can discuss the variety of difficulties they face in a society where well established institutions and social and moral norms are in a state of flux.

In E.P.A.s and similar areas throughout the country the problems of bad housing and poor schools are exacerbated by the breakdown of established communities. A situation may well exist in many working-class areas in the large cities where parental control and authority has been seriously undermined and the family unit weakened. Any attempt to encourage an interest in children's education in E.P.A.s must be seen against such a background. If schools are to encourage and assist parents in helping their children they must engage in the sort of projects, activities and discussions outlined above. At the moment numerous organisations, formal and informal, local authority, governmental and voluntary are attempting to solve the issues facing E.P.A. parents, but often their activities are unco-ordinated.

The school offers a natural point for bringing together these activities within a community school context. Adult education defined and understood as in the Liverpool E.P.A. experience, would be a necessary and vital part of that context. As well as "educating" the community it would provide an important link between the community and the various social service agencies.

However it would be foolish to underestimate the difficulties in the way of establishing such a community school. Experience has shown that community schools in working-class areas have often failed because of the narrow, formal and traditional approach adopted by those in charge. The community side of such schools is often nothing more than the ordinary further education centre attached to the existing school building. Parents have little say in the running of such centres nor in the activities offered for their benefit.

The community school must be prepared to listen to parents, to advise and assist, rather than tell "them" what "we" think they should do. Community and social workers have learnt this lesson, and adult educationalists must do likewise. This is no easy task. It may mean a new type of professional, a Community Adult Educationalist attached to community schools. A special course for this purpose has been drawn up by the E.P.A. tutor-organiser and it is, at present, under discussion with the Liverpool Institute of Extension Studies.

Given the possibility of such a course in the near future, the home-school links already formed in many Liverpool E.P.A. schools and the wide experience gained in adult education in the area, all the components are present for the establishment of an E.P.A. community school. The fact that the Liverpool E.P.A. team will continue to operate in the city after the project has formally finished could, it is hoped, be the deciding factor in dovetailing all these elements together to create a radically new type of school.

Part Three

Conclusions

CHAPTER 13

E.P.A. Action–Research[1]

This book, the first of five volumes on our work in educational priority areas, is focused primarily on the implications for policy and practice of our attempts to change the districts and their schools in the direction broadly indicated by the recommendations of the Plowden Report. We draw our policy conclusions together in the next and final chapter. But we have also been engaged in a novel type of research—one specifically linked to the formation and development of public policy. Many of our detailed research findings are reported in subsequent volumes; here, however, we attempt to summarise the general lessons to be drawn about action–research from our experience—especially because we wish to advocate the further use of this type of research not only in the E.P.A.s but also more widely in the study of problems of social policy.

What is action–research? We may begin with a conventional definition, namely, small-scale intervention in the functioning of the real world, usually in administrative systems, and the close examination of the effects of such interventions. Action–research attempts to bring together two professions, social research and administration, which have traditionally been kept apart and which have developed their own separate methods. They are drawn together, in what we can call experimental social administration, by a shared interest in some public or political problem to co-operate, so to say, to change the world by understanding it. But their interests differ. Research values concepts such as precision, control, replication and attempts to generalise from the observation of specific events. Administrative action is concerned with the operations of the real world and by inclination translates generalisation into specific instances. Both usually, and certainly in our case, fall under the patronage of government. Either may be fitted into a programme of what we described in our first chapter by the phrase "futurology as design".

The term "action–research" has been used for many different kinds of intervention programme: we shall therefore try to classify possible types of action–research so as to distinguish them from other and from more conventional forms of social planning, in order to contribute to a more sophisticated understanding of the general phenomenon and reveal some of the implications for its participants. In the British context it is particularly relevant to look at our E.P.A. organisation for the lessons it may contain for the Community Development action–research projects recently launched under the Urban Programme.

Social planning provides one context for action–research. The opportunity for the central planner to obtain "field-tested" information on the effect of prospective centrally directed change is powerfully attractive. The outcome looked for in the planning approach to action–research is a set of

---

[1]This chapter is developed from and incorporates a paper by George Smith and Jack Barnes presented to the World Congress of Sociology, 1970, under the title "Some Implications of Action–Research Projects for Research". Volume III contains further reflections on action–research directed particularly to the Deptford Project.

field-tested proposals for action on a wide scale. The function of this type of action–research is therefore primarily for policy and the action is seen as a pilot for future national effort. Clearly this is a possible way of describing our study. The Plowden Report, after recommending the allocation of a variety of increased resources to areas of "educational deprivation", suggested that ". . . research should be started to discover which of the developments in educational priority areas have the most constructive effects, so as to assist in planning the longer-term programme to follow".[1] Our programme, financed jointly by the D.E.S. and S.S.R.C., arose partly out of this recommendation and partly from the association between the National Director, the then Secretary of State for Education (Anthony Crosland) and the then Director of the S.S.R.C. (Michael Young).

The motives then were primarily those of social planning but equally it must be stressed that action–research is attractive to the social scientist concerned with the development of theoretical knowledge. He finds in it an escape from the normal constraints in which he examines present conditions and speculates about their likely causal relationships and he has the opportunity to manipulate these relationships by inducing change. This may be called the research approach, where causal information can be added to correlational study. "To some extent evaluative research may offer a bridge between pure and applied research. Evaluation may be viewed as a field test for the validity of cause–effect hypotheses in basic science whether these be in the field of biology (i.e. medicine) or sociology (i.e. social work)".[2]

Of course both the planning and the research approach may define an action project with little reference to the outside world in general or to governmental plans for change in particular: the project is a test-bed and while theories or programmes are being tried the external world is temporarily held off. It is standard procedure to avoid undue publicity in order to minimise Hawthorne effects. Only after the experiment are the findings to be revealed and wider action taken. Meanwhile the emphasis is on minimum publicity and on insulation from public pressure.

Other approaches have a different relation to the external world. Thus one thing that must be said about our study is that it grew partly out of frustration with the inability or unwillingness of the government of the day to implement the Plowden proposals as they stood. This suggests a third possible context for action–research where the objective is to "get something done" in response to a recognised social problem. The emphasis here is again on action. We may call this the political approach. The tactics are to keep the issue in the public eye, both to enlist support for future large-scale action, and as a holding operation until further funds become available; such projects will deliberately seek publicity and canvass support by demonstrating how more widespread programmes would be received. For example there will be emphasis on the response that parents in depressed areas make to new educational programmes as contrasted with the assumptions often held by teachers or educational administrators that the reaction in such areas will inevitably be one of apathy. From a different point of

---

[1]Plowden, paragraph 117.
[2]E. A. Suchman, *Evaluative Research—Principles and Practice in Public Service and Social Action Programmes*, Russell Sage, New York, 1967.

view, however, such a project could qualify as a fourth type, the "diversionary approach". Here the project serves as an opiate to placate political pressure for more radical change; the major assumption is that one knows what should be done, but one cannot or will not do it at the moment. This point was widely made immediately after our grant was announced. For example John Mays wrote of the E.P.A. project as a "research smoke screen"[1] and decried the fashionable tendency to divert reforming zeal into the obscurities of unnecessary investigation.

In both of these latter approaches research is essentially a public relations exercise; in the third, seeking to demonstrate that the proposed action is popular and well received, and in the fourth erecting a plausible façade of serious enquiry. Doubtless there are examples of these approaches; indeed the Liverpool project certainly had an eye to action which would attract both attention and resources to the general handicaps suffered by children and their families in E.P.A.s. But from our point of view in this chapter they are not particularly interesting because they turn mainly on the external relations of an action–research project as an element in the process of social change. In our case we would assert that neither a search for publicity nor compliance with diversion affected the actual planning and content of our programme. We concentrate therefore on the planning and research approaches as those in which attention is focused on the internal structure of the action–research organisation, though this is not to say that political analysis of the external relation of an action–research project could not fruitfully be undertaken.

A fifth approach may be identified which combines a number of elements from the other four; unlike the planning model it seeks to use the social context of the project to increase its own effects; though the resource inputs are small-scale, it is anticipated that the outcomes could be substantial, if attitudes are changed and participants mobilised for wider action. It may be termed the "multiplier" approach. The function of research here will be largely a search for likely "multiplier" effects, and an attempt to identify the outcomes that occur.

The five approaches outlined certainly do not exhaust all possible types, particularly if the "political" functions that such projects could play are taken into account. Whether a project is placed in a particular category may well vary with the position of the person making the judgment and the relative importance they attach to the different outcomes. If we turn to examine the planning and research approaches in more detail, these different standpoints may become more evident. Criticism of action–research is typically launched from one or the other of these two positions.

Action–research projects, particularly in education, associated with the American "war on poverty", have received an unfavourable press. Many critics have concentrated on the relatively low level of research techniques employed in them. Travers for example writes:

"The purpose of such educational studies differs fundamentally from the purpose of most scientific research. There is almost no attempt to build each study on the work which has previously been undertaken. The writer's evaluation of the last fifty studies which have been under-

[1]*The Guardian*, 2nd May 1969.

taken which compare the outcomes of one teaching methodology with another is that they have contributed almost nothing to our knowledge of the factors that influence the learning process in the classroom. Many of them do not even identify what the experimentally controlled variables are and indicate only that the study compares the outcomes of educational practices in the community where the study originates with educational practices elsewhere. Such studies if they are conducted by scientists would probably start with a theory of learning in classroom situations which would postulate that certain changes in learning conditions would result in certain changes in performance. Within such a framework, hypotheses can be tested and the body of organised knowledge slowly built. The typical study which compares two teaching methodologies is not pursued along lines which scientists have found to be useful procedures for building an organised body of knowledge. They represent efforts which the scientific community would be unlikely to endorse."[1]

Travers' argument is that, for satisfactory results, the control of such studies must lie with research. Such control would ensure procedures that were acceptable to the "scientific community". Whether such control would produce the type of information about expected outcomes that would satisfy the planning element in the project is a separate question.

Other writers are less pessimistic about the possible co-existence of the research and planning approaches, though considerable vigilance is urged on the researchers. "Once the impact model is formulated, the researcher must continue to remain within the environment, like a snarling watch-dog ready to oppose alterations in programme and procedures that would render his evaluation efforts useless."[2] Marris and Rein, however, conclude from a review of the action/research relationships in American community action programmes that the principles of action and experienced research are so different and so often mutually exclusive that attempts to link the two processes in a single project are likely to produce internal conflict or the subordination of one element to another.

"Research requires a clear and constant purpose, which both defines and precedes the choice of means; that the means be exactly and consistently followed; and that no revision takes place until the sequence of steps is completed. Action is tentative, non-committal and adaptive. It concentrates upon the next step, breaking the sequence into discrete, manageable decisions. It casts events in a fundamentally different perspective, evolving the future out of present opportunities, where research perceives the present in the context of the final outcome. Research cannot interpret the present until it knows the answers to its ultimate questions. Action cannot foresee what questions to ask until it has interpreted the present. Action attempts to comprehend all the factors relevant to an immediate problem whose nature continually changes as events proceed, where research abstracts one or two factors

---

[1]We have drawn this quotation from a paper by Alan Brimer and Roger Dale of Bristol University, 1968, "A consideration of the Problems of Evaluating the Outcomes of the Educational Priority Areas Programme".

[2]H. E. Freeman and C. Sherwood, 1965, quoted in P. Marris and M. Rein, *Dilemmas of Social Reform: Poverty and Community Action in the United States*, Routledge & Kegan Paul, 1967, p. 201.

for attention, and holds to a constant definition of the problem until the experiment is concluded.

"Each seeks to limit the ignorance of which it must take account, the one shortening the time span, the other arbitrarily excluding factors and purposes which may also be relevant."[1]

As we noted earlier, such characterisations emphasise the difference between action and research and therefore their probable incompatibility. As the two components are often represented by different groups of people, each with their own audience and model of project operation, it is perhaps not surprising that differences in standpoint are stressed. The position taken by Marris and Rein makes it clear that the research approach is, *par excellence*, the social scientist's method of tackling futurology as design. At the extremes action and research have fundamentally different aims. But, before dismissing the viability of action–research, it is worth examining a range of possible types, to see whether the characterisation of action and research put forward by Marris and Rein necessarily holds in all contexts. Projects could vary along a number of dimensions, such as the degree of control exercised by the action or research components, the amount of knowledge about the means of achieving the desired outcomes, and the level of co-operation between action and research. A classification of these dimensions would be linked to the kinds of action–research project that we have distinguished. The classification might suggest what combinations of action and research were most appropriate for particular conditions. It might also indicate more clearly that critical discussion of action–research has at times chosen examples of action where the combination of action and research was inappropriate for the context of the project, or for the degree of knowledge about how the required outcomes were to be obtained. Thus it is clear that Travers, for example, is partly criticising projects embodying a planning approach for failing to follow the procedures of the research approach.

If the two approaches were so distinct in type that different procedures of operation were required for each, then little further discussion would be needed. Each particular type of "action–research" would be free to develop its own methods. Yet in practice supporters of both the planning and research approaches argue that their own model must play an important role if appropriate and reliable findings are to be achieved. Thus a project where the action control is high may not produce outcomes that stand up to serious research examination; and on the other hand, the project where research control is high may present a very limited set of findings which are of little direct value from the planning point of view though they may well produce a further set of questions for research investigation.

The belief that one component will act to constrain freedom of action by the other leads to attempts to minimise the influence of the rival component by emphasising a particular role for it in the overall project. Thus in a project dominated by the planning approach, where action control is high, the tendency may be to assign a largely evaluative role to research. The function of research is to indicate how successful the action has been in achieving the predicted outcomes, an essentially technical problem. It

---

[1]Marris and Rein, *op. cit.*, p. 203.

is possible that in certain contexts, this division of labour may work effectively, that the researcher may be content to accept the status of technician. Here it may be possible for both action and research to exercise a high degree of control over their own activities, and to remain reasonably independent. The field-testing of a reading kit might be a case in point. However such contexts may not be typical of action–research for a number of reasons.

First the researcher, as evaluator, cannot in many situations act as a "statistical school inspector" if he is to meet the required standards of the research approach. He has to be involved at the outset in the selection of objectives and appropriate measures to assess the effects of the programme. Again, he has to press for certain conditions of action, for comparative groups, for stability of treatment, and so on. Where action programmes are more tentative than the introduction of a kit, the role of research in pushing for objectives to be clearly specified may tend to introduce an element of uncertainty into the programme. This may increase the range of alternative hypotheses available to explain successful outcomes, further weakening the findings for future large-scale action.

Secondly, the setting up of many action–research projects results from a complicated interplay between action and research, rather than simply the mounting of action programmes of which evaluation is thought to be an important element. Thus the concentration of action–research on the problems associated with poverty, and the way the issues are approached—largely through the educational system—are, at least in part, the result of research studies. The expected outcomes from the programme are as much those of research as they are of action. The researcher does not begin as an impartial evaluator of the action; for his discipline has contributed to the conceptualisation of the problems in question and has adopted a stance towards them. The designation of an "educational priority area" for example, is for the researcher not simply the attachment of an administrative label, but an indication that a range of research hypotheses and evidence are to be considered relevant in any attempt to solve the problems. In so far as the action is not informed by the same evidence, it is likely that the researchers will try to influence the course of action to make it comply with their own standpoint. To accept a neutral evaluative role here would be to sacrifice a major advantage of participating in action–research, the chance to test research hypotheses in action.

The research approach appears to meet a number of objections to the planning model of action–research, though as we have noted its findings are often too tentative or small-scale to guide future action programmes. In practice, however, it is questionable whether there are many action–research projects that genuinely represent the research model. For in an action situation it may be impossible to simplify the treatments adequately to be sure which elements in the programme were responsible for the effects observed. For example, educational programmes have to operate over a period of time; thus it is difficult to replicate the purity of treatment that might be achieved in a short, small group study. To obtain the necessary control over a reasonable length of time, the programme may be forced to operate, for example, outside the formal school system. Thus, quite apart from any theoretical reasons for using pre-school programmes as a means of overcoming educational deprivation, the relative freedom from control by the formal school system at pre-school level is clearly an aid to experiment. A review of exemplary action–research projects in education for the disadvantaged in the United States[1] shows that it was mainly pre-school research programmes that satisfied high research standards. In ordinary schools the problem of finding treatments simple enough to work within the constraints of formal requirements, where the outcomes can be confidently linked to the programme rather than to other intervening factors, may be almost insurmountable. Where such treatments may be devised to meet precise research criteria, it may be that their very simplicity limits their effectiveness. Thus the experiment reported by Rosenthal and Jacobsen[2] where teachers were informed that certain of their pupils, selected at random, were in fact "late bloomers" and would show sudden progress, meets the criterion of simplicity of treatment; but the analysis of results by Jensen[3] suggests that the children so selected did not show significantly greater progress on strict statistical criteria. It may be that the treatment was not in fact adequate to change teacher expectation, which was strongly influenced by previous observation.

Similarly in research on pre-schooling there may be a tendency to extend the curriculum beyond the areas initially covered. In this particular case, a commitment to produce a satisfactory outcome may override the need from the research point of view to keep the programme within specified limits. Equally there may be tension between the general prescriptions of research that specify curriculum content, and the needs of particular children who are selected to take part. As the American experience with educational programmes for the disadvantaged has shown, the characterisations of such groups built up from research studies and used as evidence for particular programme contents sometimes offer a general prescription which is not appropriate to the actual groups selected. Research studies tend to emphasise differences between groups, even where the characteristics in question are found only among minorities of both disadvantaged and normal populations and thus do not necessarily provide a useful basis for action programmes.

In reviewing examples of the interplay between action and research in our own study, it becomes clear that the action and research approaches have underlain some of the positions adopted or argued for by the action or research staff. In practice, where action and research staff have to co-operate, some form of compromise between the two positions will be developed.

We may look now at certain aspects of the functioning of the E.P.A. programme on which we have been engaged, in the light of our classification of possible types of action–research.

To which type do we then belong? The first point to be made in an answer is that our form of organisation was unitary—we were all formally

---

[1] D. G. Hawkridge *et al.*, "A Study of Selected Exemplary Programs for the Education of Disadvantaged Children", U.S. Department of Health, Education and Welfare, Washington D.C., September 1968.

[2] R. Rosenthal and L. Jacobsen, *Pygmalion in the Classroom—Teacher Expectation and Pupils' Intellectual Development*, Holt, Reinhart and Winston, New York, 1968.

[3] A. R. Jensen, "How much can we boost I.Q. and scholastic achievement?", *Harvard Educational Review*, 1969, 39(1), 1–123.

members of the Oxford University Department of Social and Administrative Studies. But we recruited people of two kinds; the "researchers"
with academic experience and the "action men" with practical experience in
education. The general objectives of the programme, it will be recalled, were
(a) to raise the educational performance of children, (b) to improve the
morale of teachers, (c) to increase the involvement of the parents in their
children's education, and (d) to increase the "sense of responsibility" for
their communities of the people living in them.

But from the beginning the four teams in different parts of the country
and a parallel fifth one in Scotland were given considerable autonomy in
translating these general objectives into operational goals, both because of
the broad nature of the objectives and in view of the varying characteristics
of the districts in which the work went on, which ranged from small town
poverty to immigrant concentrations in the conurbations. There was a strong
working principle of local diagnosis. The relationship between the action
and research staff was initially left unspecified so as not to undermine that
principle. At the same time the unitary organisation based on Oxford and
our early plenary discussions were used by the national director to encourage some tipping of the balance towards research control.

Nevertheless, this being said, it must be pointed out that the main
thrust of the programme was towards "action conclusions" and its general
conception was closest to the planning approach. Thus our application to
the S.S.R.C. for resources to finance the programme used the term "demonstration project" which was to be a "preparation for later advance", so that
there would be "evidence on which to draw when (and if) the time comes
for a more general advance in the nineteen seventies".

This however is to look at the programme as a whole. In fact the circumstances and personalities of each local team produced further significant
variations. In the planning approach research is largely evaluative. In our own
case however the researchers, especially in the West Riding and Birmingham,
helped to formulate the plans as well as providing the action with information
on its evolving programme. Here we see the difficulty of assuming that
research can play a subordinate, evaluative role. The concepts used in the
discussion of the project—"disadvantaged", "deprived area", "depressed
area", "children's context-bound operations", "sense of community",
"power"—were very much those of social science. The researchers had
identified and analysed the issues; and the initiative for the programme came
from a national director who was a social scientist, albeit interested in
social policy. In so far as the researchers were more familiar with an
approach using social science frames of references, there is a real sense in
which the expectations of the project, as expressed for example in its general
aims, largely reflected a research point of view.

Though the role of the researchers in formulating action proposals had
not been clearly foreseen, it became evident that many of the ideas involved
in the project sprang from a research approach; thus the belief that intervention at pre-school level with particular curriculum devices might lead to
significant improvements in intellectual functioning is essentially based on
current research findings rather than an outcome of present educational
practice. Both parties, action and research, may come to the study with the
conviction that something has to be done, but their different ideas about

what is wrong may lead to different prescriptions for action—the action teams being more concerned with providing additional resources, the research groups with the effects that such provision might have.

In this situation it is hardly surprising that the researchers attempt to influence the type of action programme set up, where the organisation of the project makes this possible. Clearly, despite any claim that may be made for the indifference of pure sociologists to the value concerns of the real world, many social scientists like to believe that their findings have significance. R. K. Merton has characterised neatly the opposite theoretical and empirical poles in this continuing debate. "For the first group the identifying motto would at times seem to be, 'we do not know whether or what we say is true, but at least it is significant' and for the radical empiricist the motto may read, 'this is demonstrably so, but we cannot indicate its significance'".[1] Although the charge of social insignificance may not damage the research worker's findings, it is highly likely to bruise his social conscience. A "neutral" evaluative role in this context implies that the researcher is able to accept a wide gap between the findings of his own discipline and their significance for action. He is able to accept that they are true but insignificant.

Our unitary organisation, with district teams combining action and research staff, encouraged both groups to share in the planning of action programmes. The research group's participation, often strongly influenced by the research approach, had a number of implications for the project in general. Inevitably there was discussion of detailed objectives. The action staff pressed for an exploratory approach, and were reluctant to specify goals too closely in advance. The researchers on the other hand needed a clear statement of outputs that could be assessed; their influence tended to focus attention on ways of improving educational attainment. For this was an objective that all parties could agree was important—and from the research point of view it was relatively easy to assess. There was a tendency for researchers to stress the "final" importance of educational performance and to reduce other changes to stages on the way to improved achievement. Thus participation by parents and the community was linked to the effects it might have on improved performance. Similar arguments can be identified in the debate that followed the findings of the Westinghouse Report on Head Start in the United States;[2] the project is described as unsuccessful because it failed to make significant long-term impact on children's performance, even though there were changes in other areas and a degree of parental and community involvement was achieved.

Though all may agree as to the "final" importance of educational output, it may be that to set this as the main objective of a short programme will tend to direct the action in conservative directions. The pressure from research to specify the links between action and required outcomes may concentrate attention on traditional areas of reform such as curriculum change. Changes in the institutional structure of schools, or their relations

---

[1] R. K. Merton, *The Bearing of Empirical Research on Sociological Theory: in Social Theory and Social Structure*, Free Press, New York, Revised edition 1968, pp. 156–171.

[2] V. Cicirelli *et al.*, "The Impact of Head Start: an evaluation of the effects of Head Start on children's cognitive and affective development", Westinghouse Learning Corporation, Maryland, 1969.

with other institutions, may receive less attention if only because the relationship between these changes and improved educational performance is less clearly understood.

Fantini and Weinstein[1] have argued that compensatory education projects in the United States have been conservative in outlook, providing "more of the same". They attribute this to the restricted frame of reference used in compensatory education, which worked with a model of disadvantaged children suffering from "learning deficits" that had to be made good in the classroom. We suggest that certain approaches to research reinforce this tendency by insisting on action programmes where clearly articulated relationships between intervention and outcome are formulated and by pressing for a design where the contribution of a variety of elements to the eventual output can be disentangled.

A second area of debate between research and action personnel at the outset of our study concerned the degree of inter-project co-operation and the need for findings that were generalisable across districts. Pre-school appeared to offer the best chance of achieving this. The research designs that are required to produce such findings again indicate the influence of research on action. Light and Smith[2] have pointed out how the apparently appropriate research procedure of drawing a random sample of children from a large population and enrolling them in a pre-school programme may produce results that cannot be replicated in full-scale programmes. For the group created by random allocation is likely to be different from any subsequently formed according to normal practice; children attending a normally formed group will be drawn from neighbouring streets and houses, whereas those in the randomly composed group would be dispersed throughout the town. In such a group it is possible that the effects of neighbourhood and peer group influence would be minimised.

It was agreed, as we saw in Chapter 7, to examine the effects of structured language programmes on the linguistic development of children living in disadvantaged areas, in such a way that nationally valid conclusions could be achieved. As existing pre-school groups were to be used in the experiment, any allocation of children to treatments at random would have been impossible. The method adopted was thus to allocate treatments randomly to pre-school groups in the project districts involved. Immediately a problem arose over timing. When were the groups involved to be informed of what was happening? If they were informed after the decision about allocation was made, there was the risk of selective drop-out by groups who were not prepared to take part, given that they had no control over the experimental practice they were to adopt. To inform them in advance, however, was equally difficult, for the group had to be prepared to accept any one of a number of treatments that might be offered: again there was the risk of selective drop-out. It is to be noted here that apparently good research practice not only conflicts with "real world" procedures and relations but also neglects one important aspect of many poverty programmes —that people in these areas should be given power to control their future.

---

[1]M. D. Fantini and G. Weinstein, *The Disadvantaged: Challenge to Education*, Harper & Row, New York, 1968.

[2]R. J. Light and P. V. Smith, 'Choosing a Future: Strategies for Designing and Evaluating New Programs', *Harvard Educational Review*, 1970, 40(1), 1–28.

Additionally it is clear that the method of random allocation proposed for the pre-school experiment probably imposes a sterner test of the effect of any innovative practice than is likely to occur in real life. In the experiment, groups only participate if the treatment happens to be assigned to them; normally, however, groups adopt new practices because they are enthusiastic about them. Research seeks by random allocation to demonstrate the effectiveness of a particular approach even with an initially "disinterested" group. For action conclusions, such a procedure may be too rigorous; for if the effects are not discernible, it is not clear whether this is the result of an inadequate programme or of ineffectiveness in the teachers who did not choose to use it initially. This model of research-sponsored innovation clearly minimises the effects of teacher/programme interaction. Yet some findings suggest that different types of curriculum which teachers themselves have chosen, and where other conditions are equal, have very similar effects as measured by pupil performance.[1]

We have indicated that participation by research in the formulation of action programmes can have implications for the direction of the project. Similarly, what are defined as research rather than action activities may also influence the development of the project; some of the findings uncover assumptions that underlie the research position. In any project of this kind, a form of "Hawthorne effect" would be anticipated in action programmes. What we did not fully realise was the extent to which research in an action–research context creates action situations. A concentration of research activities within a small area in a short period of time—testing children, interviewing parents, questioning teachers—may uncover information which itself leads to action. For example, measures of the reading ages were taken of the children in the E.P.A. study schools as part of an attempt to provide a descriptive context for the projects. But the results caused a number of schools to review their teaching of reading. The possession of a wide range of information, collected by the project for research purposes but available to action personnel, may well affect the project's relationship with people from whom this information has been collected. Unlike a normal research project which may end once the data has been gathered, the action–research team are only at the beginning of their work, which may depend for its success upon the goodwill of the community.

Besides the neutral collection of information, which some people may find threatening in itself, research instruments inevitably reflect certain prejudices. The instruments we used were usually versions of those in general use, and were not in most cases developed from scratch; they can, therefore, be said in some senses to embody a position commonly held among researchers. In the action–research context this general research position was clearly revealed. To oversimplify, it became apparent that research instruments were generally favourable to parents, seeking to elicit their educational interests; the interviews were well received and elicited a high response rate. However the attitude to teachers implied in the teacher questionnaire was by contrast fairly hostile; and though response was also high, a number of unfavourable comments were made by teachers.

[1] D. P. Weikart, 'A Comparative Study of Three Pre-School Curricula', Ypsilanti, Michigan.

These attitudes appear to show a relatively well documented hostility between researchers and teachers. The controversy over the evaluation studies of the More Effective School programme in New York City[1] provides evidence for this hostility in the context of programmes for the disadvantaged. The project embodied what were essentially the ideas of teachers and teacher unions, particularly for smaller classes, on the needs of schools in disadvantaged areas. The evaluation revealed, however, that these changes were apparently not effective in improving pupil performance. Similarly Arnstine and Arnstine[2] suggest that the researcher is almost in competition with the teachers; action–research projects may allow the researchers to deal "directly with children in order to try out their own views of successful teaching".[3] The way that the project is organised will clearly influence how far intervention of this direct kind is able to develop. Where the purpose of the project is to produce evaluated proposals for future action on a wide scale in accordance with the planning approach, or where the project seeks to elucidate cause–effect relationships following the research approach, it is likely that the project staff will be driven increasingly to intervene directly, so that they can achieve the control necessary to derive valid conclusions. In both cases, the success of the project is largely determined by the nature of these conclusions. To work through existing educational institutions and teachers is thus to put a major feature of the project at risk. Proposals may not be carried through into action, and there is no guarantee that once a particular programme has got under way it will be continued without modification. More direct intervention by the project—recruiting teachers and setting up its own institutions—is a likely development where the "planning" or "research" approaches are being followed.

These few examples of interplay between action and research appear to indicate that any simple division of responsibility between the two components will not work in practice. The idea that the research element could adopt a purely evaluative role, as outlined by the planning approach, is impractical in a context, such as E.P.A., where research findings and expectations play an important part in determining objectives and strategies to achieve them. Equally any belief that research can monitor action programmes without influencing their direction cannot be sustained. Though theoretically the differences between "action" and "research" have been clearly emphasised, in practice, at least in our case, these activities were often interwoven and at times hardly distinguishable.

Conclusion: some implications for research

We have looked at a few concrete examples of the role that research may play in an action–research project. Though the organisation of the project we have described was primarily aimed at action conclusions, we have noted the reluctance of researchers to accept a purely evaluative role.

---

[1]D. J. Fox, 'Expansion of the More Effective School Program of', Center for Urban Education, September 1967; "A Reply to the Critics", *Urban Review*, 1968, 2(6), 27–34.
[2]B. and D. Arnstine, "Social Problems of School Reform: a critique", *Teachers College Record*, 1968, 69(7), 711–17.
[3]*Ibid.*, p. 177.

However, in trying to make the action programme approximate more closely to the criteria of the "research approach", the influence of research was at times to constrain the flexibility of action, though the emphasis of research on the need for clear objectives was clearly beneficial to the project. In activities strictly defined as research rather than action, there was evidence that researchers were using instruments that represented a particular value standpoint. Research, in this sense, was no neutral bystander monitoring the action, but an equal participant with interest in both the design of the action and its outcomes. Thus, in the practice of action–research, a number of assumptions that underlie the "planning" and "research" approaches are not supported. Both models allocate fairly precise areas of responsibility to the two components of the project; in the planning model research is largely restricted to evaluation and in the research model action is confined within strict limits. However, our experience suggests that when either of these approaches is followed closely there are implications for the direction and development of the project. It may be concluded that action–research is impracticable, as Marris and Rein appear to imply; or it may be that alternative approaches to "action–research" have to be emphasised and developed, perhaps relying on different research strategies from those entailed by the research model we have outlined.

This may be the long-term answer. Nevertheless, at this stage a number of implications for research can be derived from the examples of interplay between action and research we have described. A major reason for researchers being drawn into action programmes is the lack of clear prescription from research studies. In part this may stem from the general nature of research, but in part it may also derive from the sharp distinction made between action and research, implying that it is not the function of research to make clear the conclusions for action from its findings. In so far as prescriptions from research are unclear, the researcher is continually drawn into action in an attempt to clarify his own findings. Like the physical scientist, the social scientist cannot avoid the fact that his work has social significance and that he has some responsibility for its proper interpretation and use.

The model of research that lies behind much research intervention in action–research has a tendency to push action in relatively conservative directions; at times it created potentially unreplicable situations. Even its own activities depend in part upon certain value positions which the action–research context makes plain. This is to say not that present procedures should be abandoned but that their effects in particular situations have to be weighed against other aspects of the programme.

These implications indicate that a slightly less "ideal" type of research may have to be adopted in many action–research contexts. Where projects have little clear knowledge about how objectives are to be reached, the research approach as we have outlined it is either ineffective, failing to constrain the action to its own design, or else it turns the action away from exploration. Clearly in such a situation more exploratory research strategies are required that help to identify profitable courses of action, for example along the lines implied by the fifth type of action–research project identified at the outset, the multiplier approach. Light and Smith[1]

---

[1] *Loc. cit.*

have suggested some alternative ways of identifying successful projects in a programme such as Head Start. In the more effective projects the emphasis of research is not purely on outcomes and a comparison of tests before and after but is also on the processes which take place during the project, on changes of attitude among the people involved and on the particular events which are connected with the action. Generalisable research data may then be reinforced by case-study material which gives at least an impressionistic indication of how observed outcomes may have occurred. Thus to suggest that the only research model capable of distinguishing successful strategies is the one we have termed the research approach is to adopt a very narrow definition of research. It may be that in fact there are few cases where the research approach can be used without considerably distorting the course of the action. As Merton notes in his discussion of the relation between empirical research and sociological theory, the sole purpose of empirical work is not the testing of hypotheses; for empirical research may uncover unexpected relationships: it may indicate the importance of information that has previously been neglected, direct theoretical attention to new areas, and aid in the clarification of theoretical concepts. Though it would be rash to claim this as a programme for action–research, it may be taken to indicate that the importance of action–research does not lie purely in its ability to provide reliable field-tested information for planners, or to test research hypotheses in a context which accords with the requirements of the experimental method.

The organisation of many action–research projects, where the action and research components are represented by separate staffs, may emphasise, rather than reduce, differences of standpoint between action and research. Thus, each group may tend to argue, at least initially, for a project strategy that minimises the role played by the other in the programme. Though co-operation between action and research may develop as the project progresses, the early planning stages are likely to be marked by conflict as each group tries to get its own approach accepted. The characterisations of action and research which find favour with each group at this stage are those that contrast the two activities; yet the examples we have drawn from our own experience suggest that in practice the division is not so clear cut.

The traditional separation of action and research as separate activities with their own ideologies is in part responsible for the confusion over the nature of action–research. Obviously there is no automatic identity of interest between the two spheres though it may be that the differences have been overemphasised. There has been a tendency to see facts and values as different social objects with different procedures of investigation necessary to each one. This approach cannot be sustained: social science which is to be significant must be value based. It cannot be a value-free collection of facts. The action–research context exposes this truth—perhaps unpleasantly.

A realistic view of both action and research reduces the difference between them and casts doubt on the validity of the pure models of the planning or the research approach. Variables are difficult if not impossible to control fully in practice and results depend heavily on the particular local context of action: hence, incidentally, our insistence on local diagnosis in any E.P.A. policy. The co-operation of research in policy formation has to develop "organically" rather than "mechanically". Action–research is unlikely ever to yield neat and definite prescriptions from field-tested plans. What it offers is an aid to intelligent decision making, not a substitute for it. Research brings relevant information rather than uniquely exclusive conclusions. We base our own policy conclusions in the next chapter on our experiences over three years with action–research in four E.P.A.s. But these conclusions are also based on the wider experience of ourselves and others and on general priorities which we have not tried to disguise. It follows that our recommendations are neither the conclusive authority of social science nor beyond challenge on political or social grounds.

CHAPTER 14

E.P.A. Policy

Our major conclusions from the four English E.P.A. action-research projects are that:

(1) The educational priority area, despite its difficulties of definition, is a socially and administratively viable unit through which to apply the principle of positive discrimination.

(2) Pre-schooling is the outstandingly economical and effective device in the general approach to raising educational standards in E.P.A.s.

(3) The idea of the community school as, put forward in skeletal outline by Plowden, has now been shown to have greater substance and powerful implications for community regeneration.

(4) There are practical ways of improving the partnership between families and schools in E.P.A.s.

(5) There are practical ways of improving the quality of teaching in E.P.A. schools.

(6) Action–research is an effective method of policy formation and practical innovation.

(7) The E.P.A. can be no more than a part, though an important one, of a comprehensive social movement towards community development and community redevelopment in a modern urban industrial society.

1. *The Definition of E.P.A.*

The problem of defining E.P.A.s, i.e. of creating an instrument which turns a policy objective into an administrative practice, is not yet solved and was not part of our remit. It is important to solve it, since a rational application of the principle of positive discrimination partly depends on a workable solution. L.E.A.s varied widely in their interpretations of the guidance given to them on criteria for identifying E.P.A.s and "schools of exceptional difficulty". The I.L.E.A. index is widely acknowledged to be the most sophisticated attempt at definition so far. Clearly the attempt to designate areas of special concern by objective, reproducible criteria which are agreed before designation is a desirable one. There seems to be no rational solution of the problem of weighting the different factors which have gone into administrative definition without further work on establishing empirically grounded policy objectives. In any case no system of weighting is likely to be satisfactory for every local area in the country. While the attempt to obtain more general agreement as to criteria is certainly worth pursuing, and is a first step in the rational allocation of resources, there must always be, in the end, room for adaptation according to local conditions.

Three particular points may be made about defining educational priority areas. First, measures of pupil and teacher turnover taken from *schools* may be useful indicators of the multiple problems of *areas*; and measures of language difficulty are neither synonymous with officially defined immigrants nor accurately reflected in school records. There is a case for regular and systematic testing as an element in defining E.P.A.s.

Second, judged by some of the criteria of what constitutes an E.P.A. the West Riding district hardly qualifies when its problems are compared with those typically faced by inner city areas. The inner rings of the conurbations, for example those we have studied in Birmingham and Liverpool, suffer far more from such social stresses as overcrowding and multi-occupation. It is only on the criterion of economic prospects that the West Riding district and similar towns are in a worse position. But it is important to note that several of the criteria used to indicate where positive discrimination should be applied are to some extent positively related to economic prospects. Thus one reason why inner city areas suffer from overcrowding is that they form part of areas where there are better prospects of employment. Other indicators, such as the number of recent immigrants, may operate in the same way: many immigrants at least initially move to areas with high employment prospects, and not into areas with stable populations and dying industries. The results of our enquiry in the West Riding suggest that we ought to look more closely at a different form of urban problem than that of the inner rings of the conurbations, namely the collapse and decay of small towns based on a single industry now in decline. We ought to look closely at groups who are forced to leave these small towns by industrial and economic change, to see whether their displacement from one area does not in fact increase overcrowding and social pressures in others, possibly the centres of large cities where they may end up in search of employment.

Third, while insisting on the claim that the E.P.A. is a viable administrative unit for positive discrimination, we would not wish to deny that, in the end, the appropriate unit is the individual and his family. In other words the use of the district as a means of identifying problems and allocating resources is held by us to be no more than a convenient framework within which closer and more detailed work has to be done with schools, school classes, individuals and families in order to realise a fully effective policy of positive discrimination. No one, presumably, has ever supposed that all social deprivation with educational consequences can be neatly delineated on a map. Nor does anyone suppose that all the worst schools are concentrated in E.P.A.s nor all the pupils of lowest attainment in the schools identified as E.P.A. Nevertheless we do not reject the notion of educational priority *areas* as distinct from schools or individuals. On the contrary, we argue, the locality focus is essential to the general character of our policy for community schooling.

Our view is that the geographical definition should be retained and widened to include a greater number of schools than the present official list of 570 and that the criteria of definition should be sufficiently flexible to take in a wider variety of multiply deprived districts not only in the inner rings of the conurbations but in small economically declining urban centres, in redevelopment housing estates and in some rural areas.

2. *Pre-Schooling*

We have come to three general conclusions about pre-schooling from our experience over three years in the four districts. The first is that pre-

7EP

schooling is *par excellence* a point of entry into the development of the community school as we conceive of it. It is the point at which, properly understood, the networks of family and formal education can most easily be linked. It is, by the same token, the point at which innovative intervention can begin in order to break the barrier which, especially in E.P.A.s, separates the influence of school and community; the point where the vested interests of organisation and custom are most amenable to change.

Second, we have concluded that pre-schooling is the most effective educational instrument for applying the principle of positive discrimination and this conviction rests partly on the theory that primary and secondary educational attainment has its social foundations in the child's experience in the pre-school years and partly on the evidence that positive discrimination at the pre-school level can have a multiplier effect on the overwhelmingly important educative influences of the family and the peer group to which the child belongs.

Third, there is no unique blueprint of either organisation or content which could be applied mechanically as national policy. On the contrary, the essential pre-requisite is correct diagnosis of the needs of individual children and of particular E.P.A. conditions (which it cannot be too often repeated vary enormously) with all that this implies for a flexible provision of nursery education for the under-fives in the E.P.A..

The recommendations which we advance below should be understood within this threefold framework. Thus some possible policies for nursery education are ruled out. We would regard a nationally standardised provision for the reduction of the school starting age to four years as irrelevant to the development of community schooling, of no contribution to positive discrimination and offensive to the principle of local diagnosis.

We must moreover emphasise that we regard our recommendations as operating within a severely limited conception of the possibilities of formal nursery education. Even for that minority of children who enjoy membership of playgroups or nursery classes, educational experience in the narrow or formal sense adds up to less than ten per cent of the total waking hours of the pre-school child. The idea of parental involvement in a child's education can be inappropriate and misleading. In a sense it has to be reversed. The home is the most important "educational" influence on the child. Formal pre-schooling is marginal. It cannot in this sense be compensatory. It can however define its role as supportive to family influences where support is most needed. And given that support is most needed under E.P.A. conditions a limited national budget for nursery education should be concentrated in the E.P.A.s.

We advocate a hybrid form of *nursery centre* which is neither the expensive professionally run nursery school nor the cheap and parent-run but amateur playgroup. The hybrid may be expected to inherit the vigour of both stocks. It is focused on learning and therefore needs professional guidance, a carefully worked out curriculum and organised links to the infant school, but at the same time it needs parental co-operation and local community involvement.

These proposals have their background in the experience and experiment which we have reported in Chapters 6, 7 and 8. It is well known that the main thrust of the playgroup movement has been, hitherto, in prosperous neighbourhoods. Despite the successes of our efforts in the four experimental districts the general fact is that, in areas of urban decay, neither the money nor the initiative are so easily found. The Save the Children Fund and other bodies have concentrated some of their energies in the educational priority areas but their finances and powers are limited and there is need for more statutory support.

The Plowden Report had relatively little to say of the playgroup movement and indeed devoted only three paragraphs to their work under the title of "The Future of Voluntary Nursery Groups". The cautious approach of the Committee was that:

"We understand that the Pre-school Playgroups Association wish to continue and extend their activities and the Save the Children Fund wish to continue to provide groups in especially difficult situations where experimental methods are needed, at least until maintained groups are generally available. . . ."

"Until enough maintained places are available, local education authorities should be given power and be encouraged to give financial or other assistance to nursery groups run by non-profit making associations which in their opinion fill a need which they cannot meet. Voluntary groups, with or without help from public funds, should be subject to inspection by local education authorities and H.M. Inspectorate similar to that of the maintained nurseries."[1]

However one looks at this, the Plowden acknowledgement of the playgroup movement was but lukewarm; partially, perhaps, because playgroups are usually of middle-class origin and therefore the movement seemed to add little to the concern of Plowden with the areas of deprivation. Since Plowden there has been at least some further development of playgroups in E.P.A.s and this movement is gathering momentum. It may be that the underlying reason for Plowden's minor acknowledgement of the playgroup movement was the suspicion that exists in the professional nursery world, ranging from Nursery H.M.I.s to nursery teachers, of the play-group movement as a whole. The Plowden Committee was largely made up of professional educationists; the amateur in education attracts increased suspicion and there is a reluctance to see the playgroup as having a significant part to play in pre-school education in E.P.A.s and a tendency to rely on an assumed increase in the number of nursery places.

We thus have two contrasting traditions of pre-schooling: the nursery class and the playgroup. The disadvantages of the first are its high cost and a professional orientation which, on the whole, discourages parental involvement: but it also has the advantages of high standards of organisation and content. Playgroups have reciprocal qualities: they are cheap, albeit typically ill-equipped in miserable premises, but they encourage co-operation from parents: they are often poorly organised and, particularly when introduced into E.P.A.s, are run at a low level of unprofessional skill unless training can be introduced. Inspection is normally on medical and social rather than educational grounds.

---

[1] Plowden, paragraphs 323 and 343.

It is important therefore to be clear that we have no wish to perpetuate the less attractive features of the playgroup or to dissent from the legitimate suspicions of the professionals towards what, in popular conception, is a part-time group for toddlers run by the vicar's wife in the church hall. We are advocating a well-organised pre-school provision run by professionals with the co-operation of trained parents, with curricula designed to meet the needs of children in particular E.P.A. conditions and with resources primarily from the state through financial formulae of strong positive discrimination.

Coming then to our own recommendations in respect of organisation, what we advocate in general is the creation of a statutory framework within which the very considerable energies of voluntary organisations like the S.C.F. or the P.P.A. can most effectively be harnessed to solving the problems of families in the E.P.A. areas. We would not presume to prescribe the details of organisation at the national level but our experiences at the local level strongly suggest the desirability of a responsible branch within the D.E.S. having close links with the relevant functions of the D.H.S.S. and the Home Office in respect of pre-school children and through which funds could be channelled to support inspectorial services, the local authorities *and* voluntary groups. We recognise, of course, the recency of Seebohm reorganisation of the local personal social services and the established interests of the children's departments in the welfare of children. We are aware also that pre-schooling is not usefully thought of as serving only narrowly educational needs, and that therefore the traditions of the child care officer and the health visitor have something to contribute to a successful method of preparing children to take full advantage of the opportunities to be provided later in schools. Nevertheless the educational function of the nursery centres is, in our view, paramount. Education, especially for the under-fives, must be widely defined and it must be linked to medical guidance and skilled attention to cases of social breakdown. The trick is to integrate these essential features of upbringing. Administrative barriers and rigidities are not far to seek, especially among the poor, as we saw in our discussion of Red House in Chapter 9. They need to be overcome both centrally and locally. Urban aid grants have, in our experience, already made useful contributions along these lines.

At the local level the organisational recipe is again one of partnership between statutory and voluntary effort. We advocate a co-ordinated format of pre-school provision, under the guidance and help of local authority advisers, and including a variety—in style, location and time—of playgroups grouped around the L.E.A. nursery schools, classes and primary schools and also the day nurseries. Such a system of nursery centres is an immediately practical way forward to giving every child under five in E.P.A.s the opportunity of some pre-school experience. There are precedents from our four districts to support the hybrid form and the statutory/voluntary partnership which we have in mind. Thus for example we have claimed that the three finest precedents in the Liverpool project were the industrial funding of a playgroup organiser, the deployment of the Playmobile and the use of a primary school, its reception staff and student help for playgroup purposes. Similarly, in the West Riding a side effect of the urban aid grant was the formation of a local branch of the P.P.A. and the appointment of a part-time locally based playgroup adviser. In this latter case the final development was the transfer of responsibility for playgroups from the Health Department to the new Social Services Department. This administrative development is debatable, but far from being incompatible with an educational role it could be held to encourage a wider definition of education itself.

The Playmobile, despite its publicity as something of a gimmick, has shown itself to be a highly successful organisational device, expressing a remarkably successful level of co-operation between the local education authority and voluntary effort. This bus has already travelled, so to say, beyond the boundaries of Liverpool 8 to several other local education authorities.

Again and similarly, the development in the West Riding of a market stall illustrates the possibilities for statutory/voluntary co-operation and also the breadth of the definition of pre-schooling which must encompass more than formally organised educational experience in the narrow sense. The remarks of the West Riding team on this bear repeating. There are alternative ways of operating such schemes. One is for education authorities to play some role in supporting them. If we are thinking of educational development in E.P.A.s, we must think in broad terms, not just new educational provision, but the kind of reinforcement to such provision that may come from such other educational influences as libraries, toy and book shops. In a typical E.P.A. such developments will not occur as a result of market forces. Yet, the demand is there, and should be met; but initially and perhaps indefinitely, this demand is not sufficient to alter patterns of supply which are shaped in part by past demands from the area and in part by the commercially correct assumptions of wholesalers that "educational" materials are not profitable lines in E.P.A.s. Yet if such materials can affect the rate of child development by influencing the relation between parent and child, should such provision be left to commercial principles? There should be greater participation by education in the "market place" —making education more accessible and therefore more effective.

We have mentioned the Urban Aid Programme. Again the West Riding local experience of a grant of £1,000 for a period in the first instance of three years up to 1972 with possible further extensions later is instructive. The grant was administered locally by a management committee with representatives from the Health and Education Departments, the local branch of the Pre-School Playgroups Association, local playgroups and the E.P.A. project. Different viewpoints as to the function and distribution of the grant were apparent from the start. On the one hand there was a strong feeling that the grant represented long-awaited official recognition of past work by the playgroup movement, and should be distributed equally in the form of support grants for groups which had struggled for years to maintain good standards. This view was given additional strength by the fact that some other local authorities already gave official financial support as a matter of course to voluntary playgroups in their areas. On the other hand there was the clear statement that the grant had been made for deprived groups or areas, a view that was strongly in accord with the E.P.A. team's standpoint. The decision was finally taken to distribute the grant in the form of a pool of equipment to be loaned to all playgroups in the area; starter grants for new groups; and free places for children recommended by the health visitor.

The question of free places caused considerable local discussion and proved exceedingly difficult to administer in practice. It was felt by many that free places were being offered to the least deserving—yet another welfare benefit being exploited by the "scroungers"; and that such families in any case would not take up the offer, and could not be bothered to bring the children. This was a clear example of the difficulties encountered in the scheme involving a selection of children or families, and of the necessity for a very high level of intensive and concentrated support for groups in the greatest need if they are to take advantage of benefits offered. Positive discrimination is not simply a matter of selective monetary relief or cash payments. Here it was evident that in many cases the financial inducement of a free pre-school place for the child was insufficient without a carefully thought out programme of information, advice, and support for the family, probably including regular home visiting and possibly the transporting of the child to the playgroup. All of this would have taken far more resources of time, staff, and skill than a voluntary group possessed; and indeed presupposed acceptance that such a programme of action was necessary, which was far from being the case.

A highly successful innovation of the type we are advocating has been the Red House in the West Riding. This idea originated in Sir Alec Clegg's call for the setting up of hostels to provide short-term residential care for school children during periods of crisis in the home. It was not, as such, a scheme confined to pre-schooling—it was not, in other words, only a nursery centre—but was developed to include a range of community educational services. The E.P.A. team in fact built up Red House into a multi-purpose centre serving as an adjunct to schools in the immediate area and including pre-school work. In the course of a year it is estimated that about a thousand different children have been involved at the centre for various lengths of time. Red House is used throughout the day and in the evening as well by small groups. Children of pre-school, infant, junior and secondary age have been involved as well as parents, teachers and other members of the community. Students from local teacher training colleges have worked there and a number of people in the social service departments have used it as a contact point for the area. In the evenings parent groups have come together for sessions such as cookery demonstrations, and at times for meetings with teachers about education.

With regard to the pre-school element, Red House may be seen as incorporating a possible form of the nursery centre we advocate. There was an afternoon group run on nursery lines with strong parental involvement. As the children approached school entry, preliminary reading work was introduced. Experiments have been made with individual language work of a structured kind to see whether short sessions in a one-to-one situation would help children to take advantage of a less structured setting. Parents have taken part in the pre-school group and also in the individual sessions. The teacher in charge has also made home visits and from this a parents' group developed which has met regularly in the evenings. Children from the secondary school also have participated in the pre-school work; initially groups of girls who leave at the minimum age have worked there for a term or so in their final year; and for some of the older girls this has developed into part of a course in child care, involving a week's residential stay in the centre and visits to see the local provision for very young children, as well as taking part in pre-school work. Recently boys have become more active in the group; previously they had made equipment at the centre, but now they take part in the group work, and sometimes bring in a specialist skill such as guitar playing. These activities can provide strong motivation for teenage children who have little interest left in school and look forward to leaving early. The Red House education centre, in short, successfully and dramatically illustrates the incorporation of pre-schooling in a community organisation formed by co-operation between statutory and voluntary bodies. It suits the local character of a relatively isolated mining town. In other E.P.A.s alternative forms may be more appropriate, perhaps attached to a primary or secondary school or perhaps, as the experience of the Deptford project suggests, to a college of education like Rachel Macmillan.

Finally, among the variety of pre-school provisions with which we have experimented and which we advocate, we may mention the Home Visiting Programme instituted in the West Riding. The aim in this instance has been to take educational materials into the home and demonstrate how they can be used by mother and child. The scheme is at present operating intensively with about 20 families, focusing on the child before he joins a pre-school group; visits are made regularly by a worker each week, and material is left in the home. It is essential to involve the mother in this programme if its effects are to last. Evaluation by formal testing has supported our hopes for this particular variety of pre-school provision. Success with this work no doubt depends on recruiting highly skilled and motivated educational visitors who are knowledgeable about both the theory and practice of learning and sensitive, as the best social case workers are, to the nuances of family relationships. Nevertheless, compared with traditional nursery schooling the cost is not great because overheads are largely eliminated and the method seems to offer powerful reinforcement to the other elements of what must always be a complex and varied programme of pre-schooling.

These examples must suffice to sketch the organisational framework. Turning to our recommendations as to content, perhaps the most encouraging single finding of our researches is also from the West Riding. It is that of the follow-up study of children who attended pre-school for a full year. Our findings show that the gains made during the pre-school years are maintained in the reception year. In fact in certain cases where groups had made limited progress in the nursery, they made substantial progress in their first year of infant school. These findings are generally contrary to those of many American compensatory programmes, where children who have made gains in the pre-school year tend to fall back once they enter the elementary school. There may be several reasons for this result in the West Riding, including the stable population, the carefully fashioned link between nursery and reception class, and the fact that it was possible to offer all children entering these schools a chance to attend the nursery. Obviously follow-up work is required to check whether the gains are sustained. Meanwhile the least that can be said is that the case against Head Start cannot be applied automatically to the proposals we are making for Britain.

Our national (i.e. inter-project) pre-school experiment was designed to test whether following a structured language programme in short daily sessions would help children's oral language development. Because no British programme was available at that time the one we used—the Peabody Language Development Kit—was imported from America. We are not advocating this kit as such, but the progress we measured among the children using it should encourage the analogous development of British programmes. Although such programmes may be superfluous in some L.E.A. nurseries with high reputations for language work, in other nurseries and in playgroups it could be of great benefit to hold a special "language period" in which the material was co-ordinated in a systematic way and each child received individual attention. Moreover our experience suggests that this could be done without infringing in any way upon the contribution which pre-school education undoubtedly makes to children's social and emotional development. We therefore think it desirable that British programmes, of which those described in Chapter 8 are illustrations, should be developed, tested and disseminated.

In the related field of concept learning the number programme evaluated in Birmingham showed that E.P.A. pre-schoolers could make considerable gains. Since the programme had to be prepared under great pressure, this finding is heartening. Very radical changes were also observed in the children's capacity to concentrate on a task—a better programme could contribute more. But it is wise to interpret the findings with caution in view of the complexity of the motivations and skills involved. Piaget used three criteria in his own evaluations and our experimental procedures have not allowed any of them to be met in full. His criteria were: does the reorganisation stand the test of time, what degree of transfer is there across tasks, and what evidence is there of the acquisition of new, more complex cognitive operations? There is a need for investigations which would meet these rigorous standards. What is not in doubt is that children within the E.P.A. pre-schools respond enthusiastically to the systematic introduction of cognitive stimulations in a positive and benign environment. The benign environment remains as important as ever; but those children whose trust in verbal communication has been impaired might find the structure of a *subject* useful in achieving security and the peace in which to learn how to learn—as useful as the structure of the pre-school *situation* upon which so much reliance is traditionally placed.

What happens to the pre-school child in his group or class is important: hence our discussion of content. But finally we must return to the main theme. The vital task is to extend pre-school provision in the educational priority areas. Our policy is to give this high preference in future allocation of statutory resources. Our method is to multiply these resources by encouraging voluntary activity within a framework of statutory provision and so to develop in all E.P.A.s a variety of pre-school provision grouped around nursery centres and depending on diagnosis of the particular needs of each district.

3. *The Community School*

The Plowden conception of the community school was rudimentary and easily dismissed by Bernstein and Davies as "merely a new name for play centres, youth clubs and evening institutes, with lip-service to Henry Morris, meeting in school premises. It is difficult to see them making any significant short-run contribution to education itself in the E.P.A."[1] We, by contrast, have developed the idea to the point where we regard it as the *essential* principle along with that of positive discrimination in a policy for educational priority areas. We have conceived of the community school initially, as did Plowden, as a primary school, though we are not unaware that secondary schools frequently suffer from the same problems. But our experience has gradually re-defined it as a broad aspect of the community itself—viz. the organisation and process of learning through all of the social relationships into which an individual enters at any point in his lifetime. Thus the community school seeks almost to obliterate the boundary between school and community, to turn the community into a school and the school into a community. It emphasises both teaching and learning roles for all social positions so that children may teach and teachers learn as well as vice *versa*, and parents may do both instead of neither. It insists on seeing the whole of the social organisation of a locality from the point of view of its educational potential, whether positive or negative. Thus the family, the school, the workplace, the W.E.A. class, the public bureaucracies, the public house, the holiday camp and the street are all both potential resources and potential barriers to the educational development of the child.

We are not, of course, after three years with the realities of schooling in E.P.A.s, naive about the meaning or meaninglessness of community. Our West Riding mining town is a community with its stability of membership and "common consciousness" in a way that Balsall Heath is not, and neither resembles that stereotype of arcadian *gemeinschaft* which may be conjured up by references to the Cambridgeshire village. There is therefore no national blueprint for the community school. As we have emphasised in the case of pre-schooling, local diagnosis is a *sine qua non*.

Nevertheless we are convinced now of the possibility and urgency of using the community school principle in its appropriate local form for the educative development of the E.P.A.s. Organisationally the key is *linkage*, of school to family, school to teacher training, school to economy and school to school. Linkage we believe can be achieved partly by the initial intervention of task forces and partly by extending the administrative principles of statutory/voluntary co-operation to which we have referred in laying out our policy for pre-schooling. But the community school is more than a device for co-ordinating and concentrating separate educative forces. It has also to be informed by a relevant conception of the curriculum required for the education of E.P.A. children which depends in turn on standards of teaching.

We will take up these issues of teaching quality and community links in separate sections below. Meanwhile, we must point to the need for reform in school governance and management. The community school requires

---

[1] Bernstein and Davies in R. S. Peters (ed.), *Perspectives on Plowden*, p. 77.

community management: at present school managers do not link the school to the community it serves except in very rare cases. It is frequently difficult to find one parent who can name one manager of his child's school. Eric Midwinter's suggested panel of managers for the community school would be a parent, the head teacher, a teacher representative, L.E.A. officer, L.E.A. elected member, an industrial or commercial representative, a college representative (perhaps replacing the university delegate) with powers to co-opt up to three others able to meet or speak for interests especially relevant to the particular school. Managers should have obligatory training courses and their names should be widely publicised in the school catchment area.

4. *The Partnership between School and Family*

Turning now to the first and essential link of school to community, we can sketch the meaning of the community school in terms of improved relations with the families from which the children are drawn. The first step is to improve the visibility of school and education in the eyes of parents. It may be taken by attracting parents to schools in the manner described by Plowden and demonstrated in Deptford, or it may be taken, under suitable circumstances, through the education centre or Red House as already described in our section on pre-schooling. In Liverpool this visibility aim has been much emphasised through three devices. First, professionally produced publications have been distributed among parents. The Liverpool project experimented successfully with a teacher-centred newsletter, the child-centred magazine, the prospectus, the calendar and the booklet. These products ought to be disseminated. It is an obvious task for the Schools Council, the L.E.A. and the community managed school which we are recommending to produce such materials. As Eric Midwinter has suggested, the publications might be produced on a national basis and in a tripartite form, with a national cover, a local contribution and a school insertion.

Second, there is the exposition. There are natural focal points in the community at which the school can advertise its wares—shops, department stores, public houses, doctors' surgeries, the local market, community centres, churches and factory canteens. There are two major forms of exposition—exhibitions and live demonstrations. Nothing could more strikingly illustrate the possibilities than the combination of both types of exposition which was staged in Liverpool at a large departmental store and which was attended by no less than 10,000 people. The concept of the exposition leads naturally to the education shop of which the West Riding market stall is an example already mentioned and of which the Liverpool project has produced useful prototypes. This idea could advantageously be taken up by large chain stores and also possibly used in the large holiday camps.

A third device is the site improvement scheme, in effect a declaration of war on the chaos and greyness of the typical E.P.A. environment. Again there is a fine example from Liverpool where a huge wall mural of the "Merseyside scene" became a tourist attraction. But there is also the possibility of litter campaigns, reclamation of bits of land as children's play centres, roof and playground gardening and interior decor.

Ideally these schemes draw curricular and communal concerns together. But their main function is to inform the community of the content and the relevance of schooling for communal life. It is, in essence, a public relations venture and, as such, resources need to be diverted for the purpose. We would recommend that each E.P.A. school should be subsidised with an annual public relations grant of £150 or 50p per capita, whichever be the greater.

But the nub of it all is to encourage parents to join in the educational process. To foster the partnership between home and school it is necessary to move in both directions—to take education into the home and to bring parents into the school. We have noted the outward reaching potential of the community school in its most direct form in our reference to the West Riding Home Visiting programme. We have used the phrase "educational visitor" and beyond this lies an instructive historical parallel. Earlier in this century the health visitor service bridged a gap between advances in medicine and the health culture of the population. It was intrinsically a positively discriminatory service concentrated on those families with least appreciation of and capacity to use the new opportunities provided by new medical and hygienic knowledge for a healthy physical life. Education now offers "life chances" similarly important and similarly badly distributed in the population. The educational visitor may therefore be seen as a historical parallel to the earlier health visitor, with the task of raising standards of life by carrying new knowledge and new methods from the frontiers of educational skill in the teaching professions to the family which is remote from and unknowing about the pedagogical mysteries.

Another element in establishing a firm and constructive partnership between school and family is the work of the home–school liaison teacher. Just as work with pre-school children at the Red House was extended and supported by visits to children and their parents in their homes, so the activities aimed at making the schools more visible to parents—magazines, expositions, invitations to parents to come to school—can be valuably complemented by teachers, or a specialist teacher, deliberately cultivating a relationship with parents on a more individual basis.

The job of the home-school liaison teacher, as we see it, is essentially educational. It is concerned partly with explaining the aims and methods of the schools so that parents can better understand the nature of the experience their children receive within them, and partly with encouraging parents to recognise and have confidence in their own capacity to teach. But it is of first importance that this kind of home–school work should be the responsibility of qualified teachers who have a thorough understanding of pedagogical methods and of the special challenge presented by the educational priority areas.

Arrangements for home–school liaison need to be flexible. Discussions with parents may arise in the school when they are attending some school activity, or they may stem from a home visit; some parents have to be encouraged to come to the school and others may not come at all. And although home visiting may in some instances be best organised through the appointment of a special teacher on the model of our Birmingham experiment, in some circumstances the ordinary teaching staff may be able to

share the home liaison work between them. Much must depend on the interests, enthusiasms and circumstances of the staff of each school.

We want to emphasise that the liaison teacher would, in principle, be
concerned with all parents, explaining and encouraging participation in and
even planning with them a whole range of school and school-linked activities. But it is also possible for the liaison teacher to exercise positive discrimination by concentrating attention on families and groups with special
problems. It is always possible that a teacher's understanding and handling
of a difficult child will be transformed by awareness of the home situation.
Ignorance of a child's particular circumstances may result in disastrous
failure of communication. In Birmingham the simple device of translating
letters of invitation to a school outing into three Asian languages doubled
the response from Asian parents.

Our projects and especially the action taken in Deptford raises the
question of the need for school social workers and of the role of education
welfare officers in providing links between schools and homes. We want to
distinguish clearly between the liaison teacher and the social worker. The
former, we have argued, is essentially concerned with education and works
within that context however broadly defined. The social worker is essentially concerned with social breakdown, with families who are handicapped
physically, socially or economically to a degree necessitating public support.
It is perhaps a pre-condition of success for the liaison teacher that the
social worker and the social services should be adequate. *A fortiore* the
educational priority area can only succeed in the context of a wider programme of community development in which the social worker and the
social services are no more than one among many links.

Promoting the partnership on the school premises completes the link
between school and home. Parents involved in pre-school or evening
activities or accompanying children on the Deptford environmental studies
programme are all moving towards understanding the educational process
through which their children have to pass. Full participation may be thought
of as experience of both learning and teaching by the parent in partnership
with teachers and children. In Liverpool the most profitable focus for this
participation was found to be the school classroom, with teacher and children inviting parents to join them regularly for half-day sessions. These
began in Liverpool as "coffee mornings" but widened encouragingly into
the afternoon and evening, with parents joining their children working in
groups. The success of the evening efforts, when fathers and working mothers
had an opportunity to engage themselves, also points to the possibility of
weekends as well as evenings as a viable time for schooling. Of course, if
such schemes are to be realistic, they must avoid imposing an increased
overall burden on teachers and to this point we shall return. The need for
holiday programmes in educational priority areas also deserves mention.
Given the lack of leisure facilities and the paucity of traditional educational
achievement in such areas, a strong argument can be made for holiday
schooling, again provided teachers are not overburdened. The ultimate aim
of parental involvement in the school is that of mutual teaching and learning
in parent-child projects. Experience with these has been limited but hopeful.
Certainly it is the placing of fathers and mothers in the learner role that

requires urgent attention; as such the teacher must be seen as critical. If one teacher can be converted to good home–school practice, 30 pairs of parents and their children can benefit.

5. *The Quality of Teaching*

One of our basic aims in the E.P.A. action–research projects was to improve the morale of teachers. There is ample evidence from Deptford, Birmingham, Liverpool and the West Riding that this aim is achieved by action–research projects of the type we have undertaken. Though the characteristics of E.P.A. teachers vary both within and between districts, the following summary of replies to a questionnaire in London may be taken as the starting point.

"The Deptford teachers saw their teaching job as relatively badly paid, with limited salary prospects. Salary detracted from, rather than contributed to, general satisfaction. Physical conditions of work were thought poor, the neighbourhood was seen to be extremely unfavourable and a majority thought they received less parental support than other teachers received. The children were thought to be less able than those taught by other teachers and they generated more discipline problems. On the other hand, the work was seen to be worthwhile and generally satisfying. Although the pressure of work was thought to be high, relatively less time was spent at work than was spent by friends, security was seen to be good and there were better opportunities than were generally available to improve qualifications."

In order to realise our aim which is to develop the community school and to fashion the E.P.A. as an effective instrument of positive discrimination, it is necessary that teachers be adequately motivated, equipped and supported to be effective partners with the parents and other potentially educative forces in the community, and to this end it is necessary to give them smaller classes, adequate curriculum materials, teachers' aides, teachers' centres, effective links with colleges of education and with any sources of information about successful E.P.A. innovations which become available.

A major initiative from central government in respect of E.P.A. was the institution of a £75 per annum increment (later raised to £83) for teachers in schools of exceptional difficulty. Alan Little and his colleagues in the London research team evaluated the impact of the E.P.A. salary increment. Their findings, as we saw in Chapter 11, were: There was an initial decrease in resignations from schools receiving the £75 allowance. There was no marked increase in resignations from schools receiving the £75 allowance. After only one year of operation the initial impact of the scheme was not only lost, but the rate of resignation became higher than in the year prior to its introduction. An explanation of this result might be found in the temporary impact of the strategy for E.P.A. schools that focuses attention on the morale of the teachers. Small increases in salary may have a small initial impact on morale, but will have limited long-term impact. Head teachers' views on the existing scheme were mixed. Most, while approving of the idea of extra allowances for E.P.A. schools, also thought that the Present scheme was ineffective partly because the amount of money was small and partly because of the way it was administered. Perhaps the most disappointing finding of the head teachers' interviews was the suggestion that they could not discern any impact on schools receiving the allowance, but did feel that there was a negative influence on schools not receiving it. Assistant teachers' views were similar to those of head teachers, in that those who thought extra allowances should be given also thought that the present amounts were inadequate. Both assistant teachers in schools receiving and those not receiving the extra pay thought that the existing scheme had no impact on the schools or staff.

But these gloomy findings should not be misinterpreted. The responses of both heads and assistant teachers were almost universally in favour of the principle of salary differential for teachers working in E.P.A. schools. Indeed we would argue along with many others in the teaching professions that such salary differentials should be used to mark the superior professional challenge of such teaching and not as a kind of compensation (what some of the Liverpool teachers habitually refer to as "dirt money").

It should also be noted that the limited character of the differentials introduced on a national footing was bound to produce local anomalies which created tensions and thereby inhibited their impact. In any case it is not to be expected that short-term measures taken in isolation will have striking long-term effects. The raising of the quality of the teaching force is not simply a function of salaries but also of class sizes, relevant curricula, college links and in general the conditions under which the teachers work. In other words the morale and effectiveness of teachers in E.P.A.s are functions of the degree of success with which our notion of the community school is introduced. Of course questions of salary and qualifications have their place in this broader context. We want to see the E.P.A. differentials increased. But we also want to advocate that plans be introduced in colleges of education and in-service courses such that after a period of five or seven years there can be a prescribed qualification for the E.P.A. teacher which would enable him to earn a higher annual increment than has yet been considered. On the one side, this would give the E.P.A. teacher a well-deserved status and bonus; on the other side, it would assure a modicum of specialised training for those attempting probably the most arduous of all teaching jobs.

The testing programme which we conducted in all the projects' primary schools showed that levels of attainment are disturbingly low, and the problems are complicated by the special difficulties of non-English speaking immigrants. New teaching methods can help to attack them.

In Birmingham "Breakthrough to Literacy" has been an important contribution to classroom practice and especially valuable in providing a structure for the reading process without radical alteration in the classroom milieu. This kind of work is obviously of crucial importance in schools with a high proportion of immigrant children. In the West Riding the audio-visual reading scheme for children who had reached the end of primary school or had begun secondary education but were still unable to read has shown itself to be successful in raising reading levels substantially, and incidentally pointed to the benefits to be derived from extra help in the classroom for special programmes for a minority of the class group.

But beyond this there seems to us to be a general curricular principle. It is that the curriculum should be aimed primarily at the critical and constructive adaptation of children to the actual environment in which they live. This principle is essentially a long-term aim and is not adequately encompassed in the conventional measures of educational attainment.

Eric Midwinter has argued that the balance of the curricular diet should change from "academic" to "social" with reality-based themes forming the staple. These should become what teachers now call the "basic" or "bread-and-butter" subjects, with all else feeding in and growing out of them. There is a firm case to be made for extensive language programmes, but here again, it is important that these are imbued with a high sense of social purpose and that reading and writing are exercised on socially relevant material. This is not to advocate a modern form of parochialism ("television", for example, is a non-local theme highly relevant to the urban child) and every opportunity should be sought to widen the outlook of the children. Indeed our impression from the West Riding project is that some E.P.A. conditions may induce a constraining over-identification with the local community. Nevertheless, a careful study of their immediate environment should form the primary school child's chief fount of enquiry and it should remain at the centre of their social learning. This in turn is the more likely to engage parental interest and it is a truism of home–school practice to observe that curriculum choice is probably as meaningful as any other feature in cementing links between teacher and parent.

Moreover social environmental or communal studies should concentrate on skills rather than information. Teachers have traditionally noted the maturational rates of children in reading and number, but this has been less marked in humanities teaching. Similarly, relatively little effort has been made to see these subjects developmentally, with due regard paid to the evolution of concepts about time, space, society and the like along the same lines as number or word skills. We often hear of teachers using geography and history lessons to "help" reading and writing or as the basis for art and craft work. This needs largely to be reversed, with both verbal and creative methods placed at the disposal of social purpose and expertise.

Above all, and most difficult, there must be change of teaching attitudes. Historically, the teacher has been cast as the defender of the status quo and, indeed, the one found culpable if social unrest, be it juvenile delinquency or drugs, threatens. E.P.A. community education, as an element in community development, is about moving on, not standing still. It is about the formation of social personalities with the attributes of constructive discontent. It is about children who are made eager apprentices of community life. It presumes that an educational priority area should be radically reformed and that its children, as junior citizens, should be forewarned and forearmed for the struggle. Teachers need to be sensitive to the social and moral climate in which their children are growing up. The application of teaching virtues to a compassionate, tolerant and critical examination of all social, political and moral issues is the highest hurdle along the road to a community-oriented curriculum. It could take years and it will require a generous and sympathetic change of heart, not only among educational authorities but in society at large.

The kind of curriculum we have in mind requires supporting resources. A schedule of courses and publications is needed in the schools and here again project teams of the type we have formed would be ideal for the purpose. Such a team or, failing it, each L.E.A. (or, for scattered E.P.A. schools, several L.E.A.s in concert at suitable vantage points) could establish a teacher resources centre, similar to the one being created in the Liverpool E.P.A. These centres would have two allied functions. They would introduce teachers to the principles and methods of community-based studies by courses, seminars, exhibitions and discussions, and provide opportunities for teachers to prepare their own related materials. They would produce locally-based or otherwise relevant materials for the teaching service, thus meeting the valid complaint of teachers who, while accepting the need for this kind of work, point out that educational publishers must perforce provide for a much more general and abstract market. The Liverpool project's "Projector" series were promoted as examples of this function and included kits, games and work books dealing with all levels from preschool to adult. Eric Midwinter's *Social Environment and the Urban School*[1] is an example of a teachers' primer on junior school community-based studies and linkages. A four-volume social studies work book is now being prepared in Liverpool. It is flexible enough to be used in any area for local investigations and also "developmental" in that succeeding volumes are geared to the average social maturation rate of the junior child. L.E.A.s might well be advised to appoint an E.P.A. adviser/organiser or E.P.A. teacher resources warden, or both, to co-ordinate this and other internal school action.

The quality of teaching in E.P.A. schools may also be considered from the point of view of teacher training. The College of Education is probably the most under-used potential resource for positive discrimination and community schooling in the E.P.A.s. There are only three E.P.A. schools for every teacher training institution in the country. Thus in principle the establishment of a continuing link between every E.P.A. school and a teacher training institution is clearly feasible, though varying in convenience because of the differences in geographical spread. The potential of colleges of education as resources for both positive discrimination and the development of the community school are enormous. For example the various elements of action in the Deptford project sometimes involved as many as 300 college of education students simultaneously in work with the project schools. Moreover the material cost of mobilising them is minimal. The widely expressed opinions of E.P.A. teachers and of the college of education tutors and students who have been involved suggest that the development of continuous college-school links has been a most successful component of the London, Liverpool and West Riding projects, giving mutual benefit to the schools and the colleges, an exciting and effective training for students and an invaluable contribution to curriculum development and task forces for special ventures.

The paradox here is that while some colleges or college tutors have responded to the approach of the E.P.A. teams (e.g. Rachel Macmillan in London, St. Peter's, Saltley in Birmingham or Edge Hill and others around

---

[1] Ward Lock, 1972.

Liverpool) the general impression is one of remoteness or indifference. Whatever the other implications of the James Report, it is urgently necessary to launch a national initiative towards integrating colleges of education with the work of every E.P.A. school. The Area Training Organisations could offer a strong lead in promoting E.P.A. option courses of the type pioneered at Edge Hill, and university education departments could advantageously appoint tutors, to be responsible for developing the relevant links between colleges and schools and for the proper construction of E.P.A. optional coursework in relation to teacher certification. Similarly each college needs a tutor qualified for E.P.A. work and must find ways of circumventing the rigidity of existing timetables so as to accommodate the need for students to attend E.P.A. schools where the continuous link system is instituted.

6. *Action–Research and Innovation*

In Chapter 13 we tried to draw some lessons from our experience about the character of action–research. We are aware of the conflicts which may arise between social science and policy interests in this context. Nevertheless we believe that the form of organisation that we were able to build up in our study is a serviceable one for partnership between social scientists and administrators in the formation of public policy. Partnership rather than domination by either side is essential to success and to this end we were much helped by a unitary organisation and by that optimal degree of financial independence which enabled us to place minor resources directly where they were needed while at the same time compelling us to face the realistic tests of dependence on the willingness of public and voluntary bodies to provide the major part of the budget.

But within the context of planning for educational change distinctions have to be drawn between three functions—discovery, innovation and dissemination. Action–research can serve the first two functions if the partnership between social science and administration is realised. Our projects have had successes in both these directions. Nevertheless we can by no means claim to have settled all the issues in studies so limited in number and duration. There is a case for further research studies, not necessarily using the action–research method, for example of the changes which take place in the organisation of E.P.A. schools during the course of redevelopment and population change in the surrounding district. There is a case also for more action–research projects of the type we have undertaken but in districts of a different social character, like new housing estates. And the E.P.A. secondary school needs further study. We would like to see the D.E.S. take the initiative here, setting up working parties to specify the most urgent E.P.A. research and action–research problems.

The third function—dissemination—requires different methods. Both the successes and the failures of research need to be known by all L.E.A.s and schools. A private venture—*Priority*—based in Liverpool but national in aspiration has evolved from our action–research programme. It has support from the Liverpool Corporation and deserves more from other public bodies. Again we hope to see central initiative in examining the general arrangements for improving the spread of tested E.P.A. practice. Educational change is a notoriously slow process. The task force might

well be more widely used. A team of six or seven (for instance, a co-ordinator, a pre-school adviser, an adult educationist, a home and school
relations officer, a curriculum development/teacher resources organiser, a
teacher-education adviser, and so on) could channel materials and funds,
establish networks of action and communication and create the essential
impetus for change and innovation. If large L.E.A.s or smaller L.E.A.s
in consortia could, heavily backed by central sources, undertake to operate
such semi-independent, locally based and partly autonomous teams, and
if they could grant them freedom from too many administrative and political constraints, then the catalytic agent released could be a major factor
in the establishment of community education.

7. *E.P.A. and Beyond*

We must return finally to the fundamental question raised in Chapter 1—
the limits of an educational approach to poverty. These limits cannot be
removed by any kind of E.P.A. policy. But within them we think we can see
a viable road to a higher standard of educational living for hundreds of
thousands of children in the more disadvantaged districts.

We have outlined a wide range of policies around the development of
pre-schooling and the community school, and we have called for a co-
ordinated advance of statutory and voluntary effort. The action-research
project method, adroitly constituted to work with "the system" but with a
small but essential element of independence from the normal administrative procedures, has proved itself to be an effective agent of educational
change and a magnet for voluntary effort from a wide range of public and
private organisations. Such projects, perhaps linked in some cases to the
current Community Development Projects, could carry forward the development of E.P.A. policy as we have done in three years from its incep-
tion in the Plowden Report. At the same time we would hope that there is
sufficient confidence in our results from the first projects for the Government and the local education authorities to create the framework of
organisation for pre-schooling and community schooling that we have
advocated. If so there will be a new landmark in British educational
progress.

APPENDIX I

E.P.A. CONFERENCE
Thursday, 2 January—Saturday, 4 January 1969
Oxford

I am hurriedly setting down a summary of the conference proceedings and the conclusions which I think we reached, before going off to the New York conference with our counterparts in the U.S.A.

1. *Aims of the research as a whole*

The impetus for our E.P.A. research programme arose from the discussions which followed the Plowden Report about what could be done to carry out the proposals the report contained. It was taken for granted, or very quickly had to be taken for granted, that very little money would be forthcoming and that serious action to carry out the recommendations would probably have to wait until economic growth had permitted a very large increase in educational resources. Our research, then, has been framed in terms of political and administrative expectations. From Whitehall's point of view our aim was to discover how to improve education in schools in slum areas. But we did not think we should reach any firm conclusions about this. A great deal is already known about what is needed. Not perhaps as much as some imagine, but nevertheless there is a great deal that could be put together by a canvass of existing knowledge, including research knowledge. We ourselves shall not be able to contribute very much that is new to this question.

A second, and more ambitious, way of describing our aim which again has a Whitehall tang about it is to say that we are trying to find the most economical way of getting the best results. How can we order the various kinds of additional allocation of resources to education in such a way as to maximise marginal productivities? This is a real and serious problem; it is a way of looking at education which is rather new and rather suspect. But we are passing through a revolution from this point of view in that the need to define what is being done and what is the relation between inputs and outputs is increasingly recognised. This kind of approach to educational administration is gaining a foothold in the Department of Education and Science as it has in other countries. But again I think our capacity, given the frame of research in which we are working in E.P.A., is not likely to offer very serious additions to our knowledge in this direction. We shall have very strong moral arguments, which are usually extremely weak arguments with the Treasury, but we shall not have the sort of cost and benefit studies which will enable us to make much contribution to policy decisions.

If these two possible aims of the research are to be discarded what then is it that we are after? I suggest that we are asserting that there are educative forces in society which under the present dispensation are not in fact utilised for educational purposes. We believe that a lot of those forces are suppressed. We think that children perform badly in schools because of the

199

relation between those schools and the communities and families in which the children live. We think that education is often a less effective instrument for the development of individual personalities than it could be because there is not the kind of partnership between parents and teachers in relation to children that there should be in an ideal community. We want to say, therefore, if we have to translate it into economic terms, that we are looking for ways in which an input of resources has a multiplier effect, releasing energies of educational value in the communities in which the input is made which will be much larger than the input and which will persist after the input itself has been withdrawn. I would like to look at every particular element that is proposed in our action programmes from the point of view of whether it does or does not conform to fit with this multiplier notion. It would be a criterion of action programmes which would enable us to decide which was relatively more valuable and more attractive. What are the implications of this approach for the action programmes?

2. Implications for action

First, it means a very strong focus on community action and in this sense it follows very much the spirit of what Plowden had to say. Perhaps the most essential theme in Plowden is the idea of mobilising the community and of relating the school to the community in ways in which it has not been related before. The second implication is that we shall be in danger, if we are not careful, of having too much scatter in our activities. Our resources are small. It is very tempting in view of very different local circumstances to initiate all kinds of different activities. We could have an enormous list of rather small and rather scattered projects which, quite apart from looking rather a ragbag to the critics, would be fundamentally unsatisfactory in being too random, small and unco-ordinated to provide much guidance to an overall attack on the Plowden problem when large funds are available. We must, then, both emphasise community projects and at the same time beware of too much dispersion of our efforts.

Perhaps I can emphasise this and make a fourth point by referring to George Smith's paper on parents and community. He argues that a likely implication of accepting the proposed research design is "that the projects selected will be those that are additions to the system"—that is to say more of the same kind of thing—"rather than those designed to promote institutional change"—that is to say to redefine the aims of education. And he goes on to argue in favour of the second type of project or, as I think of it, the community type of project on research grounds—"it would be wrong to rule out the second type of project on the grounds that they cannot be evaluated adequately if it seemed likely that by mounting such projects we would acquire more knowledge about the relationship between objectives, processes and outcomes in these areas which could be fed back into further research". And there is another very good reason for favouring the second type of project, apart from the research reason, in that they could have an impact on educational thought and educational policy which from an action point of view is what we are concerned with. I conclude that we must have in our baseline information some kind of general survey of parents and teachers to serve as a set of indices for measuring what we may call the "educative potential" of the community in which the research is going on. And this should be as broadly defined as possible to emphasise that the sort of aims we are interested in go beyond the traditional aims of education.

The fifth point that I want to make, and this is perhaps the most important thing that I am going to say, is that the most important integrating focus for all the local studies should be the community school. Some conception of the community school should be right at the centre of the whole programme. The idea could be extremely varied in its definition, according to local circumstances, and there are many ingredients or elements in the idea of the community school which would not be found in each local project. But if we can have one single focus to convert what could otherwise be unrelated local case studies into a national action programme, this I believe is what it ought to be.

Such a plan would also probably make it easier to get more money for our research. It is likely that the next parliament will vote a fairly large sum of money for the so-called urban programme. This will mean extra resources for areas which are not just educationally poor but which are, in a more general sense, defined as underprivileged. The programme will be directed not only at the education service but at the social services generally and there is already in process of formation a community development area project which is rather like E.P.A. writ large. In so far as we accepted the idea that the community school, or a variant of it, was the central focus of our action programme and in so far as each of the localities happens to be in an urban programme-type situation, and I think that applies to everyone with the possible exception of the West Riding, it is possible that we might get more funds from that urban programme. And the more ambitious we were about the interpretation of the notion of the community school, the more we went into problems of families which went beyond purely educational ones to include housing and family income and things of this kind, the more we would need such extra resources. We have both the need, and I think the opportunity, of collecting them if we go in that direction. Perhaps some of you may see this as a frightening expansion of a programme which is already scarcely within either the research workers' or the project directors' control. I well understand these feelings but nevertheless I believe that such an extension would be valuable.

3. *Implications for evaluation*

In our discussions we have posed a kind of challenge to ourselves. We have said that if the worst comes to the worst we have a team of people in five different localities who will be able to produce a series of case studies which would at least contain some evaluation locally based. That is the minimum starting point. How much further can we go? How far can we turn the local studies into a single programme as if we had selected a random sample of populations to which we applied a random set of Plowden ameliorative action programmes and evaluate the output in relation to the input by careful control grouping and all the rest of the social science apparatus which is at our disposal? We know that we shall not be able to make any very exact evaluation of this kind. Alan Brimer has suggested the lines along which we might attempt it and we have prepared three papers framed in terms of the theoretical layout in Alan Brimer's original model. How far have we got?

I want to leave the discussion of this question and conclude with three general points. First, if we adopt a set of community aims then evaluation is going to be far more complicated than it would otherwise be. It is intrinsically very much more difficult to specify aims and then go through the process of relating inputs to outputs if we go in the direction I am advocating. Second, the attempt of the Dundee and Liverpool teams to prepare a national proposal for pre-schooling has raised a dilemma of another kind. Dundee has argued strongly that a close experimental design is not within the scope of a particular locality since it needs to be repeated in other areas. This is challenged by Liverpool who are not so much concerned with the type of provision as with provision itself. The problem in educational priority areas is not one of method but of getting something done. Liverpool want to concentrate on investigating ways of encouraging pre-schooling and argue that only when programmes are established is it worth worrying about what kind of pre-schooling is best. This is perhaps an oversimplification of the Liverpool position but it seems to me to raise a dilemma that is related to the first problem of community aims as opposed to narrower aims. I do not think that this is an insoluble problem but it does bring out the question of what we are trying to do. Are we aiming at a very careful 'scientific' evaluation of different types of programme or are we deliberately exploring the unknown—trying to simply get things started where they were not started before? I am aware that the remarks that I have made about the Alan Brimer models are very partial in that he himself has patiently explained that there is another way of using the word evaluation which means a careful description of what actually happens as opposed to an input-output measurement model.

This brings me to my third and final point. It will be vital to build into the description of our E.P.A. research an assessment of the impact the project director himself has had on the action programmes. I am not here thinking so much of the personality of the man involved: I am rather more concerned with the fact of the existence of the role. Things will happen as a result of the playing of that role. It is an interference in the very situation which is being set up to be studied. This is perhaps the most obvious example of the need for a self-conscious recording of the research which might then be used as material, presumably by someone outside any local team, to say something about the impact of the role of the project director. May I then emphasise and extend a suggestion I made much earlier. We anticipated a communications problem between the local teams and I propose that I should be the co-ordinator, receiving a regular "stream of consciousness" from the localities, editing and sending it round to everybody else, and at the same time corresponding with the individual project teams myself in this way. I want to repeat this suggestion and turn it into an urgent request. It should be of very great value for communications and of even greater value in writing the general account of the E.P.A. project which has to follow each of the individual local accounts. I also think my original proposal should be extended. We must now urgently consider whether the research teams should write an account of the "before" situation of the relation of the schools to their administrations and the schools to each other. We ought to have this kind of systematic description before the action programmes go any further. Things may happen simply because a project starts and the local teams should attempt right away to try to describe the situation that they saw or that existed before they came in. We shall have to do the same thing at the end as well as accumulate, through what I originally referred to as a Finnegan's Wake, an account of the impact of the team on the network of authority, communication, influence, opinion and so on in the school system and its administration.

Conclusions

Some conclusions emerged from the seminars. It should be remarked that we had the Chairman of the National Steering Committee, Michael Young, with us until Friday evening and thereafter one of its members, Professor Jack Tizard.

The first conclusion was that the stress laid by me on the community school and the multiplier aim of releasing previously untapped resources in the community were on the whole strongly endorsed by the group. Nevertheless an essential modification was introduced, especially stimulated by Jack Tizard's contributions, which had the effect of relating these principles primarily to the action side of the project, i.e. as criteria for innovations rather than as objects of experimental research in the full and rigorous sense.

Second, our research intentions were clarified and concentrated by strong pleas, again led by Jack Tizard, that we should not put an impossible load on our slender resources and research staff by too much scatter of effect in the evaluation of a large number of elements in the action programme. Instead it was decided that research effort should be concentrated primarily on a simplified version of the Dundee pre-school experiment with replications in all five areas. This would be carried out and written up as a rigorous experimental research report on each district by the relevant research officer.

Two implications flow from the above two conclusions. First, a distinction will be drawn between "educational writing" and "research reporting". Under the first heading we shall look for an orderly and detailed account of the project as a series of innovations and actions. Under the second we shall look for research monographs directed primarily at the educational research world. The audience for the first is, of course, a much wider one including Whitehall, the L.E.A.s and the interested public at large. The audience for the second no doubt overlaps with that of the first but would presuppose in the reader a capacity to read professional, psychological, sociological and statistical writing. All of this writing must be completed by the end of the three years for which the project is scheduled. Authorship of both the action and research reports is to be determined locally but my presumption is that the primary responsibility for the action report will be taken by the project director and the primary responsibility for the research report by the research officer. In addition we shall have to agree on the character of the action and research reports on the national scheme as a whole. I expect to take major responsibility for this myself but I think we must leave open the question of participation by others who will have taken part in the programme either locally or nationally or both.

APPENDIX 2

A SELECTED BIBLIOGRAPHY

Acland, H., What is a "bad" school?, *New Society*, 9 September 1971. Does parental involvement matter?, *New Society*, 16 September 1971.

Barker Lunn, J. C., *Streaming in the Primary School*, National Foundation for Educational Research, Slough, 1970.

Barnes, D., *Language, the Learner and the School*, Penguin Books, 1969.

Bernstein, B., *Class, Codes, and Control*, Vol. 1, Routledge & Kegan Paul, 1971.

Bereiter, C. and Engelmann, S., *Teaching Disadvantaged Children in the Pre-School*, Prentice-Hall, New York, 1966.

Birley, D. and Dufton, A., *An Equal Chance: Equalities and Inequalities of Educational Opportunity*, Routledge & Kegan Paul, 1971.

Blackstone, T., *A Fair Start: The Provision of Pre-School Education*, Allen Lane, The Penguin Press, 1971.

Bloom, B. S., *Stability and Change in Human Characteristics*, Wiley, New York, 1964.

Boaden, N., *Urban Policy-Making*, C.U.P., 1971.

Bhattragar, J., *Immigrants at School*, Cornmarket Press, 1970.

Boyson, R. (ed.), *Down with the Poor*, Child Poverty Action Group, 1971.

Brandis, W. and Henderson, D., *Social Class, Language and Communication*, Routledge & Kegan Paul, 1970.

Burgin, T. and Edson, P., *Spring Grove: the Education of Immigrant Children*, Institute of Race Relations: O.U.P., 1967.

Cane, B. and Smithers, J., *The Roots of Reading*, National Foundation for Educational Research, Slough, 1971.

Cazden, C., Subcultural differences in child language: an interdisciplinary review, *Merrill Palmer Quarterly of Behavior and Development*, 1968, 14, 82–100.

Central Advisory Council for Education (England). *Children and their Primary Schools* (2 vols.), H.M.S.O., 1967 (The Plowden Report).

Centre for Educational Research and Innovation, *Equal Educational Opportunity I*, Organisation for Economic Co-operation and Development, Paris, 1971.

Chazan, M., Laing, A. and Jackson, S., *Just Before School*, Schools Council Research and Development Project in Compensatory Education, Blackwell, 1971.

Clegg, Sir Alec and Megson, Barbara, *Children in Distress*, Penguin Books, 1968.

Coard, Bernard, *How the West Indian Child is made Educationally Sub-Normal in the British School System*, New Beacon Books, 1971.

Coates, K. and Silburn, S., *Poverty: The Forgotten Englishmen*, Penguin Books, 1970.

Coleman, James S. *et al.*, *Equality of Educational Opportunity*, U.S. Government Printing Office, Washington D.C., 1966.

Corbett, Anne, Are educational priority areas working? *New Society*, 13 November 1969.

Corbett, Anne, Priority Schools, *New Society*, 30th May 1968.

Cox, T. and Waite, C. A., *Teaching Disadvantaged Children in the Infant School*, Schools Council Project in Compensatory Education, University College, Swansea, 1970.

Craft, M., *Family, Class and Education*, Longmans, 1970.

Craft, M., Raynor, J. and Cohen, L. (eds.), *Linking Home and School*, Longmans, 1967.

Creber, J. W. P., *Lost for Words: Language and Educational Failure*, Penguin Books, 1972.

Daniel, W. W., *Racial Discrimination in England*, Penguin Books, 1968.

Davies, Bleddyn, *Social Needs and Resources in Local Services*, Michael Joseph, 1968.

Deakin, N. *et al.*, *Colour, Citizenship and British Society*, Panther Books, 1970.

Department of Education and Science, *Continuing Needs of Immigrants*, Education Survey No. 14, H.M.S.O., 1972.

Department of Education and Science, *Parent-Teacher Relations in Primary Schools*, Education Survey No. 5, H.M.S.O., 1968.

Derrick, June, *Teaching English to Immigrants*, Longmans, 1966.

Douglas, J. W. B., *The Home and the School*, MacGibbon and Kee, 1964.

Douglas, J. W. B., *All Our Future*, Peter Davies, 1968.

Evans, P. C. C. and LePage, R. B., *The Education of West Indian Immigrant Children*, National Committee for Commonwealth Immigrants (now Community Relations Commission), 1969.

Eyken, W. van der, *The Pre-School Years*, Penguin Books, 1967.

Eysenck, H. J., *Race, Intelligence and Education*, New Society: Temple Smith, 1971.

Fantini, M. D., and Weinstein, G., *The Disadvantaged: Challenge to Education*, Harper & Row, New York, 1968.

Gahagan, D. M. and Gahagan, G. A., *Talk Reform: Exploration in Language for Infant School Children*, Routledge & Kegan Paul, 1970.

Goldman, R., *Research and the Teaching of Immigrant Children,*, National Committee for Commonwealth Immigrants (now Community Relations Commission), 1967.

Goodacre, Elizabeth, *Home and School Relations: A List of References*, Home and School Council, 1968.

Gordon, E. W. and Wilkerson, D. A., *Compensatory Education for the Disadvantaged*, College Entrance Examination Board, New York, 1966.

Hannam, C., Smyth, C. and Stephenson, N., *Young Teachers and Reluctant Learners*, Penguin Books, 1971.

Harvard Educational Review, *Environment, Heredity, and Intelligence*, Reprint Series 2, Cambridge, Mass., 1969.

Harvard Educational Review, *Equal Educational Opportunity*, Harvard University Press, 1969.

Harvard Educational Review, *Science, Heritability and I.Q.*, Reprint Series 4, Cambridge, Mass., 1969.

Haynes, Judith, M., *Educational Assessment of Immigrant Pupils*, National Foundation for Educational Research, Slough, 1971.

Holman, R. *et al.*, *Socially Deprived Families in Britain*, Bedford Square Press, London, 1970.

Hunt, J. McVicker, *Intelligence and Experience*, Ronald, New York, 1961.

Hunt, J. McVicker, *The Challenge of Incompetence and Poverty*, University of Illinois Press, 1969.

Jackson, B. and Rae, R., *Priority*, Association of Multi-racial Playgroups, N.d.

Kellmer Pringle, M. L., *Deprivation and Education*, Longmans, 1965.

Kellmer Pringle, M. L., Butler, N. R. and Dane, R., *11,000 Seven-year-Olds*, Longmans, 1966.

Kelsall, R. K. and Kelsall, H. M., *Social Disadvantage and Educational Opportunity*, Holt, Rinehart and Winston, London, 1971.

Kohl, H., *36 Children*, Penguin Books, 1972.

Kozol, J., *Death at an Early Age*, Penguin Books, 1967.

McGeeney, P., *Parents are Welcome*, Longmans, 1969.

McNeal, J. and Rogers, M., *A Multi-Racial School*, Penguin Books, 1971.

Marris, P. and Rein, M., *Dilemmas of Social Reform: Poverty and Community Action in the United States*, Routledge & Kegan Paul, 1967.

Mee, E. C., *Audio-Visual Media and the Disadvantaged Child*, National Council for Educational Technology, Councils and Education Press, 1970.

Ministry of Social Security, *Circumstances of Families*, H.M.S.O., 1967.

Midwinter, Eric, *Social Environment and the Urban School*, Ward Lock, 1972.

Midwinter, Eric, *Projections: an Educational Priority Area at Work*, Ward Lock, 1972.

Morrish, Ivor, *The Background of Immigrant Children*, George Allen & Unwin, 1971.

Morton, D. and Goldman, R., *The Formal Institutions of Pre-School Education in Britain and the Sociological Context of their Emergence*, Occasional Paper No. 1, Didsbury College of Education, Compensatory Education Project, 1969.

Moynihan, D. P., *Maximum Feasible Misunderstanding: Community Action in the War on Poverty*, Arkville Press, New York, 1969.

Moynihan, D. P. (ed.), *On Understanding Poverty*, Basic Books, New York, 1969.

Newsom, J. and Newsom, E., *Four Years Old in an Urban Community*, Penguin Books, 1970.

Newsom, J. and Newsom, E., *Patterns of Infant Care in an Urban Community*, Penguin Books, 1965.

Passow, A. H. (ed.), *Education in Depressed Areas*, Teachers College Press, Columbia University, New York, 1963.

Passow, A. H., Goldberg, M. and Tannenbaum, H. J. (eds.), *Education of the Disadvantaged: A Book of Readings*, Holt, Rinehart & Winson, New York, 1967.

Patterson, S., *Dark Strangers: A Study of West Indians in London*, Tavistock, 1963.

Peaker, G. F., *The Plowden Children Four Years Later*, National Foundation for Educational Research, Slough, 1971.

Peters, R. S. (ed.), *Perspectives on Plowden*, Routledge & Kegan Paul, 1969.

Pidgeon, D. A., *Expectation and Pupil Performance*, National Foundation for Educational Research, Slough, 1970.

Razzell, A., *Juniors: A Postscript to Plowden*, Penguin Books, 1968.

Richardson, K., Spears, D. and Richards, M. (eds.), *Race, Culture and Intelligence*, Penguin Books, 1972.

Robinson, W. P. and Rackstraw, S. J., *A Question of Answers* (2 vols.). Routledge & Kegan Paul, 1972.

Rubenstein, David and Stoneman, Colin (eds.), *Education for Democracy*, Penguin Books, 1970.

Schools Council, *Cross'd with Adversity: the Education of Socially Disadvantaged Children in Secondary Schools*, Working Paper 27, Evans/ Methuen Educational, 1970.

Schools Council, *Enquiry 1: Young School Leavers*, H.M.S.O., 1968.

Schools Council, *English for the Children of Immigrants*, Working Paper 13, H.M.S.O., 1967.

Schools Council, *Teaching English to West Indian Children: the Research Stage of the Project*, Working Paper 29, Evans/Methuen Educational, 1970.

Schools Council, *Immigrant Children in Infant Schools*, Working Paper 31, Evans/Methuen Educational, 1970.

Schools Council Project in Compensatory Education, *Field Report No. 6*, Schools Council, n.d.

Schools Council Project in Compensatory Education, *Compensatory Education—an Introduction*, Occasional Publication No. 1, University College, Swansea, 1968.

Schools Council Project in Compensatory Education, *Children at Risk*, Occasional Publication No. 2, University College, Swansea, n.d.

Schools Council Project in Compensatory Education, *Compensatory Education and the New Media*, Occasional Publication No. 3, University College, Swansea, 1971.

Seabrook, J., *City Close-Up*, Allen Lane, The Penguin Press, 1971.

Sharrock, A., *Home and School: A Select Annotated Bibliography*, National Foundation for Educational Research, Slough, 1971.

Shea, K., *Liverpool and its Under-Fives*, Association of Multi-Racial Playgroups, 1970.

Silver, H., *The Concept of Popular Education*, MacGibbon & Kee, 1965.

Smilansky, S., *The Effects of Sociodramatic Play on Disadvantaged Pre-School Children*, Wiley, New York, 1968.

Smith, G. A. N. and Little, A., *Strategies of Compensation: A Review of Educational Projects for the Disadvantaged in the United States*, Centre for Educational Research and Innovation, Organisation for Economic Co-operation and Development, Paris, 1971.

Social Science Research Council, *Research on Poverty*, Heinemann, 1968.

Suchman, E. A., *Evaluative Research—Principles and Practice in Public Service and Social Action Programmes*, Russell Sage Foundation, New York, 1967.

Taylor, G. and Ayres, N., *Born and Bred Unequal*, Longmans, 1969.

Taylor, L. C., *Resources for Learning*, Penguin Books, 1971.

Townsend, H. E. R., *Immigrant Pupils in England: The L.E.A. Response*, National Foundation for Educational Research, Slough, 1971.

Townsend, Peter (ed.), *The Concept of Poverty*, Heinemann, 1970.

Tyermann, M. J., *Truancy*, University of London Press, 1968.

Wiseman, S., *Education and Environment*, Manchester University Press, 1964.

Young, M. and McGeeney, P., *Learning Begins at Home*, Routledge & Kegan Paul, 1968.

APPENDIX 3

FURTHER PUBLICATIONS

The full list of publications from the E.P.A. programme is:—

Volume I — *Educational Priority*, edited by A. H. Halsey.

Volume II — *E.P.A.: Surveys and Statistics*, edited by Joan Payne.

Volume III — *E.P.A.: Evaluated Action in London and Birmingham*, edited by Jack Barnes.

Volume IV — *E.P.A.: A Case Study in the West Riding*, edited by George Smith.

Volume V — *E.P.A.: A Scottish Study*, edited by Charles Morrison in collaboration with Joyce Watt and Terence Lee.

Volumes II–V will appear in 1973. A Penguin educational special based on the Liverpool project and written by Eric Midwinter will be published soon after the appearance of the present volume.

Printed in England for Her Majesty's Stationery Office by
J. W. Arrowsmith Ltd., Bristol
Dd. 504457 K120 5/73